Giving Up
the Ghost

Giving Up the Ghost

Spirits, Ghosts, and Angels in Mainstream Comedy Films

Katherine A. Fowkes

Wayne State University Press
Detroit

CONTEMPORARY FILM AND TELEVISION SERIES

A complete listing of the books in this series can be found at the back of this volume.

General Editor
Patricia B. Erens
Hong Kong University

Advisory Editors
Lucy Fischer
University of Pittsburgh

Barry Grant
Brock University

Peter Lehman
University of Arizona

Caren J. Deming
University of Arizona

Robert J. Burgoyne
Wayne State University

Library of Congress Cataloging-in-Publication Data
Fowkes, Katherine A., 1962–
    Giving up the ghost : spirits, ghosts, and angels in mainstream
comedy films / Katherine A. Fowkes.
        p.   cm. — (Contemporary film and television series)
    Includes bibliographical references and index.
    ISBN 0-8143-2721-4 (pbk. : alk. paper)
    1. Ghosts in motion pictures. 2. Angels in motion pictures.
I. Title II. Series.
PN1995.9.S8F68   1998
    791.43'675—dc21   97-37951

CONTENTS

Contents

To my beloved
(a.k.a. KOPH)

PREFACE

Although this book covers a variety of issues in relation to film ghosts and angels, it will soon become apparent that my argument coheres around a concept that may at first be off-putting to the general reader. I use the term "masochistic" in the Introduction and continue to do so throughout the book as a counterpoint to a more prevalent term often used in discussions of mainstream films—"sadism." Such terms are the result of a psychoanalytic perspective, and do not have anything to do with actual sexual or offensive practices in either the films or the analysis. Rather, these terms are used to refer to the narrative, visual, and auditory operation of cinematic stories. As applied to films then, these terms are less literal than metaphoric, and their use should not discourage the reader from pursuing their application to the subject at hand. (The films in this study are quite tame. Their content and tone is generally comic and romantic, rarely "sexual," and not offensive.) In addition, although I am expecting this book to attract mostly film scholars and students, I have attempted to clearly lay out the important "theoretical" concepts so that any interested reader will be able to follow the argument with a minimum of confusion.

The following pages stem from work that I began as a graduate student at the University of Texas at Austin. As such, many of my assumptions and arguments were formulated within the context of theories and ideas popular at that time. While the field has grown and become more complex in the intervening period, the observations tendered in this book are still highly relevant and the majority of theories from which I draw continue to carry much currency. Having said that, I do wish to concede that there may be omissions or blind spots that are a direct result of the time lag between the initial ideas and the publication of this book. I believe that the time is ripe for a book about ghosts and angels in film and that this book has much to offer despite possible omissions or oversights. In the absence of similar scholarly works, this book represents a step toward redressing a larger oversight within the field of film studies itself—namely, a recognition of the phenomenon of mainstream comedy films populated by ghosts and angels.

I would like to acknowledge several people for their role in the writing of this book: Janet Staiger for her ongoing enthusiasm, support, and advice—including her comments on the earliest versions of this manuscript; Tom Schatz, Mary Desjardins, Charles Ramirez-Berg, and Doug Kellner for their readings of the earlier version; and Joanne Hershfield for her friendship and for her comments on the final chapter.

I would also like to thank Jennifer Backer, my editor at Wayne State University Press. She has been a pleasure to work with and has made the publishing process considerably less stressful than it might otherwise be.

Lastly, my tremendous and heartfelt thanks goes to Pranab Das, who has been my most enthusiastic supporter, my amanuensis, my unofficial copy editor, my computer whiz, and my most favorite all-around partner in crime.

INTRODUCTION

Over the last several decades gender has become one of the most important topics of debate and exploration in both the academic and nonacademic communities. Within the field of film studies, critical and cultural theorists have argued that gender is a structuring influence on both the formation and consumption of mainstream films. The most widely accepted arguments contend that mainstream films are inherently sadistic and misogynistic both in their visual coding and in their narrative trajectories. Critics of this framework have largely resorted to analyses of avant-garde or experimental films, arguing that alternative narrative or filmic strategies are necessary to subvert what is seen as an impenetrable and monolithic ideology. Overlooked, however, are the many mainstream films that do not adhere to the traditional model of sadistic climax, closure, and voyeurism. Comedy ghost films, as a case in point, appear to elicit and are structured around a different type of pleasure.

Film scholars might not be surprised to learn that the majority of recent ghost films feature male ghost protagonists, which would seem to harken back to the traditional arguments about gender in film. Whereas many film theorists have suggested that mainstream films involve the mapping of sexual difference and that narrative and filmic processes are inherently sadistic, I argue that ghost films dramatize an explicitly masochistic fantasy in which the desire to switch genders is part of a desire to achieve sexual sameness. In most cases this phenomenon is realized through gender switching, a process directly imbricated with the figure of the ghost. In the process, they provide a substantially different approach to traditional gender roles.

Although comedy ghost films run counter to the sadistic voyeurism and closure associated with Hollywood films, they are also far from being experimental or avant-garde. It is ironic, in fact, that comedy ghost films are consistently criticized and/or ignored precisely because they are said to be too formulaic, too Hollywood.

Introduction

This book provides an analysis of a number of films that have been overlooked by academics and popular critics alike. It also offers a counterpoint to recent studies focusing on "body" genres via slasher and male-focused action movies. Ghost films employ a strategy wholly opposite to such films—ghost films engage in a denial of the physical body, whereas slasher and action films focus obsessively on it. Yet both body-obsessed films and ghost films work through difficulties related to gendered identities. Ghost films can thus be understood in relation to other Hollywood genres (horror, occult, melodrama, comedy, action), revealing that ghost comedy films are emblematic of a cultural confusion with—or an insistence on working through—problems of gender.

A related curiosity of the film ghost is that while ghosts would at first glance appear to dramatize a fantasy concerning the death of the subject, comedy ghosts are in fact more concerned with the origin of the subject and the problems of gender identification associated with this type of fantasy. The primal fantasy of origins is central to many ghost films and is inherently masochistic—in part because it involves the difficulty of assuming a stable gender configuration. Whereas mainstream male protagonists usually display their masculinity by actively pursuing and fulfilling their goals, male ghosts suffer a feminization in their inability to affect their surroundings. Male ghosts see without being seen, speak without being heard and suffer difficulties communicating their desires. The male ghost embodies a masochistic experience inflected along gender lines, dramatizing a primal fantasy in which the binary roles of masculine and feminine are impossible to realize.

In a different vein, the masochistic aesthetic applies also to the way in which the film ghost becomes a figure of delay and repetition within the narrative. While purporting to reverse the tragic pathos of death associated with melodrama, the ghost ultimately and masochistically prolongs the very difficulties it ostensibly returns to address. Both male and female viewers may find pleasure in the masochistic processes of disavowal and narrative delay, and in the reversals of gender position of which comedy film ghosts are emblematic. Thus, while the films dramatize an explicitly masochistic fantasy at the diegetic level, the masochistic scenario is not just played out between the characters, but becomes the setting or mise-en-scène of desire for the viewer. That the masochistic aesthetic is foregrounded in these so-called fluffy mainstream films (and not just in non-Hollywood or avant-garde films) suggests that the process of experiencing any cinematic narrative may be just as important as the hermeneutic solutions and cathartic endings of Hollywood films.

One of the most obvious characteristics of film ghosts is their ability to become invisible, a characteristic that will be explored at length. In addition to providing a point of reference for masochistic viewership, invisibility will become a key to understanding how the fantastic qualities of the ghost elicit a comedic rather than a horrific response. Yet while ghosts naturally seem to involve problems concerning vision and spectacle, the ghosts in these films dwell just as (or even more) insistently on problems surrounding the voice. Since the theoretical and critical literature on cinema has tended to overlook the role of voice and sound in cinema, this analysis should provide a contribution to the small number of critical discussions on this topic. By demonstrating how comedy ghost films play upon established conventions of sight and sound, I will unravel the precise way in which these films attempt to provide a compelling fantasy world. In the case of comedy ghost films, the invisible body combined with the ever-present disembodied voice provides a very different experience from that found in melodrama or horror—genres that also problematize the voice and body along gendered lines. It becomes clear that in comedy ghost films the use of voice, vision, and voyeurism is not sadistic or misogynistic, but decidedly masochistic.

Although the characteristics of ghosts and angels often overlap, the function of angels in comedy ghost films is specific and highly significant to the masochistic fantasy. Whereas most mainstream film protagonists strive to gain control of their narrative destinies, the comedic nature of the ghost-scenario provides a fantasy in which the protagonist is required, by dying, to relinquish control under the rubric of heavenly guidance or destiny. Furthermore, the comedy format provides a generic context in which the film viewer is similarly invited to relinquish control with the assurance that the outcome is "destined" to be a happy one. The film viewer is much like a ghost in that s/he observes the scenario at hand, but is unable to affect it. The framework of comedy combined with the device of the film ghost prove to be uniquely suited to a masochistic conception of narrative film pleasure.

The fact that films can be interpreted differently by different people should not discourage one from attempting to analyze films. Rather, one should remember that the range of interpretations is not infinite but is limited by the field of possible meanings generated by the film's structure, images, and by the cultural contexts that inform both the film and the viewer. Film viewers formulate their interpretations within the context of established conventions, genre being an example of just one type of conventional framework. In other words, both the film and the viewer make sense and meaning through a network of shared symbols and conventions. Although there will always be idiosyncratic responses to films, there will also remain sets of shared constructs that are evidence of certain tendencies and possible interpretations.

Because we must take into account the role that the viewer plays in relation to textual meaning, any analysis of films or film ghosts must stem from and be influenced by one or more cultural perspectives. My perspective derives not only from film theory, but also from an avowedly feminist agenda that seeks to expose, or at least illuminate, patriarchal ideology. My agenda is not to empower women at the expense of men, but rather to understand the ways in which we are all implicated in cultural and psychological processes of gender formation. Although no single feminist theory exists, one of my basic assumptions is that any reading of a text must have an explicit standpoint from which to base its interpretations precisely because meaning and pleasure do not lie in the text, but in the interaction between the text and the perceiver. My perspective includes post-Freudian, Lacanian, and feminist viewpoints, informed by film theorists such as Laura Mulvey and Teresa de Lauretis, who have attempted to expose the ways in which the cinematic apparatus and the very structure of narrative have been implicated in the subjugation of women. The book relies more heavily, however, on later theories that both acknowledge and reformulate such accounts so that processes of subject formation and cinematic identification are understood to be not necessarily or inherently misogynistic or sadistic.

In examining ghosts as character, filmic, and narrative devices, this book draws on several major strands in the field of film scholarship, including genre studies and neoformalist textual analysis, but focusing primarily on poststructural and feminist psychoanalytic theories. Such theories provide not only the assumptions and frameworks within which to formulate hypotheses, but also suggest methodological approaches to the topic at hand. For example, genre and neoformalist studies suggest that films are systems of conventions that make meaning in particular ways at particular times. These conventions are imbricated not only in the technological apparatus but in ideological constructs shared by both the producers and consumers of films. Some of these shared constructs involve culturally formulated notions of individual identity, an area of investigation that psychoanalytic, feminist, and poststructural theories address. Psychoanalytic film theory seeks to forge a link between the formulation of the human subject in society with the formulation of both the viewing subject in cinema and the construction of such a subject as a filmic representation. Because this body of theory is based heavily on the notion of gendered identities, feminists have often turned to it in their efforts to expose patriarchal oppression. Poststructural and (at least some) feminist theories may find a common point of interest with psychoanalytic and neoformalist theories when they argue that gendered identity is not an inherent or biological essence, but an ideological construct subject to deconstruction. In fact, a major assumption of this book will be that gender is not a biological state but a socially formulated concept. I argue that because gender is not innate, it is also not necessarily fixed irrevocably in childhood. Hence, the human subject might conceivably identify with or assume a variety of gendered positions over the course of a lifetime. The notion of constructed identities and realities will be, similarly, a major site of convergence in my use of these various theories.

The films considered in this book were selected, in part, because of the similarities I perceived in the functioning of ghost and angel characters. While I refer to all of these movies as comedies, my definition is a loose one, based in part on distinguishing these films from the horror genre. Specifically, the ghosts in these films are clearly not designed to evoke a reaction of fear in the audience, and none of them are marketed as horror films. Most of these films can be found in rental stores either in the comedy, romantic comedy, or drama sections, which reveals both an industrial as well as a public consensus concerning these movies. In addition, I have not included films that use ghosts or ghouls only as devices for comic antics, unless the ghost appears as a bona fide character. Thus, while *Ghostbusters* (1984) is certainly a comedy, the "ghosts" are merely special effects monsters, designed to be comically exterminated by the heroic antics of Bill Murray and friends.

To be considered for the study, the film must have a ghost who adheres to several requirements. A ghost is defined as any character who has died, but who nevertheless appears visibly or aurally as a character in the narrative. The ghost typically returns for a specific reason, such as correcting an injustice or doing a good deed, and usually displays at least some of the following characteristics: a) invisibility; b) disconnection of voice from body; c) a tendency to reveal itself to some and not to others; d) the ability to move through solid objects like doors and walls; e) the ability to float or fly; f) the inability to manipulate solid objects (or, if able to do so, is invisible to other characters when doing so; g) physically similar to itself before death; and h) the ability to enter other bodies. Although no comedy film ghost will necessarily exhibit all of these characteristics, some combination is usually present. Returning from the dead, however, is a key component of the ghost character. (As a point of comparison, I will also briefly discuss several films featuring invisible characters, even where the character does not return from the dead.)

Because ghosts and angels often seem to overlap, I also consider films that feature angels. Some angels are actually ghosts who are trying to do a good deed to "earn their wings" and go to heaven. In this case, angels are ghosts whose raison d'être is pre-defined as that of a helper to another character. In other cases, angels may be representatives of heaven only and were not human previously. Though not a ghost per se, this type of angel may display physical characteristics similar to the ghosts described above. Lastly, while ghosts often tend to have difficulty making themselves seen or heard, angels usually have complete control of their body and of the environment. In fact, angels often have magical powers and may control the physical and narrative destiny of the other characters. As will become apparent in the penultimate chapter, my own definition of angels hinges on these latter characteristics.

The focus on recent movies as opposed to all ghost films stems directly from the startling similarity among the films in this group—a trend not found as clearly in older films. Since the device of the ghost can be used for a variety of narrative and generic purposes, the similarities in recent films are all the more striking. However, I do include some of older films in the final chapter, to suggest both points of comparison as well as avenues for further exploration. By revisiting several ghost films that reveal the relationship between ethnicity and gender, the last chapter also briefly addresses the way in which racial issues have been rendered "invisible" by mainstream film. These mainstream films tend to conflate racial and sexual categories through a variety of narrative and visual strategies. Finally, while masochistic pleasures are specifically mobilized in ghost films, other mainstream films might be re-evaluated using the same set of parameters. Re-readings of classically "sadistic/voyeuristic" and action films show that the psychoanalytic paradigm traditionally used to understand Hollywood films needs to be re-examined and revised to accommodate a more flexible and "polymorphous" range of pleasures. Although comedy ghost films provide explicitly masochistic scenarios, even films that use overtly aggressive or sadistic narratives provide a space for masochistic and other fantasies. Furthermore, viewers may identify with more than one narrative and gender position even while being prompted by traditional binary categories.

During the course of writing this book it has occasionally been tempting to pursue a number of tangents relating to both film theory and film ghosts themselves. For example, the relationship between religion and ghosts is an obvious area of exploration. Thus far, critics have generally concluded that ghost films appeal to our "spiritual side." While there is nothing particularly wrong with this observation, it is not particularly fruitful either. A more interesting line of inquiry would involve a comparison between spiritual narratives and popular narratives that feature spirituality. Of particular note is the obviously masochistic figure of Christ. Such a long-standing and influential religious theme begs to be investigated and contextualized where it intersects with popular narratives and popular myths. It is important to remember that different methodologies yield distinct types of research questions and conclusions. Industrial, historical and other more empirically based methodologies might approach these films from equally valid and important perspectives. Although any of these approaches would undoubtedly yield important insight to the phenomenon discussed here, I will tender this study as merely one piece in the puzzle.

Chapter 1

The Ghost
in the Machine

Although considerable study has been devoted to ghosts and spirits as literary and horror devices, little research has been done on comedy ghost films or on comedy ghosts as narrative and cinematic devices. Literary theories of the fantasy genre do not address cinematic ghosts, while the much-studied horror genre focuses on a very different kind of ghost than those found in comedies. It is important to consider first the question of why comedy ghost films have been so consistently ignored by critics and scholars, and then to examine the scholarship pertaining to ghosts as fantasy figures, since fantasy provides a context for ghost films not only as a part of a fictional genre, but also as a psychoanalytic concept. In connection with this, a brief description of traditional psychoanalytic film theory will provide a context for the discussion that follows. The ideas presented will be familiar to many, but the anomalous position of film ghosts inside that framework is surprising. Comedy ghost films raise important questions about narrative and visual pleasure in mainstream cinema that are not adequately answered by current assessments of either mainstream films or by assessments of comedy ghost films themselves.

Silly Specters?

Although this study focuses on recent films, the comedy ghost is hardly a recent innovation in film narrative. Throughout the 1930s and 1940s

Giving Up the Ghost

Hollywood produced a number of films that dealt with the afterlife, including *Topper* (1937), *The Canterville Ghost* (1943), and *The Ghost and Mrs. Muir* (1947). Although many of these films were successful, few such movies were produced again until 1978 when *Heaven Can Wait* was released. A remake of the 1941 *Here Comes Mr. Jordan,* this film and its success appear to have spurred a new cycle of Hollywood ghost films, which the infamous *Ghost* (1990) eventually capitalized on. Between 1978 and 1995 over twenty comedy ghosts films were released, making comedy ghost films an important presence in contemporary film. The substantial number of ghost films produced over the past two decades and the runaway popularity of *Ghost* suggest that ghosts are a significant phenomenon in current films, one that has until now been little explored.

Ghost films may have been overlooked by scholars and critics on the basis that they are too conventional and too formulaic. Comedy ghost films seem to represent the epitome of "typical" Hollywood cinema, as most are schlock entertainment or mindless escapism. Particularly when such fantasy films lack a horror element or are combined with comedy, the usual response by critics is to dismiss the films as mere fluff. Critics are, for the most part, disdainful of ghost films, whose stories seem improbable when judged by normal standards of realism or verisimilitude. In fact, virtually every popular review considers ghost films to be silly escapist entertainment, designed to gloss over real problems and deny reality.[1] Such was the assessment of the movie *Ghost,* one of the most important films in this study, in part because of its huge popularity. Yet *Ghost* was similar to films that had been appearing for over a decade. Drawing on films preceding it, and influencing those following it, *Ghost* can be seen as a kind of perceptual hub around which even the most disparate ghost films revolve. Films such as *Heaven Can Wait* (1978), *Made in Heaven* (1987), *Kiss Me Goodbye* (1982), and *Always* (1986) had all employed ghost characters and afterlife images with obvious similarities to those later appearing in *Ghost.* Other films of the decade took ghosts to more slapstick extremes, notably *Beetlejuice* (1988) and *Ghost Dad* (1990). Although the tone may vary widely among films, all intersect in form and content with *Ghost,* a blockbuster hit that brought in over two hundred million dollars at the box office, making it the most successful Hollywood film that year and one of the highest grossing films ever. Its success confounded critics, however, who had previously ignored the many other films it so obviously resembled. The *New York Times* called it one of the biggest "sleeper" hits in Hollywood history, and *Time* magazine concurred, noting that the film had "marketing experts trying to figure out its success."[2] The runaway success of *Ghost* indicates that the film struck a chord with the American public. Not only did the film attract huge audiences, but exit polls indicated that many people returned to see the film again and again. Unable to account for this phenomenon, one critic claimed that "the spiritual message prompts moviegoers to see it over and over with cultlike devotion."[3]

Most reviewers attributed the popularity of *Ghost* to a desire to overcome death or escape reality. One reviewer quoted a psychologist who opined: "Ghost pictures? Hey, it's wishful thinking, a magical way of trying to defang death. We deny death by these fantasies."[4] A similar analysis has been used to explain the prevalence of ghost films during the post–World War II period. In fact, Peter Valenti coined the term "film blanc" to describe some of the ghost films of the 1930s and 1940s. Contrasting these films to film noir, Valenti argues that these sentimental ghost films became popular during World War II because they provided reassurance that deceased loved ones were going to a better place and that they were dying for a higher cause.[5]

As with the popular literature, most scholarly work dealing with fantasy (e.g., ghosts, hobbits) supports the theory that such films provide reassurance during stressful times.[6] In their discussion of fantasy and nostalgia in 1980s cinema, Michael Ryan and Douglas Kellner argue that the emergence of these films was a reaction to the turmoil of Vietnam and to the feminist and civil rights movements. Ryan and Kellner argue that most popular movies in the 1980s tended to smooth over problems, providing easy and unrealistic solutions, exemplified by such nostalgic fantasies as *Star Wars* (1977) and *E.T.* (1982)—both blockbuster hits appearing at the same time as *Heaven Can Wait*.[7] Tom Genelli and Lyn Davis Genelli link the success of *Heaven Can Wait* and *Resurrection* (1979) to America's discovery of Eastern religion and to a renewed interest in spiritualism resulting from the youth movements of the 1960s and 1970s.[8] We might add to this list of possible influences the current mainstream popularity of the New Age Movement and the "specter of AIDS."[9] On the surface comedy ghost films do seem to display the same kind of nostalgia for easy answers and good-versus-evil dichotomies that characterize the other fantasy films of the 1980s and thus may be considered part of the larger trend Ryan and Kellner discuss. But a more careful reading reveals that these films are significantly more complex than expected.

Although ghost films are certainly fantasies of some kind, they are more than mere escapism. Such characterizations are simply inadequate to explain some of the apparent contradictions inherent in the films' visual and narrative structure (as compared with other mainstream films) or to account for the profound similarities among such a wide variety of films. Many critics see the fantasy genre as simple wish-fulfillment, but a more thorough reading reveals the potentially subversive aspects of desire. Psychoanalytic theories are especially pertinent to an analysis of fantasy, as Rosemary Jackson points out in her account of literary fantasy: "Literary fantasies, expressing unconscious drives, are particularly open to psychoanalytic readings, and frequently show in graphic form a tension between the 'laws of human society' and the resistance of the unconscious mind to those laws."[10] Although Jackson focuses her argument on horror fantasies, a similar approach might be applied to ghost films. What are the unconscious drives at work in comic ghost fantasies and what "laws of human society" are at issue? Ghost films deal with ideas and characters that are not "real" or "realistic" so that psychoanalytic theory may be particularly crucial for analyzing and accounting for their ubiquity in popular narratives. A psychoanalytic approach involves examining the relationship between the individual's unconscious desires and the society that produces and perpetuates those desires. The comedy film ghost raises these issues both within the framework of narrative agency and within the framework of human subjectivity. In other words, film ghosts raise questions of subjectivity on two levels: 1) within the diegesis, as a function of their invisibility and their narrative agency within the film; and 2) as a function of the audience's perception and pleasure.

Although fictional fantasies may be particularly obvious choices for psychoanalytic readings, all literary and cinematic narratives can be described in psychoanalytic terms. The theories described below cut across generic categories and provide compelling psychoanalytic descriptions of the pleasurable processes associated with literary narrative and narrative film. The common ground between these literary and cinematic theories lies in their descriptions of purportedly sadistic operations. However, recent ghost films show repeated thematic, visual, and narrative similarities that appear to contradict qualities supposedly synonymous with mainstream films.

Sadism in Narrative

A number of well-known scholars use psychoanalytic theory to argue that narratives are inherently sadistic in nature. Well conceived and of notable descriptive power, these perspectives serve as a springboard from which to undertake an analysis of comedy ghost films. Since ghost films reveal a significant variation on such conceptions of narrative and visual pleasure, it will be useful to review the particulars of this tradition in some detail.

In a now classic text, *Reading for the Plot,* Peter Brooks discusses narrative in relation to the human life span and a psychoanalytic model of desire. He argues that the desire of and for narrative is related to the death instinct as described by Freud. According to Freud, desire in the individual is born from an original need, which is unmet, from the gap arising between need and its fulfillment—the child and the mother's breast, for example. But desire can never be satisfied because the original need was never real (i.e., the actual mother), but a fantasy (the "Imaginary" unity and plenitude Lacan discusses). Thus desire itself must be understood as hallucinatory: "It is irreducible to need, for it is not in its principle relation to a real object, independent of the subject, but rather to a phantasy."[11] The paradox of this desire is that it must constantly be activated in the search for satisfaction or else face the alternative of death (loss of plenitude). But at the same time, its satisfaction (total unity) can only be achieved in death. Narratives are thus seen as the endless reworking of an inherently unsatisfiable desire, whose ultimate goal is always for the end. The pleasure of narrative, then, lies primarily in the solutions and conclusions to the desire that the narrative has constructed at the outset.

A generic form of this desire is often expressed narratively in the form of ambition. The ambition may be mundane, but its fulfillment is inextricably linked with a desire for an ending. This is equally applicable to Hollywood narratives, where a (usually) male protagonist pursues a goal, which is fulfilled by the end of the film. In *Heaven Can Wait,* for example, the protagonist's narrative desire is to become a professional football player. Although he is killed in a car wreck, he returns to earth as a ghost to try to find a new body so that he may achieve his goal. But why kill off a goal-oriented protagonist only to bring him back immediately? Since the ghost-character continues to pursue the same goals as before death, the return of the ghost seems nonsensical if not paradoxical. He eventually achieves this goal by returning as a ghost, but the unconventional narrative trajectory suggests that the ghost fulfills a special function in this drive toward narrative resolution. What is, in fact, the relationship between this desire for the fulfillment of an ambition (the end) and the returning ghost?

The returning ghost might be better understood by considering the trajectory of the narrative as a whole. Although Brooks and others privilege the notion of endings and the narrative's relation to mortality, this is tempered by notions of delay and repetition. According to this model, repetition both of and within narratives is seen as a way of controlling and mastering choice—a desire to control being characteristic of the "sadistic" aspect of the death drive: "Repetition as the movement from passivity to mastery."[12] But since the desire to fulfill the stated ambition also signals conclusion and death, narratives themselves might be seen as a means of delaying the mortal end. They are constantly regenerated in an attempt to come to the "proper end," avoiding the "danger of reaching the end too quickly, of achieving the improper death. The improper end indeed lurks throughout narrative, frequently as the wrong choice."[13] The "improper" end is, in fact, directly related to all ghosts that haunt because of an inappropriate ending—for example, a murder, or a failure to achieve an ambition or consummate a romance.

Some feminist film theorists agree with the notion that narratives, particularly Hollywood film narratives, are expressions of sadistic impulses. More precisely, these impulses are directed at women, who bear the burden of "lack," which narratives seem designed to deny or overcome. The male in film is invariably the active narrative agent, while the female is merely the object of his gaze and hence his desires. Again, this narrative trajectory is intimately linked to sadism: "Sadism demands a story, depends on making something happen, forcing a change in another person, a battle of will and strength, victory/defeat, all occurring in a linear time with a beginning and an end."[14] In the process, narratives construct a "feminine" and passive narrative space over which the active male protagonist must cross.[15] Narrative is imbricated in an Oedipal myth in which male acts of regicide, patricide, and incest become crimes essentially because Oedipus has crossed boundaries and destroyed difference: "If the crime of Oedipus is the destruction of differences, the combined work of myth and narrative is the production of Oedipus. The business of the mythical subject is the construction of differences."[16] In narrative, the male hero's desire to control events in the achievement of desire and his penetration through a border of obstacles into a space gendered female is a sadistic endeavor designed to "map sexual difference" into the text, thereby signaling an Oedipal triumph.

But if male protagonists are usually considered to be active narrative agents, then why does *Heaven Can Wait* present us with a protagonist who is so ineffectual? While a ghost, Joe has no control over the physical world and cannot be seen or heard by other characters. The ghostly state forces him to occupy a passive and ineffective narrative position similar to that traditionally occupied by the female. Throughout the film he is unable to fulfill his ambitions and does not regain his classical male agency until the very end of the film when he finally takes over the body of another athlete. As with *Heaven Can Wait,* other recent films feature ghosts with similar characteristics. In each case a male character is forced into what might be deemed a classically female narrative position: passive and unable to make his desires known.[17]

If literary and cinematic narratives are described as sadistic mappers of sexual difference, the argument becomes even more comprehensive when combined with an analysis of the visual pleasures created by the cinematic apparatus.

Misogyny and Sadism in Film Viewing

Feminist film scholar Laura Mulvey is perhaps best known for describing the misogynistic and sadistic nature of voyeurism as constructed by the filmic apparatus for the viewing subject. In her landmark essay, "Visual Pleasure and Narrative Cinema," Mulvey proposes a theory of cinematic address in which the viewer is assumed to be male and is positioned with a powerful controlling look that reduces women to the object of the gaze. Scopophilia (the pleasure of looking) is crucial to the formation of the male child's identity in society, a pleasure replicated in the experience of viewing a film. Mulvey draws on the Lacanian stages in which the child recognizes the concept of difference and attains language (the Symbolic Stage) but in doing so represses the sense of unity and plenitude (the Imaginary phase), which then becomes the unconscious. Although desire is born from the gap between the sense of this difference and the sense of imaginary unity, the recognition of difference provides the castration fear Mulvey associates with "the look" or "the gaze" in cinema. This account of voyeurism and fetishism as key processes in cinema are predicated on the fear of castration so that scopophilia in general becomes a process of fear, control, and ultimately sadism. The look is never innocent but serves to reassure the male. The look must either control and annihilate the woman, who represents lack and castration (voyeurism), or it must glorify her in an effort to deny the lack (fetishism). The upshot of Mulvey's theory is that the cinematic apparatus is constructed in such a way that it inherently objectifies women as passive objects of the male gaze.[18]

As this well-received theory describes, mainstream films are constructed along rigidly defined gender lines, both visually and narratively. Characters fulfill gendered positions as the story progresses, but regardless of what gender the character "really" is, the desiring hero is always male and the space to which he crosses is always female: "The hero must be male, regardless of the gender of the text-image, because the obstacle, whatever its personification, is morphologically female and indeed, simply, the womb."[19] Sexual difference is mapped into the texts of Hollywood films, where women's anatomical differences from men become the sign of difference at numerous levels. The world of the female is often characterized by a lack, which surfaces in symptoms of invisible, psychological problems or in the woman's classic inability to either possess the gaze or to avoid becoming the object of the male's desire.[20] The notion of lack becomes associated with interiority, both concepts having as their model the female body, which is repeatedly shown to be a receptacle or vessel for either male fear or desire. A whole range of symbology pits the male against the female in binary oppositions stemming from the notion that the male is a subject and the woman is other, non-subject (or not-man). This fundamental opposition gives rise to a host of other dichotomies, creating homologies between biology and gender. Such dichotomies can also be seen in ghost comedy films, which draw heavily on the supposed difference between the masculine and feminine: for example, visible (penis)/invisible (lack of penis); active/passive; language/ ineffability; exterior/interior; world and business/house and home; rationality/ irrationality and emotion; and reason/intuition. The supernatural in ghost and other occult films is almost always associated with feminine emotion, intuition, interiority, and mystery, while the masculine is typically portrayed as "normal": rational, external, visible.[21] Although ghosts do take part in a traditional mapping of sexual difference, they also take part in scenarios of gender flux and a return to oneness, which differs significantly from sadistic scenarios.

The role of looking and seeing certainly pertains to ghosts, who are often invisible to the audience, other characters, or both. The ghost's ability to become invisible would seem at first glance to be a product of the sadistic scenario. Like a film viewer, the male ghost has the ability to possess the woman through his gaze but is not himself seen, thereby seeming to illustrate the type of voyeurism associated with both male characters and viewers.[22] *The Invisible Man* (1933) is an early horror film that illustrates the sadistic scenario, but it also relates to ghost films through its portrayal of an invisible character. In this adaptation of the H. G. Wells classic, a scientist develops a formula which causes him to become invisible. His narrative ambition is typical: to impress his fiancée and become rich and famous (thereby providing the financial means to consummate the marriage). The invisibility potion has the unintended side effect of exacerbating his drive to succeed, however, and he becomes a power-hungry madman. The character, Jack Griffin, uses his invisibility for sadistic purposes, terrifying the townspeople, stealing from banks, and murdering those who thwart his goal. In the end, he is captured by the police and dies an unceremonious death, much to the horror of his fiancée but to the relief of the frightened community. Though this film is very different from recent ghost films it is important to the discussion here. The device of invisibility is a double-edged sword that can be used for a variety of ends, depending upon the context in which it "appears." The invisible character in this film is used to promote a narrative of male ambition, which mobilizes the sadistic narrative and cinematic operations described above. His motivation explicitly exposes the desire to establish his sexual difference in that his goal is linked to his need to prove his worthiness to his fiancée. When Griffin's fiancée asks him why he did it, he explains: "For you Flora . . . for wealth, fame, honor . . . I was pitifully poor. I had nothing to offer you." His scheme includes selling his potion to the highest bidder. Nations will bid millions for it, he claims, and then will sweep the world with invisible armies. Thus, Griffin uses his invisibility to achieve his ends in a sadistic and manipulative way. The ghost characters in recent films, however, are perhaps that much more remarkable for consistently using the device of invisibility in the service of a completely different, masochistic fantasy.

Another interesting variation on invisibility appears in several ghost films from the 1930s and 1940s. Films such as *Topper* (1937) and *Blithe Spirit* (1945) are intriguing for the way in which female ghosts raise questions pertaining to the female body and the male gaze. When invisible, female ghosts would seem to have the potential to subvert the spectacle usually associated with film images of women. Here, what is not visible might become the target of the "gaze," but one that is either unfulfilled or else satisfied by a spectacle unassociated with the human body (e.g., flying objects manipulated by invisible hands).[23] Oddly, however, out of roughly twenty ghost films released since 1978, only one features a female ghost protagonist, a box-office bomb titled *Maxie* (1985).[24] Another important question then is, to paraphrase a female character beset by ghosts in *Truly, Madly, Deeply* (1991), Why are all the ghosts men?

If most recent film ghosts are men, and if the position of active narrative agent is gendered male, why then is the character's narrative agency thwarted so that he is, in a sense, forced to switch genders? This change in gender position is further supported even by films that do not feature a ghost per se, but do involve returning souls. For example, *All of Me* (1984), *Switch* (1991), and *Dead Again* (1991) concern the souls of deceased characters who return to inhabit living people. In all of these films the souls enter bodies of the opposite sex. Such films thus intersect in theme and content with other ghost films such as *Heaven Can Wait* and *Ghost* in the sense that these souls, like many film ghosts, display an ability to "switch" gendered positions.

The focus on both ghosts and out-of-body transformation clearly nominates these films for inclusion in the fantasy realm, thus suggesting a generic category for exploration. But the fantasies also tend to operate in the context of a heterosexual romance. Since the romance is complicated by the death of a character (hence the ghost), a melodramatic element is introduced to the fantasy scenario. The films may thus be analyzed in the context of fantasy, romance, and melodrama. However, there is also a comedic sensibility to the films, a tendency which sets them apart from both melodramas and horror films containing ghosts and ghouls. In general terms, then, I will describe these films as comedies, comic fantasies, or comedy romances. I have initially been using the term "comedy" merely as a way of setting this group of films apart from horror films, as a handy way of indicating the nature of the films to be studied. The comedic aspect is not just a random component, however, but an integral part of the narrative and thematic fantasy.

Generic Context

Although *Ghost* was often criticized for being a generic hybrid, the tendency to mix genres has become increasingly prevalent in recent Hollywood cinema. In particular, Henry Jenkins and Kristine Karnick see a recent infiltration of the comic into horror, fantasy, and science fiction.[25] The hybrid nature of the films in question (both within and amongst themselves) complicates a discussion of them in terms of traditional generic categories. The term "comedy" may be more rightly deemed a "mode" than a genre, alongside categories such as the "tragic" and the "heroic." These categories are much broader than any one genre, which individually may also belong to one mode or another.[26] While comedy may be too broad a concept to constitute a genre per se, it nevertheless opposes itself to horror or tragedy in both its "mode" of operation and in the response it intends to provoke in the audience. Specifically, the films here do not just contain comic elements—any film may contain moments of comic relief without being considered a comedy. Rather, as a mode, the comedy here seems to be part of a larger design, where the comic elements work together with the overall narrative to create a coherent dynamic that opposes both melodrama and horror in its intended effect. In comparing the films in this study to groups of other films, it may be useful to consider even so-called discrete genres as clusters of formal and thematic conventions that may overlap with one another.[27] Thus, the hybrid mixture of comedy romance and melodrama found in *Ghost* might demonstrate latent overlaps between the genres. This conception of genre is also more useful than proposing completely discrete categories in that it allows for comparisons among films that display a range of similar characteristics, but might otherwise be unclassifiable. According to this model, any representative of a genre need not display all of the characteristics of every other member. My initial strategy has not necessarily been to define a new genre comprised of ghosts, but rather to use generic categories to help explain the similar function of ghost characters across a variety of films. However, since the films in this study do seem to operate as a group either in tandem with, or in contradistinction to, other "discrete" genres, the ghost films in this study may indeed qualify as an undiscovered genre, or subgenre.

Literary conceptions of ghosts traditionally employ the categories of gothic, horror, fantasy, or the fantastic. Though problematic, these categories can also serve as generic locators for an examination of comedy film ghosts.

Fantasy and the Fantastic

The comedy ghost films of this study present fantasy scenarios that are at odds not only with the narrative trajectory described by traditional film theory, but also with the ghosts most often studied by traditional literary scholars. Much attention has been paid to the gothic horror story of the eighteenth and nineteenth centuries and on the spirits and wraiths found in modernist literature. A major focus has been Henry James's *Turn of the Screw*, a story in which ghosts appear as frightening and evil specters. Here, the critical debate has largely concerned the question of whether the ghosts are "real" or merely the hallucinations of a sexually deprived governess.[28] That is to say, the reader can never be sure whether the ghosts really ever "appeared" in the first place. One of the major movements in modern literature is associated with a shift in the narration of subjective reality so that ghosts in modern literature are more likely to be the product of the mind's subconscious. By contrast, earlier fictional ghosts are often described as existing independently of the perceiver—the embodiment of pure good or evil. This change in the ontological and epistemological status of the ghost is attributed to two major developments over the last two centuries. The first was the increasing reliance on empirical science whose instruments could not verify the existence of ghosts and whose tenets began to overshadow religious thought. The second development was the rising popularity of Freudian theory, which provided convincing psychological explanations for demons, ghosts, and apparitions.[29]

While ghost literature of the nineteenth century and before revolved around ghosts whose main purpose was to inspire fear and incredulous horror, this is not their purpose in the Hollywood films studied here.[30] In addition, ghosts in early "ghost stories" do not usually appear as full-fledged characters or narrative agents. They most often appear in short stories as specters or wraiths who do not interact with the living. Their "appearance" in the story is either to prove the existence of ghosts and an afterlife, or to create a conundrum concerning their existence.[31] By contrast, the majority of the ghosts discussed here are full-fledged characters and narrative agents. Although the reality of the ghosts is always an issue (whether explicit or not), most of the films do not revolve explicitly around this question.

The ontological and epistemological uncertainty caused by the appearance of the ghost is the primary focus of Tzvetan Todorov's theory of the fantastic in literature. The genre of the fantastic is defined by the "ambiguous perceptions shared by the reader and one of the characters."[32] Todorov is quick to point out, however, that the fantastic can only be maintained as long as uncertainty exists. "The fantastic occupies the duration of this uncertainty. Once we choose one answer or the other, we leave the fantastic for a neighboring genre, the uncanny [where the phenomenon is explained by rational means] or the marvelous [where the phenomenon is at all times accepted as 'real']."[33] The fantastic is an important element of many comedy ghost films and may account for a certain amount of humor in films such as *Ghost* and *Ghost Dad*. For example, Whoopi Goldberg's memorable performance as the reluctant spiritual medium in *Ghost* derives much of its humor from her character's incredulous response to a "fantastic" situation. Most comedy ghost films might be better described as "marvelous" than "fantastic," for often the reality of the ghosts is never questioned by protagonist or audience: "The marvelous . . . may be characterized by the mere presence of supernatural events, without implicating the reaction they provoke in the characters."[34] Since most of the films in this study are likely to be neither wholly fantastic nor wholly marvelous, the effect of their mixture will be explored. For example, the audience may laugh at the fantastic response of the characters who cannot fathom the sight of a pen writing without a hand or a tire being changed by invisible means, while accepting the presence of the ghosts—a characteristic of the marvelous.

Many ghost films may qualify as wholly "marvelous" by virtue of their generic "fantasy" status. In other words, what Todorov specifically calls the marvelous, many other writers call simply "fantasy," a genre some writers characterize as being almost the opposite of the fantastic:

> The writer of fantasy avoids prompting those hesitations, uncertainties, and perceptions of ambiguity that Todorov takes to be essential in the experiencing of *littérature fantastique*. In successful fantasy all is clarity and certainty, as far as presentation goes. Thus fantasy, though often using the same material, moves in a direction opposite to that of *littérature fantastique*. Between the two is a radical difference in the primary point of engagement: in fantasy the intellect, in the fantastic the imagination.[35]

By this definition, fantasy stories or films take place in a world of special rules, and are not subject to questioning by either the reader, viewer, or characters within the story. The worlds created in J. R. R. Tolkien's fantasies are examples of such hermetically sealed universes. The reader never doubts even the most improbable events because all rules have been meticulously and methodically laid out.

In *The Hills of Faraway,* Diane Waggoner discusses ghosts in fantasy literature and makes a distinction between "scary ghost stories" and "ghost fantasies," acknowledging that not all fictional ghosts are scary (a surprisingly rare observation). Waggoner divides the non-scary ghost stories into two opposing groups: the comic and the nostalgic fantasy.

> The ghost story means to frighten the reader or, sometimes, to convince him that ghosts may really exist. The ghost is an intruder in to the Primary World. But in a ghost fantasy, we are in a Secondary World; ghosts there are characters interacting with the ordinary human characters. In many cases the humans do not discover that the ghosts are ghosts until well into the story. Ghost fantasies are usually either comic or nostalgic.[36]

Waggoner's distinction between comic and nostalgic ghost fantasy breaks down a bit when applied to ghost films, however, since many current ghost films combine both elements.[37] For example, *Ghost,* while suffused with a nostalgic glow through its love story, also contains many slapstick comedy scenes between the ghost and the spiritual medium. Just as the marvelous and the fantastic rarely appear in isolation, the comic and nostalgic elements of ghost fantasies often appear in the same films. Despite a type of generic mixing, however, all of the films in this study fall under the rubric of comedy because they do not attempt to scare the audience but instead employ ghosts in comic situations. As with Shakespearean comedies, the films in this study end happily, and often conclude a romantic plot or subplot with a couple's union.[38] The comedic and romantic components of these films are complicated, however, by the death of a key character in the romance. Although the death of this character provides a potentially melodramatic scenario, none of the ghost films follow through on the tragic consequences in the same way as classic melodrama.

The Melodramatic Too-Late

From the viewer's perspective, genre provides a conventional framework, a "horizon of expectation," which helps to formulate an understanding of a film. While melodrama provides one set of expectations for the viewer, ghost films seem to acknowledge these expectations, only to (ostensibly) reverse them. In melodramas a romantic partner is often lost through death or other misfortune, thus thwarting the romance and causing tragedy. If *Ghost, Truly Madly Deeply, Kiss Me Goodbye,* and *Always* all explicitly concern romances cut short by the death of one of the characters, what are we to make of the fact that the dead characters subsequently return as ghosts?[39]

In ghost films, the pathos common to melodrama is invoked by the death of a character but then is quickly reversed. The particular way in which melodramas evoke tragedy and pathos will become important to understanding this reversal. In melodramas trains are missed, lovers pass in the night, or they die before fulfilling their romantic promise. In her influential analysis of the melodramatic genre, Mary Ann Doane observes that the tragedy and tears of melodrama stem from a temporal mistiming characterized by miscommunication and by consistently being "too late." This temporal thematic is described as a slippage that occurs between desire and its object: "Pathos is thus related to a certain construction of temporality in which communication or recognitions take place but are mistimed."[40] Whereas what the melodrama demonstrates "above all is the irreversibility of time,"[41] what ghost narratives demonstrate is the very surprising reversibility of time. The device of the ghost appears to thwart the melodramatic pathos of the story, and completely redirect the narrative trajectory.

Although not all ghost films foreground a romance, the narrative reversal remains the same, correcting the pathos attendant to the untimely death of the characters. For example, in *Beetlejuice,* the loss or mistiming involves the couple's inability to have a child before dying, a problem the film solves by bringing back the characters as ghosts and confining them to a domestic space in which a little girl is delivered to them. *Ghost Dad* also involves a domestic problem as the lead character dies before being able to ensure the financial and emotional well-being of his children. Here again, the character's return as a ghost deflects the obvious pathos attendant to the abandoned children and redirects the story into a different arena where the loss is eventually made good. While melodramas may end tragically, comedy ghost films use the device of the ghost to turn the tables on melodrama, providing a narrative solution designed to produce happy results.

Although the return of the ghost ultimately facilitates a happy ending, it does so in a convoluted and decidedly masochistic way. Specifically, many recent ghost films display a masochistic desire to return to the illusory oneness of the pre-Oedipal. Although this occurs most obviously through ghost films involving romance, the emphasis on oneness also occurs in the context of domestic and family affairs, which become linked to the feminine and dominate the majority of the films. Thus, although ghost comedies draw on the same gender stereotypes as many other films, they do not concern the desire to map sexual difference, but rather the desire to achieve sexual sameness.

Chapter 2

The Masochistic Contract

If visual distance and narrative repetition strike at the very heart of the sadistic interpretation of film, the notion of a masochistic aesthetic provides an analytic landmark from which to locate the appeal of ghost films. While masochism has a somewhat less illustrious theoretical lineage than sadism, several scholars have recently suggested the beginnings of a narrative and visual critique based upon it. Before constructing a novel interpretation of the comedy ghost phenomenon, this perspective should be considered with an eye toward its unification into a theory of mainstream films. Whereas a theory of masochism has not been widely acknowledged as pertaining to mainstream films, here it will become a compelling explanatory tool for understanding pleasure in ghost films. The masochistic aesthetic pertains to the way in which ghosts function as devices of distance and delay, challenging explanations that focus on sadistic mastery. And although ghost films rely on the "mapping of sexual difference" so common to Hollywood narratives, they ultimately express a desire for sexual sameness—a return to oneness.

In "Masochism and the Perverse Pleasures of the Cinema" and in her later book, *In the Realm of Pleasure,* Gaylyn Studlar reformulates the process of cinematic looking and identification as described by previous film theorists.[1] Her key move is to shift the focus of power from the Oedipal/Symbolic stage to the pre-Oedipal/Imaginary stage. Instead of seeing the mother as representing lack (the original "difference"), Studlar sees her as an omnipotent and powerful figure to the child in the pre-Oedipal (and hence pre-sexual) stage. Whereas previous theories focused on the father and the power of the phallus instituted by the Symbolic, Studlar argues that the mother is a primally powerful but also ambivalent figure. Instead of seeing the dread of woman as a fear of castration, this model sees a similar, but "masochistic" rather than "sadistic" reaction to the power of the mother. The mother is powerful because the child desires the fantasy of union and the plenitude of the breast and womb. But the child also experiences ambivalence because at the same time that it desires union, it also fears being engulfed. Rather than being controlled by the gaze, the mother is a figure to whom submission brings pleasure. The repetition of the "fort/da" game (described by Freud, in which the child throws the ball away and has it returned by a string) re-enacts the pleasure/pain cycle of union and loss with the mother—not a re-enactment of disavowal over the phallus.

An application of masochistic pleasure to film theory provides a reformulated assessment of the gaze and subsequently a new perspective on problems of viewing and seeing, critical issues for film ghosts who themselves create problems of viewing and seeing. Whereas the castration metaphor understands the distance between the viewer and the object of the gaze as a by-product of the need to remain separate (asserting control and "difference"), we can instead explain this distance as necessary for submission: "Masochistic desire depends on separation to guarantee the structure of its ambivalent desire. To close the gap, to overcome separation from the mother, to fulfill desire, to achieve orgasm means death."[2] Far from implying that the filmic gaze is sadistic, this theory suggests that the film viewer takes a certain masochistic pleasure in the prolonged submission to the images on the screen—images that he or she can neither obtain or control. The process of cinema spectatorship re-creates the disavowal of an absence, but in this case the absence is not the phallus, which the mother lacks, but the mother herself (or union with the mother). Instead of seeing fetishism as the cathexis of the phallus onto the woman, this process describes the imaginary realization of the primary plenitude with the mother. This is a profound revision to previous theories of gender in film, one that will ultimately provide a window into the logic of the film ghost.

In addition to viewing pleasure, the masochistic aesthetic also applies to narrative structures. Studlar relates the desire for unity to the notion of delay and the pleasure found in this process. We can easily reformulate Brooks's notions of endings, shifting the emphasis from endings to middles. Narratives are seen as endless reworkings of an inherently unsatisfiable desire whose ultimate goal is always for the end: "The desire for the text is ultimately desire for the end, for that recognition which is the moment of the death of the reader in the text."[3] This privileging of the ending is not uncommon and indeed the ending of a narrative provides a definitive stance by which to make sense of the events preceding it. Nevertheless, since fulfilling the desire does mean, paradoxically, virtual death, various devices of repetition and delay are instituted throughout the narrative to postpone the conclusion. But postponing the fulfillment of desire is painful and so Brooks, likening the misery to that of the child's fort/da game, asks the crucial question: *"Why does the child repeat an unpleasurable experience?"* Brooks's answer is that delay is necessary only to "ensure that the ultimate pleasurable discharge will be more complete."[4] This is consistent with the sadistic pleasure described by Oedipal-based theories that find value in the attainment of the narrative goal. In doing so, however, the process of narrative is needlessly undervalued.

Instead of privileging endings, a masochistic understanding of pleasure focuses instead on the pleasure of delay and repetition. A masochistic aesthetic sheds light on the returning ghost, which appears to be a character or a device that delays the (improper) ending of the narrative and reinstitutes a kind of a gap where transformation and gender play can unfold. This delay is one way of providing the necessary kind of gap without which narrative would extinguish itself. Within the text, delay can be seen as a value and a pleasure in and of itself, in which "dramatic suspense replaces Sadian accelerating repetition of action."[5]

As a point of comparison, the soap opera exhibits the perfect masochistic aesthetic—dramatic suspense and a complete de-emphasis on endings. Tania Modleski, for example, suggests that the soap opera is a kind of narrative whose pleasure seems to be other than that of the classic narrative. "The narrative, by placing ever more complex obstacles between desire and fulfillment, makes anticipation an end in itself."[6] Although the notion of delay in the classical narrative depends on a notion of the end, the soap opera's emphasis on the obstacles delaying the end provides pleasure—for, as Modleski points out, soap operas do not end. If truth is usually found at the end of the classically "male" narrative then "truth for women is seen to lie not 'at the end of expectation,' but *in* expectation."[7] Modleski seems to be suggesting that this is a peculiarly feminine aesthetic that plays on the woman's social condition of passively waiting ("for her phone to ring," etc.). The soap opera exemplifies the notion of delay taken to its logical extreme, almost as if to right an imbalance that normally privileges the "male" tendency toward conclusion. The notion of a feminine aesthetic necessarily hinges on a conception of the feminine, which is itself a construction of women's subjugation by patriarchy. For this reason, linking such an aesthetic to the "feminine" is potentially harmful in that it seems merely to reverse the existing binary aesthetic, and may suggest a tendency to essentialize certain modes and pleasure as inherently "feminine."

Giving Up the Ghost

In her book, Studlar applies the masochistic aesthetic only to Von Sternberg films that have been criticized for not measuring up to the usual standards of mainstream narratives. Her thesis is thus based on the argument that masochistic pleasure is mobilized in non-mainstream visual and narrative tactics. However, masochistic pleasure need not apply to only a handful of non-mainstream or avant-garde films. Films may produce multiple types of pleasure (sadistic, masochistic, and other kinds), although one type of pleasure may dominate at any given time. The pleasure described by the masochistic aesthetic is not only a condition of the soap opera or of Von Sternberg films, but is an aesthetic and a viewing position available not just in "women's genres" but in many narratives, and not just for women. The notion of a "masochistic" aesthetic allows one to focus on delay, on passivity, and on many notions traditionally associated with the feminine, and yet it avoids classifying these things as definitively gendered. In this way, what used to be associated with (and denigrated as) "feminine" now becomes both a reading/viewing position and an avowed aspect of narrative structure that permits identification and pleasure in and of both men and women. More important, it is an aesthetic that explicitly invites a play of gender because it plays on traditional notions of passivity and activity, creating and exposing the tension between them. The notion of delay creates what Roland Barthes calls a "dilatory space" and this is precisely the space necessary for both character transformation and indeed for the generation of narrative itself.

Studlar's theory of masochistic film viewing is not without problems. For example, its ahistorical mode of positing film viewership can be problematic. Furthermore, the theory draws heavily on the same phallocentric model it purports to critique. That is to say, while Freudian theories of sadism have led Mulvey and others to theorize that mainstream narrative films operate sadistically to glorify the male (father) at the expense of the female (mother), Studlar's revisions appear merely to reverse this so that the female is glorified. However, both sadistic and masochistic theories of viewership are merely that—theories. These theories are formulated within the context of existing cultural conceptions of gender and subject formation and will therefore never be totally free from the ideological milieu in which they were conceived. In other words, although psychoanalytic theories are in a sense a-historical, they also reveal their historical context through their very assumptions. Specifically, the masochistic fantasy draws its pleasure from and is the direct result of the very myths of male superiority that have permitted theories of sadism to take hold. Masochism is no less valid or real for the fact that it uses traditional conceptions of male superiority as an alibi for its fantasy scenario. Indeed, psychoanalytic theory acknowledges (or should acknowledge) that its conception of the gendered subject perpetuates—just as it stems from—pre-existing myths about gender and subjectivity. As long as patriarchal society operates at the expense of women, using them as the scapegoats for an inherent lack or insecurity (a cultural tendency psychoanalytic theory describes well), then masochism is relevant as a form of pleasure specifically in relation to this system. Not only do ghost films involve masochistic scenarios in which the feminine/mother is glorified and the masculine/father expelled, but they do so precisely in the context of traditional gender stereotypes. They could not do so otherwise, for even as Gilles Deleuze argues that masochism is completely separate from sadism, the masochistic fantasy nonetheless derives its power from its opposition to the sexual differences mapped by mainstream culture and by mainstream Hollywood films.

The Ghostly Contract

Masochism can be defined as a "sexual perversion in which satisfaction is tied to the suffering or humiliation undergone by the subject."[8] But whereas Freud understood masochism to be the turning inward of the sadistic, controlling death drive, later theories explain the etiology of masochism as completely separate. As described, masochism derives from the ambivalence associated with the pre-Oedipal attachment to the mother. Consequently, fantasies associated with masochism should not be seen as placing the masochist in the opposite position to the sadist in a fantasy of sadism. Instead, they depend on an aesthetic or structure which, while in many ways opposite to sadism, is nevertheless not the reverse of sadism, but part of a completely different fantasy scenario.

Although the two differ in numerous ways, one contrast resides in the object or nature of the desire as well as the way in which the "perversion" is undertaken. Sadism relies on the complete control and humiliation of another individual, but the sadist does not seek a masochist as his object. The sadist can glean no pleasure from inflicting pain on someone who enjoys it—this would destroy the entire mechanism of control on which the operation rests. Likewise, the masochist does not take pleasure in being tortured by a sadist. On the contrary, although it is critical that the masochist's suffering appear to stem from another, the pain is actually self-inflicted. To this end, the masochist needs to convince another to inflict the pain that he wishes heaped upon him. Thus in the sadistic scenario the tortured is by definition not a masochist and in the masochistic heterocosm, the torturer is likewise by definition not a sadist: "Just as the sadist does not wish to torture a masochist whose enjoyment of pain would undermine his/her status as true victim, so the masochist could not tolerate a sadistic partner who would undermine the masochistic scheme of mutual agreement. To control the masochistic performance, persuasion ensures mutual agreement between partners."[9] Thus instead of forcing control, the masochist requires a contract—an elaborate process by which the masochist persuades and cajoles another. The contract refers to the particular way in which the masochist devises his own subjugation and can be applied literally to an understanding of ghosts in at least four films—*Always, Truly, Madly, Deeply, Kiss Me Goodbye,* and *Ghost.* In these films, the ghosts each engage in a masochistic contract with a woman to ensure their own pain and ineffectuality.

If masochism is the "suffering and humiliation of the subject" then in *Always, Kiss Me Goodbye,* and *Truly, Madly, Deeply,* the suffering and humiliation occur when the male ghosts return from death for the purpose of causing their lovers to reject them. Each film provides an example of a classic masochistic relationship in which the male contracts with the woman to abuse and rebuff him. Contrasting masochism to sadism, Deleuze writes: "We are no longer in the presence of a torturer seizing upon a victim and enjoying her all the more because she is unconsenting and unpersuaded. We are dealing instead with a victim in search of a torturer and who needs to educate, persuade and conclude an alliance with the torturer in order to realize the strangest of schemes."[10] In *Kiss Me Goodbye,* this strangest of schemes is realized when Jolly returns from death for the sole purpose of making his bereaved wife, Kay, realize his character flaws so that she will reject him and marry her new suitor, Rupert. In *Always,* Pete returns as a ghost only to find his beloved Dorinda being courted by another man. Despite his best efforts to the contrary, Pete finally realizes that he has returned to earth, at least in part, to make sure that Dorinda will forget him and move on. In *Truly, Madly, Deeply* the ghost of Jamie returns to Nina who, initially overjoyed, spends every waking hour with him. Gradually, however, Jamie annoys Nina so much that she is forced into asking him to leave. The raison d'être of the ghost is masochistic—in each case he must force himself to be denigrated, in effect, tortured by his lover so that she will send him away and begin her life again without him.

Although the masochistic alliance between a male and a female is literally dramatized in the above films, the ghost by itself may be seen as the epitome of the masochistic contract. In almost every instance the masochistic contract is integral to the very device of the ghost, for in most ghost films, the ghost returns only under certain conditions. The very concept of the ghost contains within it not only the idea that the ghost is sent back for a specific "reason," but also the understanding that the ghost suffers a price for being allowed to return. Hence, the ghost contains within itself the idea of a masochistic contract, for the dead person is allowed to return—but not without serious repercussions.

In films such as *Ghost, Ghost Dad, Always, Heart Condition* (1990), and *Heaven Can Wait,* the price paid is the character's narrative agency, which is undermined by the ghost's inability to be seen or heard, and/or by an inability to manipulate the material world. Although not all ghosts share the problem of physical impotency (i.e., *Made in Heaven, Truly, Madly, Deeply*) the repercussions of the ghostly state in these films are similar to those in *Ghost* and many of the other movies where the male ghost appears to be a "helper" to the female protagonist. The way in which the ghosts provide this help, however, is through a masochistic alliance of rejection—truly the "strangest of schemes."

(Mis)-Communication and the Verbal Contract

In melodrama, the pathos of the too-late and the fundamental problem of mistiming usually centers around the mistiming of communication. Therefore, the tragedy of the melodrama resides not exclusively in death per se but in the fact that death prevents the expression of crucial information that would set the story straight and provide a happy resolution. The desired but thwarted communication often involves the confession of a character's feelings of true love for another.

In ghost films, the device of the ghost has the potential to thwart the pathos of the melodramatic story by bringing back the loved one, thereby completely redirecting the narrative trajectory. But in ghost films, although the dilemma of mistimed communication is eventually addressed by the return of the ghost, at the same time the very process of communication itself becomes problematic. The difficulties in communication not only provide a masochistic space of delay within the narrative, but also become a trope of the masochistic alliance. In fact, the very reason for "haunting" is to communicate something. But the masochistic restrictions of the ghost cause it to communicate only in certain frequencies, in certain places, or only through certain people, often known as mediums. Although the purpose of haunting might be to communicate with the living, the process is necessarily one of repetition and is doomed to failure. If the ghost could obtain satisfaction—if it could communicate properly—then it could rest (i.e., die), but it cannot; hence it continues indefinitely. The inability to communicate fully is one of the primary aspects of the ghost's ineffectuality.

In *Ghost, Always, Truly, Madly, Deeply, Ghost Dad, Heart Condition, Heaven Can Wait,* and *Beetlejuice,* all the ghosts suffer various degrees of ineffectuality in communicating with the living. In *Heart Condition,* the ghost of a lawyer, Stone can only be seen and/or heard by police detective Moon, which makes it impossible for him to avenge his death or contact his girlfriend without Moon's very reluctant help.[11] In *Heaven Can Wait,* Joe is unable to make his presence known while in the ghostly state. Even later, when Joe inhabits the body of another man, he succeeds only with great difficulty in communicating his true identity to the living. *Beetlejuice* offers one of the funniest self-referential examples of this tendency. Here, the ghost-couple tries in vain to scare away the new inhabitants of their house. Their moaning voices and gruesome hijinks adhere to all the standard methods of haunting (as gleaned from traditional ghost stories and films) and yet the new family completely ignores them. As the *Handbook for the Recently Deceased* explains to them, "The living won't see the dead." When the husband asks, "Can't, or won't?" his wife replies, "It just says 'won't.'" The handbook hints that it is clearly not impossible for them to reach the living if only they could haunt (communicate) more effectively.[12]

In several cases, the problem of difficult communication goes beyond the ghost itself, permeating and subtending the surface plots of the film narratives. I turn now to an in-depth discussion of several ghost films, focusing heavily on *Ghost,* because of both its popularity and its tendency to intersect in theme and content with a wide variety of ghost films. Although there are similarities between the gender of the characters and the masochistic aesthetic ("feminine masochism" as described by Deleuze and others), these similarities represent more than homologies between the role of the fictional characters and their relation to a masochistic fantasy. Although the characters fit neatly into many of the gendered stereotypes of classical Hollywood films as well as into classically Freudian categories, the very structuration of the fantasy will ultimately work against such clear correspondences. This is precisely because the fantasy provided in these films is not just a fantasy of desire played out between the characters, but a fantasy played out for the viewer. In this way, the masochistic aesthetic applies to an internal narrative thematic, as well as to a mode of film spectatorship.

Miscommunication in *Ghost* and Other Films

If ghost films have been accused of shameful sentimentality and escapism, then *Ghost* is certainly no exception. Janet Maslin remarked that *Ghost* was one of many films in 1990 to avoid "true-life experience" in favor of unrealistic, escapist entertainment.[13] Caryn James commented on the sudden plethora of sentimental ghost films in the 1990s: "They are ghost stories for a skeptical age, for on one level they suggest that we are too sophisticated to believe in some cloud-filled afterlife. But their heart-tugging endings also suggest that we long to be reassured that those we love are not truly gone and that we, too, can hope for peaceful immortality."[14]

But whose story is really being told here? If *Ghost* is about the unrealistic longing for the return of a deceased loved one, it is strange, then, that the narrative centers much more around the dilemma of the ghost, Sam Wheat, than it does on the mourner, Molly Jensen. Although the audience may sympathize with her loss we do not necessarily share her dilemma of belief—we perceive that Sam has returned as a ghost and (presumably) root for Sam to convince her of his presence.[15] Nor does the film focus on the healing process that often occurs after the death of a loved one. (It does so only inadvertently, in the context of Sam's mission to warn Molly of impending danger.) The melodrama of Molly's grief is thus deflected not only by the dilemmas attendant to the male ghost, but also transferred onto a murder/revenge/embezzlement narrative. The problem is not so much, "Will Molly recover and make a new life?" but "Will Sam complete his mission—to save Molly and avenge his death?"

A similar tendency can be found in *Always,* which, while treating the problem of Dorinda's grief, nevertheless focuses more on Pete's mission and the effect of his actions on Dorinda then it does on Dorinda's attempts to cope with her loss. Likewise *Ghost Dad* focuses (perhaps predictably) more on Bill Cosby's antics rather than on the family's grief. While *Truly, Madly, Deeply* and *Kiss Me Goodbye* do concern the ability of women left behind to put their lives back together, these women are nevertheless acted upon by the ghosts in the masochistic alliance—as are the female characters in each of the other films. The problem in determining just whose story is being told can also be observed in occult horror films to which Carol Clover applies the term "dual focus narratives." In such films, although the story often seems to be about a demonically possessed female, for example, they are perhaps more concerned with a "male crisis."[16] Similarly, even though two of the above films focus more heavily on the female's experience, the masochistic tendencies of the male ghosts—and the masochistic alliances forged—provide a narrative and thematic dynamic that is strikingly similar in design and affect to other ghost films.

In *Ghost,* although Sam is clearly the protagonist of the film, his death and subsequent return as a ghost pose serious problems. If classical Hollywood protagonists are almost by definition goal-oriented, narrative agents, then Sam's narrative agency is seriously undermined by his inability to be seen or heard, and by his inability to manipulate the material world. In *Ghost,* Sam finds himself not in the classically male position of active, narrative agent, but instead in the classically female position of passivity and ineffectuality. He has desires and goals, but he cannot make them known to the world, or to the person to whom he needs to relate most, namely Molly. Remarking on the strange inactivity on the part of Sam's character, one film reviewer blamed the director, Jerry Zucker: "Mr. Zucker needlessly defuses much of what goes on between these two separated lovers by keeping Mr. Swayze on screen too much of the time, so that he's less like a ghost than an albatross in certain scenes. *Unable to communicate with the living or even react very much, he must simply sit by helplessly until they finish talking.*"[17]

Giving Up the Ghost

Far from being a directorial snafu, this helplessness is precisely what characterizes both the ghostly dilemma and the masochistic scenario that informs it. For what Sam experiences is not bad direction but a masochistic interlude—one that has repercussions throughout the film. It has everything to do with Sam's narrative trajectory, with the way in which he attempts to communicate, and with various thematic and structural features related to his ghostly presence. It is not just that Sam, as a character, undergoes a masochistic transformation, but that the figure of the ghost in general can be seen as a kind of pure embodiment of the masochistic aesthetic, one that can potentially play itself out in myriad ways but tends to be realized in certain culturally coded structural and thematic conventions.

Specifically, the Oedipal scenario associated with sadism in most Hollywood films is reversed in *Ghost* such that the maternal and the pre-Oedipal are celebrated at the expense of the paternal Symbolic. As Deleuze writes, "sadism stands for the active negation of the mother and the inflation of the father (who is placed above the law.)" But unlike the sadist, the masochist does not seek the approval of the father, but instead seeks to expel him and all that he represents, for "the function of the masochistic contract is to invest the mother-image with the symbolic power of the law."[18]

The glorification of the mother-image at the expense of the father becomes obvious in many ghost films through the exaltation of the occult and the mystical realms traditionally associated with the female.[19] In *Ghost,* an understanding or empathy for the feminine realm is precisely what the spiritual medium, Oda Mae, refers to as "the gift"—a sensitivity to mystical and intuitive spheres passed down through the women in her family: "My mother had it, and my mother's mother had it." It is likewise the intuitive or emotional realm to which Sam must aspire in order to regain the physical effectiveness necessary to save Molly and finally to communicate and facilitate the proper closure at the end of the film. Although the murder/revenge story line structures much of the narrative, providing deadlines and plot points crucial to the action and to the resolution, the film's resolution actually hinges on the solution of an important thematic problem posed at the beginning of the film. This problem underlies much of the surface conflict in the film and is central to the masochistic ghost-character itself. *Ghost* works through the problem of Sam's fundamental inability to communicate properly with Molly, thus problematizing the same difficulties of mistimed and misunderstood communication found in melodrama.

Early in the film, much is made of the fact that when Molly tells Sam that she loves him, he can only reply, "Ditto." Right before his death, Molly complains that Sam does not seem capable of actually saying that he loves her. Sam protests that he says it all the time:

Sam: What do you mean why don't I ever say it? I say it all the time! I feel like I. . . .
Molly: No, you don't, you say ditto and that's not the same.

If Sam has difficulty expressing himself while alive, this problem becomes even worse in the ghost state—he now can neither be seen nor heard by Molly. His status as a ghost thus becomes emblematic of their relationship prior to Sam's death, while the murder/embezzlement story is the vehicle by which to force a solution to the communication problem.

In this respect, *Ghost* bears a great deal of similarity to *Always* in which, like Sam, Pete, the protagonist, is unable to articulate his love for his girlfriend, Dorinda. At the beginning of the film, Dorinda tells Pete she loves him as they slow dance together.

Dorinda: I love you.
Pete: I know.
Dorinda: So tell me you love me. Please, please, please tell me, tell me, tell me, tell me. . . .
Pete: What, in front of all these people?!

Although Pete does eventually attempt to tell Dorinda he loves her right before his death, Dorinda is unable to hear him over the noise of an airplane engine—once again signaling the problem of faulty communication and the too-late. At the end of the film, however, Pete (like Sam) is finally allowed to say the words and correct the earlier imbalance of emotion and expression, achieving the "oneness" necessary to the romance but impossible in melodrama. However, the better part of both films is devoted to the ineffectual and faulty communication processes of the ghosts. In fact, the masochistic contracts undertaken by the ghosts in these two films largely concern vocal or verbal dilemmas of communication.

In *Always,* after Pete dies in a fiery airplane crash, an angel named Hap tells him that she is sending him back to help others, in particular a young firefighter named Ted. When Pete recalls his seemingly natural ability to fly planes while alive, Hap explains that he, like others, actually received outside help.

Hap: And you think you did all that by yourself?
Pete: Well, there was certainly nobody else up there with me.
Hap: There was, Pete. There was someone like you. And behind him there was someone else. . . . It's what flyers and piano players and everyone else count on. They reach for it, they pray for it. And quite often just when they need it most, they get it. It's breathed into them. It's what the word means. Spiritus. The di-

vine breath. Inspiration. . . . And now it's your turn to give it back. That's how the whole thing works.

To provide this "inspiration," Pete must speak into the ears of the living characters who hear him but believe the thoughts to be their own. When he first discovers that he is a ghost, Pete delights in murmuring insults to people who then respond physically to his remarks. He tells one man, "I think you're a pretty silly-looking guy. What do you think of that?" The man then looks at himself in a car mirror and walks away in disgust. Later Pete is able to persuade Dorinda to brush her hair away from her face by whispering in her ear. Although Pete's ability to cause others to do his bidding may at first glance seem sadistic, this interpretation of events is undercut by several factors. Unlike the sadist who focuses on physical force, the masochist has a peculiar relationship with words, which provide him with the special power of masochistic persuasion. For the masochist, "words are at their most powerful when they compel the body to repeat the movements they suggest, and 'the sensations communicated by the ear are the most enjoyable and the keenest impact.'"[20] The masochistic aesthetic does not so much concern itself with physical force but with the words which bind the actors into the masochistic contract—a subtle network of submission: "the masochist appears to be held by real chains . . . in fact he is bound by his word alone."[21] Furthermore, although Pete at first demonstrates the power of words, this power is soon turned back upon Pete himself, binding him in the masochistic alliance that is inextricably linked to his mission as a heavenly helper. For although Pete is only permitted to return to earth because he is basically a good man who will be able to help someone on earth (as Hap says, "we don't send back the other kind"), his mission has distinctly masochistic overtones.

Pete's mission to help Ted succeed as a flyer also includes helping Ted win Dorinda's heart and helping Dorinda reject himself. Hap implies that this is actually part of the "contract" of return several times when she hints, "There's more, you'll find out," when describing Pete's mission with Ted. The verbal element of the masochistic contract can thus be seen most clearly when it comes to Pete's personal desires and his relationship with Dorinda, for here Pete is completely unable to control the effect of his words, which consistently work against him. Although Pete does ultimately help Ted become a better firefighter and flyer, he is simultaneously unable to control the relationship developing between Ted and Dorinda, a budding love affair which causes Pete a great deal of anguish. When Pete tries to help Ted get involved with another woman whom he believes has a crush on Ted, Ted ends up using the lines Pete is feeding him to talk about Dorinda rather than wooing the girl in front of him.

Later, when Ted's plane makes an emergency landing, Pete and Ted find themselves in a ramshackle building inhabited by a hobo who, inexplicably, can hear Pete. Pete decides to use the old hobo as a mediator to facilitate his efforts to fix Ted up with the other woman—anyone other than his beloved Dorinda. But each time Pete speaks, the hobo utters only part of Pete's sentences or twists their meaning so that the message has completely the opposite effect than the one intended.

> Pete: Ted, listen to me.
> Old Man: Ted, listen to me!
> Ted [to old man]: How did you know my name?
> Pete: Who knows about crazy old hobos. Maybe they're like radio stations picking up voices from people who've gone off the air. So tune in, kid. This is one thing I really want to get through to you.
> Old Man: Through to you. . . .
> Pete: With *me* it was Dorinda.
> Old Man: Dorinda. . . .
> [Ted gasps as the old man says Dorinda's name.]
> Pete: When you meet the woman you love. . . .
> Old Man: The woman you love.
> Pete: Not Dorinda! The woman *he* loves!
> Old Man [to Ted]: Dorinda, the woman you love.
> Pete: After you're dead you can never go back to her.
> Old Man: Go back to her!
> Pete: You can never turn around.
> Old Man: Turn around!

Instead of encouraging Ted to take action with the other woman as he had intended, Pete ends up strengthening Ted's resolve to proclaim his love for Dorinda, the very thing Pete was unable to articulate while alive. Thus, although the ghost's return often helps reverse the pathos and tragedy associated with melodrama, it does so only to prolong the very process of miscommunication, which it seemed to have solved.

As in both *Ghost* and *Always,* in *Truly, Madly, Deeply* the ghost, Jamie, achieves the masochistic alliance through the verbal rejection supplied by Nina. Although Nina does not want Jamie to go, she finds her patience taxed when she returns home to find that Jamie and his ghost friends have taken over her bedroom.

> Jamie: Nina, you can't come home in the middle of the night and then complain I've got company.
> Nina: It's not the middle of the night! I don't know these people. I don't even know what period they're from. This is ridiculous!

Jamie: You could try talking to them.

Nina: I can't believe this is happening! I've got ghosts watching videos in my bedroom and I'm being accused—of what? What am I being accused of? Jamie, they're dead people! The rats have gone, now I'm infested with ghosts!

Jamie: There are eight or nine people in there, they're not doing you any harm. If you want to go to bed, they'll go. Just tell them. If you want me to go, just tell me.

At the end of this sequence, Jamie attempts to provoke her into saying what it is that he wants to hear: "If you want me to go, just tell me." In this scene Jamie uses his passivity as a ghostly haunter in an attempt to elicit an abusive verbal reaction from Nina. It is crucial that Jamie appear to be reasonable, even "helping" Nina, whereas he is, in fact, designing his own demise at her hands—or rather through her voice. "The masochistic hero appears to be educated and fashioned by the authoritarian woman whereas basically it is he who forms her, dresses her for the part and *prompts the harsh words she addresses to him. It is the victim who speaks through the mouth of his torturer without sparing himself.*"[22]

A similar process occurs in *Kiss Me Goodbye,* where Jolly himself never articulates the information necessary to make Kay rebuff him (the fact that Jolly played fast and loose with other women during their marriage). The revelations are finally prompted by a friend of Kay's who had an affair with Jolly and who pretends to confront him for Kay's sake—even though she cannot see or hear him. Meanwhile, Jolly gently needles Kay into remembering for herself that he really was a two-timing womanizer. Again, the rejection of the ghost must be finally made good by the woman, but is not brought about by force, but by the passive and indirect means of the masochistic process.

In *Ghost,* although Sam cannot be heard by Molly, he can be heard by Oda Mae, whom he then uses to relay words to Molly out of seemingly thin air. The fact that Oda Mae can hear him but Molly cannot has already been partly explained by the lack of communication established between Sam and Molly. This becomes representative of a classically troubled male/female relationship, in which the male has difficulty expressing emotion.[23] The fact that Oda Mae can hear him but not see him, however, is an interesting device. A common motif of the masochistic scenario is a mediating tactic in which love affairs are carried out via messages sent through a third party. "In Masoch's life as well as in his fiction, love affairs are always set in motion by anonymous letters, by the use of pseudonyms or by advertisements in newspapers."[24] Just as Pete uses the old man in *Always,* and Jolly uses Kay's friend in *Kiss Me Goodbye,* Oda Mae serves as a form of anonymous "media" (being a spiritual medium) when she relays the disembodied voice to Molly. The words then take on a life of their own through a distance brought about through such mediation. One of the "perverse" pleasures of masochism depends on a certain amount of distance between the masochist and the desired object. Sam uses Oda Mae as a mediator not only to extend the distance which is so desired in masochism, but also to formalize the process as required by the contractual process. The masochistic alliance in this case becomes the elaborate process by which Sam uses Oda Mae to communicate. The alliance with Oda Mae guarantees and highlights Sam's pain and ineffectuality, as he is helpless without her. He repeatedly cajoles Oda Mae to take part, and he must do so ultimately to convince Molly of his very presence. In the works of Masoch, the torturer is inevitably a woman and this process of persuading the female characters to form an alliance (in Oda's case an alliance of communication, in Molly's an alliance of belief) becomes central to the film.

Ghosts as Repetition and Delay in the Narrative Contract

The masochistic ineffectuality attendant to the ghostly contract relates equally to the masochistic emphasis on delay and to a type of repetition which is anathema to sadism. The masochistic aesthetic shifts emphasis away from the desire for an ending and toward the process and pleasure in delay. Whereas Brooks, for example, sees repetition in narrative as a delaying tactic following a path of mastery and Sadian acceleration leading to the end, masochistic repetition is of a different nature. "Repetition does occur in masochism, but it is totally different from sadistic repetition: in Sade it is a function of acceleration and condensation and in Masoch it is characterized by the 'frozen' quality and the suspense."[25] The type of repetition associated with the ghost is a cyclical process which can be seen in the figure of the ghost itself, who represents a repetition of its own life and thereby delays its own mortal end. Such repetition may also occur as a tactic in the masochistic contract, where cyclical repetition equals a kind of waiting.

In *Ghost,* for example, Sam must convince Oda Mae to help him, as she is reluctant to do so. In his initial attempt to convince her to be his mediator, Sam essentially waits her out by singing an endlessly repeating song. The song's structure adheres to the cyclical repetition associated with masochism, as opposed to the goal-oriented repetition of sadism. Sam merely places himself comfortably in an armchair and sings the incessant song until Oda Mae submits to the alliance: "I'm Henry the Eighth I am. . . . Second verse, same as the First. . . . I'm Henry the Eighth I am. . . . Second verse same as the First," and so on. Just as the song's purpose and content is the same as its structure—endless or indefinite repetition—so the ghost's purpose and content are the same as its structure—indefinite repetition of its life and of the difficult communication process.

In *Truly, Madly, Deeply,* the ghost accomplishes his haunting, in part, by hanging around with other ghosts and watching old videos. He too, in a sense, waits Nina out as a key method of his own rejection. Unlike many ghosts who try to scare away the inhabitants of a house by using their ghostly powers of invisibility (e.g., *Beetlejuice*), Jamie undertakes the reverse, so that he is the one driven away. In this "reverse haunting," Jamie need not resort to ghostly hijinks to produce the result (although he often startles Nina by showing up unexpectedly—in the bathroom, bed, etc.). Instead, Jamie drives Nina crazy by crowding the apartment with annoying couch potato ghosts. This again is consistent with a masochistic aesthetic in which waiting, duration, and passivity predominate. That the ghosts barely interact with Nina is hardly surprising because it is enough to simply "wait her out." Indeed, "formally speaking, masochism is a state of waiting; the masochist experiences waiting in its pure form."[26]

The ghostly return provides delay within the narrative trajectory of the character or protagonist and is part of the masochistic ghost's internal contract. But this delay also pertains to the contract between the film viewer and the film, providing the pleasure of delay associated with the masochistic aesthetic. The viewer takes pleasure in the process of delay via the ineffectuality of the ghost and the obstacles he must overcome: "The spectator suffers with the characters and braves plot predicaments because, like the masochist, he/she knows the 'painful' experiences are based upon a contract promising pleasure."[27] Through its ineffectuality and difficulties in communication, the ghost thus provides the diegetic delay necessary to the characters' masochistic fantasies, and also becomes a particularly apt narrative device to institute the delay necessary to the audience's narrative pleasure.

If masochistic repetition can help explain a type of pleasure made possible both within and beyond the narrative trajectory, it also helps to explain two other types of repetition associated with ghost films. According to exit polls, many viewers of the film *Ghost* returned to see the film again and again, indicating a desire to repeat the fantasy experience provided by the film.[28] That viewers return to see films again and again indicates that the pleasure taken does not revolve solely around the catharsis associated with the end of the film, but also lies in the middle portions of narrative and filmic experience. In his book *Hollywood Genres,* Thomas Schatz speaks of genre films as those films produced with the knowledge of their generic intent—as virtual "contracts" between the filmmaker and the audience. The masochistic contract agreed to by film ghosts is in many ways like that which the viewer agrees to when sitting down to experience a film.

The blending of generic elements in *Ghost* may have caused a confusion in terms of generic expectations. This may account for the consternation generated by the mystery plot, whose function has been misunderstood by popular critics. For example, many reviewers criticized the film for its poorly constructed mystery plot. Janet Maslin lamented the fact that the identity of the villain in *Ghost* was too transparent and that the outcome of the mystery was too obvious: "He [Sam] discovers a terrible secret about a colleague, even though the audience is already miles ahead of him."[29] The masochistic aesthetic makes it clear that the mystery aspect of the story (i.e., solving the mystery) is not central to the viewer's enjoyment. What is central is the process of the masochistic fantasy, which becomes a significant source of pleasure for the viewer who desires to repeat the experience associated with relinquishing control to the narrative.

Many current ghost films either are avowed remakes of older films or explicitly draw on or make reference to these films. Although *Ghost* was not a remake per se, many reviewers noted its relation to previous ghost films, particularly those which originally appeared in the 1930s and 1940s. One writer argued, "The story has that edge of old movie familiarity that makes audiences comfortable right away; we feel that we've seen it before, even if we haven't, and we're ready to enjoy it again."[30] Ghost films take part in a pattern of repetition in which certain popular fantasies are revisited, not just by repeat viewings, but by repetitions of the same stories. In addition, remakes—like ghosts—revisit and work through particular fantasy scenarios again and again. In attempting to explain the appeal of ghost films, Dana Parsons writes, "People want to know there is something out there, that it's not over when it's over."[31] While on the diegetic level ghosts reflect the sentiment that "it's not over when it's over," on the extradiegetic level, ghost films reflect this same sentiment by being consumed repeatedly, and furthermore, by repeating themselves through the process of explicit or implicit remakes. In this sense, just as remakes are like returning ghosts, ghosts are likewise similar to "remakes" of individual characters or subjects. Thus the masochistic aesthetic can be applied to the ghost as a figure of waiting, repetition, and delay and to the way in which such tendencies are mimicked in the viewer's pleasure of the diegetic narrative. As the word "haunt" means "to visit often; to frequent," and "to recur continually," the very concept of the ghost is thus synonymous with repetition as the ghost recurs continually as a simulacrum of its former self. Similarly, film viewers "visit often" in their repeat viewing of films and in their consumption of remakes.

The analogy between the masochistic ghost and the masochistic viewer can be further extended to the way in which ghosts relate to the masochistic process of film viewing, an activity that requires a kind of passivity and distance. Passivity in the masochistic aesthetic does not preclude a range of interpretations by the viewer, who is not merely an empty vessel to be filled with ideas dictated by the film. Scholars threw out the notion of passive viewership in the process of theorizing that meaning is generated through an interaction between viewer and text.[32] Passivity within the masochistic aesthetic does not preclude interaction and negotiation between the viewer and the film. On the contrary, masochistic passivity merely facilitates a particular kind of interaction. The masochistic scenario is linked to the notion of fantasy as a space of dilatory and shifting pleasure which provides ample space for active spectatorship and varied identificatory positions.

Spectating Specters in the Masochistic Scenario

Though not all ghosts are wholly invisible, the majority are invisible at some point in the film. These ghosts can neither make their desires known, nor be acknowledged visually by the world. Invisibility is a double-edged sword, however. Although preventing ghosts from achieving certain goals, invisibility would also seem to afford the ghost a great deal of power. This power is most readily apparent when it permits the invisible person to eavesdrop, visually and aurally. Invisibility is a mark of ineffectiveness (particularly when part of an explicitly masochistic scenario), but it also facilitates voyeurism (usually associated with sadism) and eavesdropping (associated with an auditory regime favoring the male). In the previous chapter, I considered a version of psychoanalytic film theory which posits that the film viewer is conceived of as a male scopophilic, whose power to look is part of a sadistic regime stemming from castration anxiety—an anxiety that the presence of women provokes by reminding the viewer of the possibility of lack. In his influential essay on viewer identification, Christian Metz links the distance created by the film and the viewer to an inherently sadistic brand of voyeurism.[33] The film viewer is made to feel omniscient and omnipotent from his privileged vantage point.

Invisible characters mimic this process of viewing, illustrating an impulse realized, for example, in *The Invisible Man,* where the protagonist uses his invisibility for sadistic purposes. But invisibility itself need not be necessarily sadistic. When invisibility is combined with the ghostly state, the hero's gaze may not always be exerted from a position of power. And, like film viewers, ghosts frequently watch from a distance and cannot control events. Film viewers are more like ineffectual ghosts than invisible sadists— the distance is entirely masochistic as viewers watch but cannot control the events at hand.

A comparison of *The Invisible Man* to its loose remake, *Memoirs of an Invisible Man* (1992), reveals two versions of invisibility. Instead of using invisibility as the vehicle for the fulfillment of a goal, in the later film invisibility becomes the cause of delay in the narrative resolution. The latter updates the original invisible man scenario, and in the process reformulates the nature of the protagonist's invisibility to reflect a masochistic sensibility. Unlike the protagonist in the earlier movie, Nick Halloway does not engineer his invisible state, but is instead rendered invisible by a freak accident. Although he remains corporeally solid, he cannot be acknowledged by the rest of the world. To further complicate problems, he wants desperately to become visible, but he is chased by maniacal CIA operatives who are responsible for his condition. If he does manage to be acknowledged, he risks giving himself away. If caught, he may be killed, subjected to mad-science experiments, or enslaved as a secret invisible spy for the government. Here, the film harkens back to the earlier film, in which Griffin hopes to sell his secret to other countries for the formation of invisible armies. But in this case, Nick's invisibility will be the cause of his subjugation by others, rather than the vehicle for omnipotent power.

To further complicate matters, Nick has met the woman of his dreams just hours before the accident. Though initially portrayed as a shallow philanderer, Nick finds that Alice might be his true love. Once invisible, however, it is "too late" and his prospects for settling down seem hopeless. While attempting to elude his captors, Nick struggles just to function as a normal person (eating, getting a cab, etc.). Exhausted by his efforts, he falls asleep and dreams that he is "recognized" by everyone, including beautiful women who cluster around him. He is somewhat of a celebrity, and is applauded for his piano playing and tennis victories. When he encounters Alice in sexy lingerie, however, he suddenly realizes that he is naked and visible, but that his private parts have disappeared. The dream illustrates his desires to be recognized as a sexually potent, powerful man while revealing that his invisible state emasculates him and thwarts his desires. Eventually, Nick escapes his pursuers and consummates a relationship with Alice, but he spends the majority of the movie in an extended masochistic interlude.[34]

Masochistic ghosts mimic the role of the film viewer even in cases where the characters are not invisible, a tendency further underscoring the pervasiveness of the analogy. The similarity between ghosts and film viewers is suggested in several films. For example, the masochistic contract between film viewers is parodied in *Truly, Madly, Deeply,* where Jamie invites a horde of male ghosts over to Nina's house as part of the masochistic alliance in which he will eventually be asked to leave. This is "reverse haunting," where, instead of trying to drive the inhabitants out of the house, the ghost causes himself to be driven away. Much to Nina's chagrin, every time she comes home from work she finds a room full of shivering, handkerchief-wielding ghosts huddled around the television watching old movies in the dark.[35] The ghosts seem to mimic doubly the process of distance in which film viewers see but cannot be seen and derive pleasure from fantasy scenes that are distant and beyond influence. The ghost and viewer alike "must comprehend the images, but the images cannot be controlled."[36] At the end of *Truly, Madly, Deeply,* after Nina has finally rejected Jamie and decided to date her new friend Mark, the final scene shows Jamie and his fellow ghosts watching Nina and Mark from behind a window. The masochistic alliance has been concluded and the ghosts pat Jamie on the back to congratulate him on his success. A bluish light on their faces mimics the earlier light from the television screen, while the window separates them from Nina, recalling Jamie's earlier description of his experiences after death: "Maybe I didn't die properly, maybe that's why I can come back. . . . It was like walking behind a glass wall."

While invisible and incorporeal ghosts all share the tendency to observe events from a distance without benefit of control, the obvious reflexive qualities of distance, passivity, and waiting can also be seen in other films concerning the afterlife. In *Scrooged* (1988) (as in Dickens's *A Christmas Carol*), the protagonist witnesses scenes from his past life he cannot control. Although he desperately wants to make contact and interact with the participants, he is told that he can have no effect on the scenes before him, which are then likened to television "re-runs."[37] In *Defending Your Life* (1991), Daniel Miller dies in a car accident and finds himself in a kind of purgatory where he must defend his former life on earth. Daniel finds himself at the mercy of a trial-like process in which he is forced to watch scenes from his life as if they were scenes in a movie. The room is thus part courtroom, part movie theater. While none of the scenes is to Daniel's liking, he is unable to change the narrative and must watch in agony as it unfolds.

Hearts and Souls (1992) is a film that displays many of the themes and issues already discussed, but does so in a slightly more complicated way. This film centers around four characters, each of whom will suffer his or her own version of the too-late after dying in a bus accident. Milo wishes he could return some valuable stamps he previously stole from a child. He is about to do so, vowing then to "go straight," when he dies in the accident. He is too late. Winthrop wishes to be a singer but is unable, year after year, to gather enough courage to face the audition process. His stage fright causes him to run from yet another audition just before the accident; again, too late. Julia is a loving mother who heads a fatherless family. Her regret is that she is unable to make sure that her children are raised properly, particularly her son Billy, for whom she has an intense affection. Finally, Penny and her boyfriend, John, provide a reversal of the male/female miscommunication process described above. Here Penny, not the boyfriend, is unable to commit or proclaim her love. Here the male waits and waits, only to be disappointed one more time. At the last minute, Penny changes her mind and rushes after

John only to be killed in the bus accident. Thus as a ghost, Penny's dilemma is identical to those of the male characters already described. Although it is too late to express her love, Penny discovers later in the film that she will be given a chance to solve this problem. This gender reversal is ultimately re-reversed through a complicated process involving the corporeal protagonist of the film, Thomas.

After dying and turning into ghosts, the four characters are sucked into the body of a baby boy just born in a nearby car (the couple are on the way to the hospital when their car collides with the bus). The film then cuts to the boy, Thomas, as a toddler who can see and hear the four ghosts even though nobody else can. As might be expected, the ghosts are unable to affect their physical surroundings and are prevented from leaving Thomas's immediate area by an invisible force field. Furthermore, whenever Thomas moves, the ghosts are dragged along so that they are always near him. As with other ghosts, the four characters are supposed to resolve the problem created by the too-late but are prevented from doing so because of their bondage to Thomas. By the end of the film, they learn that they were supposed to ask Thomas to help them resolve their personal issues so that they can move on. Unfortunately, there has been another type of miscommunication in that no one has told them about this cosmic plan. Instead, they suffer for years not knowing why they are bound to Thomas and wondering if they might really be in hell. Early in the film they decide to spare Thomas the humiliation of being haunted and at a young age they decide to become invisible and inaudible to him. When the bus-driving angel discovers (too-late) that they have not been informed of the system but have been left in limbo for years, he bends the rules to give them a second chance. However, they are given only a limited amount of time to fulfill their missions. This not only constitutes the deadline which frames the narrative trajectory, but as with other ghosts, it comprises part of the requisite masochistic contract. When the ghosts finally learn that they are supposed to use Thomas to set their lives right, they must persuade him that they are real and that he must help them. Just as with other ghosts, these characters return as ghosts to correct the too-late only to masochistically prolong the problem precisely because they are ghosts. Thus the majority of the ghosts' experience within the film consists of prolonging the narrative trajectory, which will be terminated upon the completion of their mission.

Although Thomas does not become a ghost, he is the protagonist of a story that involves him in the problem of miscommunication and the too-late in a convoluted but substantial way. When the film cuts to Thomas as a young adult, he is portrayed as a wheeler-dealer with little heart. He coolly threatens his business clients with bankruptcy and climbs the corporate ladder with little thought as to whom he has ruined along the way. Despite repeated encouragement, Thomas is unable to commit to his girlfriend, Anne, and is unable to express his feelings for her. The ghosts thus become the frustrated audience to scenes in which Thomas is unable to further his romantic relationship. The ghosts complicate his problems by persuading him to help with their various missions. In doing so, Thomas becomes involved in situations that are difficult to explain to the evermore frustrated Anne and thus exacerbate the communication problem. Although Thomas creates the initial problem, the ghosts inadvertently assist him in driving Anne away. (By becoming invisible and inaudible to him as a child, they cause him to feel abandoned. As Thomas explains in the final scene, the fear of losing loved ones has caused his emotional distance.) Soon, as with Penny's boyfriend, Anne finally tires of waiting for Thomas and drives off.

At the end of the film Milo, Winthrop, and Julia are all able to resolve their problems just before being whisked away by the cosmic bus driver. Penny's resolution is thwarted, however, when she discovers that her boyfriend has died during the time that she was bound to Thomas. She will now never be able to express her love for him. As it turns out, however, the resolution to her personal narrative has nothing to do with her own life, but Thomas's instead. She witnesses Thomas mend the faulty communication process with Anne.

> Penny: Thomas, it's you!
> Thomas: What's me?
> Penny: You and Anne. That's what I'm supposed to do. . . . I made the same mistake with John that you're making with Anne. I pushed him away, I kept him at arm's length and finally he just left. Only you've got the chance to fix it.
> Thomas: No, see Penny this isn't about me.
> Penny: Yes it is. I've watched you all these years. You know how painful it is to know who you really are and watch you keep it hidden from people?
> Thomas: I don't hide. I protect myself. I'm cautious.
> Penny: You're so afraid of being hurt you're gonna end up all alone. It doesn't matter if she says yes or no. Don't let her go without telling her how you really feel. Promise me you're gonna go to her. Promise me you're gonna live the life that I didn't get to live.

While simultaneously appealing to the ghostly aesthetic of taking pleasure from viewing at a distance, the film now shifts the communication resolution to the male protagonist who makes good in the final scene by expressing his love to Anne. The closure to the story thus hinges on a shifting of the female's too-late problem to the male protagonist, thus mimicking the dilemma described in *Ghost* and other films and recalling a tactic described by Clover in her discussion of dual-focus narratives.[38] Furthermore, the device of the ghost once again emphasizes the masochistic pleasure in witnessing (but not participating directly in) a dramatic and narrative process—first as the frustrated audience to the earlier miscommunication and later to the resolution. In expressing the twofold process of frustration and pleasure gleaned from witnessing the protagonist's life, the ghost is emblematic of the process experienced by the film viewer, who watches a film which (to paraphrase Penny) "promises to live a life we can't live" and whose narrative trajectory is dominated by the painful prolongation of the miscommunication dilemma.

The ghost's process of mastering communication is essentially masochistic in its passivity and in its role as a device of subject-humiliation and of narrative delay and distance. The process is not mere ineffectuality, however; the distance created by film ghosts and experienced by film viewers is part of the very structure of fantasy, one which pertains to the desire to glorify the mother and expel the father.

Chapter 3

Accessing the Feminine/Maternal

While the inability to communicate makes the ghost a humiliated and impotent subject and becomes a delaying tactic in the narrative, it also illuminates another important element of the masochistic fantasy. The masochist seeks to expel the father and glorify the mother, a drive apparent in many ghost films through an emphasis on voice, music, domestic issues, and other symbolic arenas traditionally associated with the feminine. Whereas horror films attempt to use fear and horror to map sexual difference, comedy ghost films draw on the same sets of stereotypes to promote a fantasy of sexual sameness. While horror films associate abject terror with the mother and transfer this terror to all things female, ghost films deny or refute this association. Instead ghost films engage in a masochistic process whereby the father is vilified and blamed for standing in the way of the desired oneness.

Masochistic Fantasy

To understand why the masochist seeks to glorify the mother at the expense of the father it will be useful to explore further the nature of fantasy. The link between fantasy as a genre and fantasy as a psychoanalytic concept can be made by drawing on the work of Laplanche and Pontalis, who consider fantasy a "framework" or "structure" in which desire may be engaged. Thus, instead of seeing fantasy as the object of desire, it is instead characterized as the setting or mise-en-scène of desire. Fantasy originates in an autoerotic moment in which the child lacks the desired object (e.g., the mother's breast). However, at some point in its development, the child becomes capable of compensating for this lack by re-creating the satisfaction of desire as a hallucinatory experience: "The origin of fantasy would lie in the hallucinatory satisfaction of desire; in the absence of the real object, the infant reproduces the experience of the original satisfaction in a hallucinated form."[1] For example, an infant may engage in a sucking motion that mimics the suckling of the real—but now absent—breast. The child is now able to re-create fulfillment in a fantasized form. The child's first fantasy experience is one in which the real object of desire is transferred to a hallucinated object, which is then conjured up through acting out the process that originally fulfilled the desire.

Because fantasy depends on a lack, it is intimately linked to disavowal, a term which takes on slightly different connotations depending on whether it is framed within the sadistic/Oedipal theories of Mulvey and others, or reformulated in terms of a pre-Oedipal dilemma. The proponents of the traditional model would argue that the child disavows the mother's anatomical lack (lack of penis) resulting in the fetishistic glorification of the mother—or failing that—in her vilification. Disavowal in this model is seen merely as a mechanism to cover over knowledge of the mother's imputed inferiority.

By contrast, proponents of the pre-Oedipal masochistic scenario associate disavowal with the loss suffered through the lack of the mother's presence—not her anatomical lack. The process of disavowing the loss of the mother's plenitude becomes synonymous with the origin of fantasy as defined above. Furthermore, the glorification of the mother in the masochistic aesthetic is tied to this same disavowal of the loss of the mother: "Rather than relegating the woman to a position of lack, it exalts her to an idealized wholeness imitated in the son's fetishistic wish to restore identification and oneness with her."[2] Masochism is thereby linked with fantasy through the process of disavowal. As Laplanche observes, "fantasy . . . is thus intimately related, in its origin, to the emergence of the masochistic sexual drive."[3] Because fantasy arises in response to the loss of the mother, it is linked to a utopian desire that precedes the Oedipal interdiction. D. N. Rodowick notes that "the logic of phantasy derives from the simultaneous and paradoxical expression of desire and its interdiction. The utopia expressed in phantasy life, regardless of the sexual identification of the subject, is for a sexual world ungoverned by the constraints of phallic desire."[4] Thus fantasy is, by definition, linked to masochism in its renunciation of the law of the father and return to the utopian world of pre-Oedipal plenitude.

Unlike sadism, which seeks mastery and then destruction of the object, masochism employs disavowal to displace a certain recognition about the object, a process which occurs, for example, in fetishism.[5] The sadist seeks absolute negation (death); the masochist "does not believe in negating or destroying the world nor in idealizing it: what he does is to disavow and thus to suspend it, in order to secure an ideal which is itself suspended in fantasy."[6] Masochism is intimately linked to the psychoanalytic conception of fantasy through the process of disavowal, providing a compelling link between the ghost as a generic fantasy figure and the ghost as a "phantasy" in the psychoanalytic sense. At the heart of the masochistic aesthetic is an emphasis on delay, suspense, and distance—all of which is seen in abundance in the delay caused by the ghost's transitional and ineffectual status as it attempts to communicate with the living. Just as the masochist suspends belief through fantasy, the ghost is suspended both temporally (through its repetition) and spatially (through its incorporeality).

Although the "suspension" of the ghost is often physical due to the ghost's immaterial nature, it also concerns the nature of the fantasy itself. Fantasy requires the kind of disavowal known so often to film viewers as the "willing suspension of disbelief," a phrase reflected in the advertising slogan for the film *Ghost,* whose marketing approach was summed up in one word: "Believe." The disavowal necessary to accept the ghost is similar to the disavowal necessary to the masochistic fantasy (indeed to all fantasy), a disavowal also necessary to the film viewer's pleasure. The connection between the disavowal associated with ghosts and that associated with film viewing was not lost on the makers of the film. When asked what the viewer was to "believe" in (Lazarus? Casper? Patrick Swayze? Eternal Life?), screenwriter Bruce Joel Rubin and director Jerry Zucker replied, "Believe in a movie."[7]

Whereas all films require a certain disavowal on the part of the viewer ("I know it's not real, but, . . ."), the suspension and distance desired in masochism makes the connection between fantasy and ghosts particularly compelling. Contrasting the focus on distance with the opposite tendencies in neighboring genres reveals that melodrama and horror genres provoke a certain over-identification and closeness (resulting in the viewer's physical reactions) as well as an emphasis on bodily excesses, while comedy ghost films center around a fantasy of distance and an almost literal suspension of the subject.

Corpus Delicti

Ghost films bear resemblance to women's melodramas in that both types of films address problems of death, miscommunication, and a temporal thematic known as the too-late, a problem which the ghost returns to address. Linda Williams compares the problem of the too-late to the temporal schematas employed by other "body genres," a term she borrows from Carol Clover to describe film genres that both represent and provoke reactions from the human body, notably pornography, horror, and melodrama. Both Doane and Williams argue that such emotional excess is often characterized by an over-involvement of the spectator to the point that the spectator mimics the diegetic excess. Thus, a successful pornographic film is intended to arouse the viewer to the point of orgasm, a horror film should result in the audience's screams, and melodrama should evoke tears.[8]

The overwhelming pathos in the woman's melodrama is portrayed by the excessive bodily fluids of the weeping woman—an excess of tears. What is interesting here is that although melodramas are often known as "weepies," many ghost films first elicit but then stem the tide of tears they have created. Although several films contain scenes of crying widows, *Truly, Madly, Deeply* provides a textbook case by focusing intensively on the grief of the female protagonist.[9] In the beginning of the film Nina mourns the loss of her boyfriend Jamie. At several points, usually in sessions with her analyst, Nina becomes overwhelmed by grief and bursts into uncontrollable tears. As she attempts to describe her difficulties in facing the loss of her loved one, Nina's grief becomes almost palpable—the emotions are intense, excessive, and powerfully realistic—despite the fact that the character being mourned is (so far) absent from the diegesis. The effect stems not so much from who is lost, but merely that there has been a loss. As noted, the tragedy and tears of melodrama are attributed to a temporal thematic in which a slippage occurs between desire and its object, thus suggesting that the tears are the direct result of the temporal too-late.[10] In the process of transforming the too-late, thus revising the classic melodramatic trajectory, the ghost thereby stems the flood of tears evoked by tragedy and mistiming. The bodily excess found in melodrama is obviated in these films by the return of the ghost which, usually lacking a solid "body," opposes itself to the excesses found in all "body-genres." Thus, in reversing the pathos of the too-late, ghost films not only dry up the tears, but oppose themselves to the over-identification that produces bodily reactions in the audience.

In the "body genre" of horror, binary oppositions are used to solidify the feminine gender as monstrous or Other, which may result in either the glorification or vilification of women. In the primal scene, the child initially associates its newfound subjecthood in the Symbolic with a renunciation of that which preceded it, particularly that which is linked to the mother. In this process, certain bodily functions and parts become vilified as a way of distancing them from the Symbolic realm. That which is rejected can be characterized as the "abject."[11] Whereas the Other (Symbolic) is necessary to define the subject, the abject now takes on the role of Other, an expulsion of all that seems alien and simultaneously serves to mark the boundaries of subjecthood. Lacan coined the phrase *objet petit a* to refer to that which is rejected.[12] The *objet a* includes blood, feces, mother's milk and other body fluids and parts that the child originally did not distinguish as Other. By relinquishing items originally thought to be part of the self, the child begins to attain a recognition of its separateness from these things and of its separateness from others. At the same time, however, since the expelled parts are so much a part of the child, feelings about this loss become highly ambivalent and amount to a kind of castration. The expelled objects now may come to be vilified as Other, and this type of vilification is signaled as the horrific in the horror film.

Although the horror film preys upon the disgust and horror for bodily secretions associated with the engulfing mother, the horror film does not create this association (although it may perpetuate it). The process whereby the mother becomes associated with the abject is a product of the Oedipal phase in which the father comes to represent valuable autonomy and the mother comes to represent that which the child must relinquish in order to attain subjecthood. In other words, the Oedipal scenario pits the mother against the father in the attainment of subjecthood. In upholding and mapping sexual difference, horror films portray motherhood and femininity as the horrific Other which must be vanquished for the child to remain separate. The conflation of the maternal and the feminine in these films is the result of a transference from the original knowledge that the mother is Other and different, to the socialized roles which stem from sexual difference. The male child's sense of masculinity and selfhood depend upon repudiating the mother, and hence all things associated with her.[13]

Comedy ghost films oppose themselves to horror films with regard to death and the concept of the abject, which defines the boundary between life and death, between meaning and the collapse of meaning. Marking the other side of bio-cultural boundaries, the abject represents all that is anathema, loathsome, and threatening to the living subject. The corpse becomes the ultimate in abject and hence a common figure in the horror film, which focuses precisely on the borders between the realm of living and that "other" realm which must constantly be expelled. "The ultimate in abjection is the corpse. The body protects itself from bodily wastes such as . . . blood, urine and pus by ejecting these substances just as it expels food that, for whatever reason, the subject finds loathsome. The body extricates itself from them and from the place where they fall, so that it might continue to live."[14] The many horror films that revel in graphic displays of bloody excess, as well as the popular "zombie" films (e.g., *Night of the Living Dead*), play on the abject as a threat to the symbolic order.

While many horror films focus on the abject nature of death through "undead" zombies and vampires, comedy ghost films present an inverse version of the "undead." The corpse of the horror film is abject because it lacks precisely what the returning dead possess in ghost films—a soul. The corpse "signifies one of the most basic forms of pollution—the body without a soul. As a form of waste it represents the opposite of the spiritual, the religious symbolic."[15] But in ghost comedy films, the abject is elided, and the *objet a* retains its status as a fantasy object of an impossible but urgent desire. In ghost comedies the figure of the ghost rejects the abject corpse as a thematic of death, and instead plies the possibilities of connecting across forbidden boundaries by erasing, expelling, or disavowing the abject.

Although ghost films portray the aftermath of death through the simulacrum of a body, the abject horror usually associated with dead bodies is either avoided or displaced in ghost comedy films. For example, in *Kiss Me Goodbye,* reference to the abject body is used only as a tactic of comparison to the otherwise incorporeal ghost. Here, Kay's mother unfavorably compares Kay's new fiancé, Rupert, to her dead husband, Jolly. Whereas Jolly's reappearance as a ghost and his career as a singer and dancer/choreographer all evoke spirit and soul, Kay's mother condemns the Egyptologist Rupert for his association with the abject: "He scrapes in the ground for dead people; he's a grave digger." In this film, as in most of the other films that contain a non-corporeal spirit character, the abject qualities associated with the bodily corpse are glossed over and replaced by an idealized version of the body, one physically resembling the living body but representing the non-material "spirit" of the individual.

In *Truly, Madly, Deeply* the abject is erased by simply retaining the living soul inside of the body of the dead man.[16] But this erasure is also marked by the expulsion of a kind of abject house-haunting, which in the beginning of the film takes the form of rodent infestation and a domestic decrepitude signaled by broken structures (doors, foundation) and brown tap water—a water supply polluted by rusting pipes, or worse. The rats and the brown water that plague Nina's house invoke precisely that which is abject: decay, infection, and disease. Although at the beginning of the film, Nina's house shows all the signs of abject decay, it is finally Jamie's appearance as a ghost that coincides with the expulsion of the abject through the simultaneous disappearance of the rats. As Jamie explains to Nina, "the rats are terrified of ghosts." Just as the cultural rejection of the abject is signaled by the terror so often evoked by gory bodies in horror films, the ghosts in these films quite clearly reject the terror associated with the abject. In these films, the ghost is anathema to the abject, which instead is often expelled, displaced or disavowed.

In *Ghost,* the abject is also displaced onto other characters. The abject is displaced away from the site of Sam's bodily death and comes to reside instead in the evil characters of Carl and Willy. For as Barbara Creed notes, the abject also concerns the social realm "where the individual fails to respect the law and where the individual is a hypocrite, a liar, a traitor."[17] The traitorous friend Carl is clearly all three of these things, while Sam by comparison is portrayed throughout the film as "good." In *Ghost,* the abject is transferred away from the dead body—as a spirit Sam sheds his abject corporeal self—to the immoral and treacherous qualities of an opponent who must be battled and ultimately excised. "Any crime, because it draws attention to the fragility of the law, is abject, but premeditated crime, cunning murder, hypocritical revenge are even more so because they heighten the display of such fragility. He who denies morality is not abject; there can be grandeur in amorality. . . . Abjection, on the other hand, is immoral, sinister, scheming, and shady."[18] The narrative struggle in *Ghost* hovers on the edges of the abject dilemma, which is characterized by a threat to the symbolic order, but takes a completely different turn than that of the horror film.

The foray into the occult, embodied by Sam and accessed by Oda Mae, introduces a fantasy scenario representing a return to the realm of the maternal—a return to the pre-Oedipal which, like the abject, threatens the Symbolic as defined in Oedipal terms. However, the threat of the horror film is not felt in these films. The ghost takes part in a masochistic scenario in which the expulsion of the Symbolic is desired, since the return to the pre-Oedipal celebrates the maternal and expels the father. So whereas horror films may map sexual difference through their emphasis on femininity as monstrous, ghost comedy films seek to overcome sexual difference by glorifying the feminine and the maternal. This celebration of maternal and the feminine is also part and parcel of the desire to vilify and reject the father. In essence, the male masochist's desire to be rebuffed and denigrated stems not from a lack of self-esteem—as might be posited for female masochism[19]—but from the male's identification with the too-powerful and hence guilty father. One of the ways in which the guilty father is both invoked and rejected is through the aforementioned difficulties of communication—difficulties that often stand between the male ghosts and their female companions.

Emotion

As noted, the ghost's problem of communication and physical ineffectiveness is addressed through a masochistic process focusing on the feminine realm. In *Ghost,* the murder/embezzlement storyline overlays a problem of faulty communication between Sam and Molly. (Sam is unable to articulate his love for Molly at the beginning of the film.) However, even though saving Molly from evildoers makes it necessary for Sam to communicate with Molly, it does not enable him to do so. Sam must first find the means to do so—through a spiritual medium and through his eventual mastering of the physical world. The various ways in which Sam accomplishes his mission are particularly illustrative of the masochistic dilemma and of the desire to access the feminine.

After having been shot and killed by a mugger, Sam becomes a ghost and realizes almost immediately that he is unable to have any effect on his physical surroundings. His inabilities are made most clear in a scene where the mugger, Willy, enters Molly and Sam's apartment to steal Sam's little black book (the original intent of the mugging). Sam's attempts to warn Molly of the intruder's presence are useless and his attempts to stop the intruder are futile because he lacks substance: when Sam throws himself at Willy, his body falls right through the prowler to the floor. Later, when Sam meets a tortured soul on the subway, he discovers that this ghost has the ability to move physical objects through sheer "will power." Sam remains physically impotent until one day, in a fit of anger and jealousy, he knocks a picture over in Molly's apartment. In this scene, Sam has already discovered that his former friend Carl is responsible for his death. As Carl tries to seduce Molly, Sam throws his body at them to prevent a kiss and inadvertently knocks a picture off the table. Unable to repeat this performance, but having realized he is on to something, Sam returns to the subway. Here, he pressures the subway ghost to instruct him in physical effectuality. The ghost reminds him that they have no substance and that therefore trying to move objects with arms and fingers is bound to fail. A different tactic is necessary. The secret is to focus: "You gotta take all your emotions, all your anger, all your love, all your hate and push it way down here into the pit of your stomach and then let it explode like a reactor. Pow!" Only after Sam finally learns to tap into his emotions is he, too, able to manipulate the physical world.

The focus on emotion and Sam's initial inability to express it becomes a key problem of the film, reflecting a tension that stems from and is reflected by gendered identities under the classic Oedipal configuration. Although the equation of emotion with femininity is a well-worn stereotype, male difficulty with emotional expression is often understood to be a side effect of male gender formation under patriarchy. Jonathan Rutherford writes about just such a problem, quoting an article in *Brothers Against Sexism,* a magazine devoted to exploring masculinity in relation to feminism. "One men's group identified the missing element of emotion from their lives: 'As men in the "Men's Movement" we recognize that we have to retrace our steps and rediscover in ourselves those traits that we have called "feminine" ... passivity, warmth, intuition, love, EMOTION.'"[20] Similarly, in *Ghost,* Sam returns from death to "retrace his steps" and correct this failing. It is not just a problem of feeling but also of expressing emotion. The male subject lacks the language to express emotion and thus also lacks access to the emotional realm. The problem occurs because the male is exhorted to define himself precisely through his difference from a mother associated with emotion and dependency. Traditional psychoanalytic theory usually describes the female's position as merely "not-male," but, in a parallel fashion, the male defines himself as not-female. Male identity is formed through an opposition to that which the mother represented in the pre-Oedipal.

Several scholars have analyzed this repudiation. Nancy Chodorow argues that "a boy must learn his gender identity as being not-female, or not-mothers. Subsequently, again because of the primacy of the mother in early life and because of the absence of concrete, real, available male figures of identification and love who are as salient for him as female figures, learning what it is to be masculine comes to mean learning to be not-feminine, not womanly."[21] Consequently, the male child forms his identity by repudiating the emotional bond with the mother, a repudiation that comes to encompass all emotional bonds. Jessica Benjamin has written of the way in which emotion and femininity become simultaneously denigrated and associated with one another in the formation of masculine identity: "The denial of identification with the mother also tends to cut the boy off from . . . [e]motional attunement, sharing states of mind, empathetically assuming the other's position and imaginatively perceiving the other's needs and feelings—these are now associated with cast-off femininity."[22] Ghost films address the fact that the patriarchal system denies men the pleasure of emotional expression precisely because emotion is associated with the maternal bond and is thus, by definition "not-male"—hence undesirable.[23]

Feminism and other changes in the cultural climate have recently engendered both a scrutiny and a confusion about traditional gender roles. At the same time that many men have begun to concede that their gender has long been the beneficiary of cultural and economic privileges they also have acknowledged that this lopsidedness of gender roles is not necessarily to their benefit. Referring again to the men's movement, Rutherford writes that many men have come to see a lack of emotion as a liability rather than a sign of strength. Hence, for these men "the primary concern was a search for an interior realm of feeling in male subjectivity and a language with which to represent it."[24] In ghost films, this "interior realm of feeling" aligns itself with the feminine and opposes itself to the masculine world just as it does in both the melodrama and the horror film. However, both the melodrama and horror genres externalize the relationship between the physical female body and the emotional or intuitive side. In the melodrama, the emotional/intuitive realm gushes forth physically in tears of sorrow and tragedy. In the occult horror film, the mystical realm (an outgrowth of the intuitive, non-rational sphere) is expressed physically either on or in the female body (*The Exorcist*) or through similarities to the female body—bloody, gaping holes and engulfing tunnels (*Poltergeist*): "Film after film interrogates . . . the 'physical presence' of a woman: forces it to externalize its inner workings, to speak its secrets, to give a material account of itself—in short, to give literal and visible *evidence*."[25]

But whereas *Ghost* and similar films play out these same dichotomies, opposing the rational male world with the intuitive feminine, here the feminine realm remains incorporeal and ineffable and so poses a dilemma of accessibility for the male. In occult horror films, the male disregards the supernatural at his peril for the occult film equates the hero's success with his ability to access those qualities associated with the feminine/occult.[26] In their emphasis on the need to access the feminine realm, ghost films share marked similarities to the occult horror film. But although melodrama "weepies" approach the feminine realm with sorrow and horror films with dread, films such as *Ghost, Truly, Madly, Deeply, Kiss Me Goodbye, Heart Condition, Made in Heaven, Heaven Can Wait,* and *Always* actively seek access to it through a process of masochistic fantasy.

In *Ghost,* Sam attempts to communicate and find a language to bridge the gap between the masculine and the feminine. Oda Mae becomes the vehicle through which communication is made possible, precisely because Oda Mae possesses the female "gift" necessary to help channel Sam's messages to Molly. That neither Molly nor Oda Mae can see Sam is consistent with the traditional conception of the woman as lacking sight. But this, again, only serves to highlight the mystical realm which opposes itself to that which can be seen. Visual images constitute proof of the phallus (in the Freudian/Lacanian scenario) and thus cannot be privileged in the masochistic expulsion of the father. The voice, then, is crucial, and indeed one of the most interesting characteristics of film ghosts is the tendency to split the ghost's voice from its body. According to Mary Ann Doane, sound and image belong to different ideological regimes that reflect classical gendered stereotypes: "Because sound and image are used as guarantors of two radically different modes of knowing (emotion and intellection), their combination entails the possibility of exposing an ideological fissure—a fissure which points to the irreconcilability of two truths of bourgeois ideology."[27] This ideology is precisely the binary basis of knowledge and identity that underlies gender formation and defines male as the diametrical opposite of female, just as rationality opposes itself diametrically to emotion.

In *Always,* Pete's disembodied voice is privileged, as is Sam's in *Ghost,* because he is invisible, and because his voice is the means by which he concludes his masochistic alliance. In *Truly, Madly, Deeply,* Jamie attempts to force Nina to "tell" him to leave. In this film, a further emphasis on speech and mediation derives from the fact that Nina works at a translation agency. Here, as in *Ghost* (and to some extent in *Always*), the female becomes the vessel of mediation for speech, providing an extra layer of distance in the communication process. Despite the fact that her boss, Sandy, speaks dozens of languages, it is Nina who must translate the postcard his son sends him in Spanish. Although Sandy's ex-wife is Spanish, Sandy has inexplicably never learned her language.

> Nina: It's so perverse to run a language agency [and] speak. . . .
> How many languages do you speak, but not . . . I mean it's your
> son, you've got to understand what he's telling you . . .
> Sandy: I know.
> Nina: I mean, in the end, that was the problem with you and
> Gabriella, you couldn't say anything to each other.

Sandy's linguistic blind spot (to mix metaphors) ties in with other problems of male/female communication.[28] As in *Ghost,* the male needs a female mediator to overcome any association with the father. In this case, however, it is not just the punishing law of the father that is being rejected, but a repudiation of the absent father—the result of the male's preoccupation with things outside the home. The father's physical absence relates back to the problem with male emotion and the way in which boys are socialized to value independence and external success, often at the expense of their families: "But fathers, in contrast to mothers, are comparatively unavailable physically and emotionally. . . . A father's main familial function is being a breadwinner, and his own training for masculinity may have led him to deny emotionality."[29] In *Truly, Madly, Deeply,* the bad or guilty father syndrome shows up in several places. When Sandy learns (through Nina's translation of the postcard) that his son is having a good time with his wife's new boyfriend, Sandy now has misgivings about his adequacy as a father. He attempts to overcome his previous paternal failings via Nina, whom he asks to help him write back in Spanish.

The absent husband/father syndrome also applies to Nina's sister, Claire, who is pregnant but whose husband is too busy to be present for the birth of their baby.

> Nina: How's Nick?
> Claire: He's busy. Do you know about Everest?
> Harry: Dad's going to climb Mount Everest.
> Nina: You're joking. . . . When?
> Claire: Well, after Christmas sometime.
> Nina: When's the baby due?
> Claire: Oh no, no, the baby'll be two or three months by then. It's
> fine. It's fine. He probably won't go. He's hopeless with babies
> anyway.

Claire's husband fulfills the classic stereotype of the goal-driven male, obsessed with success to the point of neglecting his family, including the birth of his upcoming child. Later Nina describes the situation: "She has a family and a husband I can't stand who keeps climbing everything—climbs socially, in business, and now—finally—has started climbing mountains." Chodorow discusses such behavior, drawing on anthropological accounts of "father-absent" societies to explain the male compulsion to engage in daring pursuits: "Gang and delinquent behavior among American youth often includes strong denial of anything feminine, with corresponding emphasis on masculinity—on risk and daring, sexual prowess, rejection of home life."[30] This behavior is seen as an expression of the male's desire to denigrate ties to the mother in an assertion of difference and thus manliness.

In *Truly, Madly, Deeply,* just as both Sandy and Claire's husband are examples of absent fathers, Nina's suitor, Mark, appears to have suffered himself from such a situation. In a remarkable scene in which Mark proposes that he and Nina each hop on one foot and quickly relate their life stories, Mark cites breathlessly: "parents alive, retired, *father silent practically completely silent, eighteen years older than my mother who is not, completely silent,* . . . amateur magician, father that is, and I was his assistant at Conservative Club Dinner Dances, *regularly sawn in half from the age of seven, and made to disappear in ideologically unsound circumstances*" (emphasis mine).

While the male is usually invested with language, with a powerful voice (the law, the phallus), many of these films involve problems of the male voice (Jamie dies of a "sore throat," Sam cannot make his voice be heard, Winthrop cannot sing) and male communication (Sam, Pete, and Thomas's inability to say "I love you," Sandy's inability to speak or read Spanish, Mark's silent father, and Jamie's sudden ability to speak Spanish only after his death). The "ideologically unsound circumstances" to which Mark refers, in which he is made to disappear, might refer here to the way in which the male is somehow severed (sawed in half) from his feminine side. The problem of male silence relates to the ghost's difficulty in communicating, for it is not just the male voice which is at stake, but the voice which connects the male to the female sphere. In the masochistic world, which seeks to glorify the oral mother and expel the father, Mark's father and Sandy in *Truly, Madly, Deeply,* Sam in *Ghost,* and Pete in *Always* all exhibit symptoms of this disconnection and the subsequent privileging of the feminine sphere as a corrective. In a reversal of classical Hollywood's tendency to privilege the male voice, here it is Mark's mother who speaks, it is Oda who hears, it is Nina who translates. In *Ghost,* Sam's lack of voice becomes both a symptom of, as well as the masochistic antidote to, the father who is always absent but ever-present. The woman's feminine qualities of mediation are now celebrated in their own right, rather than merely valued as the vehicle through which the fearful father can be approached.[31]

Giving Up the Ghost

If the masochistic ghost becomes associated with a kind of rebirth into the realm of the mother (Deleuze speaks often of the "new man"), then Sam, Jamie, and Pete experience this at least partly through the voice. Only by virtue of Pete and Sam's "rebirth" as ghosts do they finally learn to say "I love you," and only in Jamie's "rebirth" does he begin to speak Spanish. This information is revealed via voice-over at the beginning of the film when Nina cannot see him, but hears only his voice. He tells her things in Spanish occasionally, a fact to which Nina attributes little significance, despite the fact that Jamie never knew Spanish while alive. She is pleased, however, and later tells Jamie that she is touched by the gesture. Jamie's effort to speak Spanish is an effort to communicate with Nina although she is surprised by the mundane things he says to her. In the very first scene of the film, Nina tells her analyst that she has been hearing Jamie's voice.

> Nina: You see, he never says anything profound or earth-shatter-ing, you know, he doesn't say, well, God thinks this or . . . or about the planet or world events or, or there's no God . . . it's all go to bed, brush your teeth, or the way I'm brushing my teeth, because I always brush them side to side and I'll be doing that and he'll say down at the top, come on, down at the top, up from the bottom, or lock the back door, cierra la puerta de atras.

The words spoken by the masochistic ghost concern "trivial" domestic issues associated with women, not world events or issues associated with the male sphere. Doane remarks that in melodramas the domestic arena consistently serves as a symbol of femininity: "In a patriarchal society, women's genres are characterized by a kind of signifying glut, an overabundance of signification attached to the trivial. In the woman's film there is a hyper-signification of elements of the domestic—doors, windows, kitchens, bed-rooms."[32] Similarly, In *Truly, Madly, Deeply* the ghost-voice of Jamie ob-sesses about such "trivial" domestic items such as how Nina brushes her teeth and whether the door is locked. The ghost's ability to walk through doors may be another sign of this desire to cross over the boundaries that symbolically separate women from men, thus breaching the distinction between the external world and internal domestic spheres. Thus, although Jamie at first tells Nina to lock her doors, as a ghost he is later able to ignore them.

In *Always*, the rift between the masculine and feminine sphere is obvi-ous in Pete's daredevil stunts and in Dorinda's position of anguished waiting. Dorinda's desire to be a firefighter is tempered by her desire to have a do-mestic life with Pete and by her delight in looking feminine when Pete buys a pretty dress for her at the beginning of the film. Furthermore, the film viewer is led to believe that what is truly on Dorinda's mind is what she says when she talks her in sleep. Yet just as Jamie gives only trivial domestic advise to Nina, Dorinda's "subconscious" is inhabited only by a grocery list, an endless recitation of household goods she needs to buy.[33] Pete calls it "shopping" in her sleep, but it is during such an episode that Pete (as a ghost) initially communicates with Dorinda. As Dorinda recites her grocery list, Pete finally tells Dorinda the things she wanted to hear while alive and Dorinda actually hears him and responds to him. For Pete, this scene marks the turning point in the resolution to his narrative dilemma.

The desire to access the feminine/maternal crops up in other films through various strategies associated with a focus on either emotions or domestic and family issues. *Heart Condition* begins with Moon telling a colleague that the point of a ball game is not winning: "It's not about winning ball games, it's about emotion. You know what that is, emotion?" The words come back to haunt him when the ghost of a dead lawyer, Stone, forces him to confront his problems with Chris, whom Stone had also dated while alive. In one scene, Stone proves to Moon that he has been an inattentive, uncommunicative boyfriend by asking Moon for personal information about her—which, of course, he cannot provide. Throughout the film, Moon's lack of interest in Chris as a person is represented by his inability to take her photography seriously and by the many rolls of film she gives him, which he never bothers to develop.[34] At the end of the film, it turns out that Chris is pregnant with Stone's baby, a fact that eventually causes Moon and Chris to get back together. The title of the film, *Heart Condition,* gives away the message of the movie despite its cops-and-robbers plot. Just as Moon must physically accept the heart of another through a transplant, so must he learn to accept the conditions of the heart, which will allow him to reunite with Chris at the end.

Both *Beetlejuice* and *Ghost Dad* approach the feminine through an emphasis on family issues. In *Beetlejuice,* the ghosts return to create the family they were unable to establish in life. In *Ghost Dad,* the father, Winston, must return to make up for his poor performance as a family nurturer. At the beginning of the film, with Winston working late at the office again, the motherless children tuck themselves into bed while listening to a pre-recorded tape of their absent father's voice. The next morning, while the kids prepare their own meager breakfast, Winston forgets his oldest daughter's birthday and even forgets her name.[35] Before his death, Winston is anxious about clinching a business deal, which will assure the financial security of his family. Although he returns from death to make good on this promise, Winston's slapstick efforts to execute the business deal as a ghost are sidetracked, leading instead to a better rapport with his children and a relationship with the woman next door. As a ghost, Winston learns to become a better dad not by "being absent" in order to make more money, but by becoming "a mom"—tending to his children's personal problems and school projects.

Giving Up the Ghost

Near the end of the film, Winston's daughter Diane suffers an accident that permits her spirit to leave her body temporarily to join Winston in his ghostly state. Much to Winston's distress, however, he is unable to convince Diane to get back into her body.

> Winston: What are you doing?!!
> Diane: Taking after my old man, I guess.
> Winston: Get back in your body . . . before something serious happens!
> Diane: You mean like having a father who's always away?

Later Winston convinces her to get back in her body in a brief exchange reminiscent of scenes in *Always* and *Ghost*. Winston tells her, "I want you to live because. . . ." Here Winston's body begins to flicker and fade away. Diane now rushes in to give him the words: "Because you love me." A triumphant family scene ensues, for as it turns out, Winston was never really dead, just scared out of his body because of a car accident. At the end, a reporter asks Winston about whether he will publicize his adventure, to which Winston replies, "Not until I've spent time with the family."[36] *Ghost Dad* dramatizes the relation between the ambivalent ghost and the desire to repudiate the absent father. Just as Sam's inability to communicate with Molly in *Ghost* becomes magnified in the ghost state, so Winston's fatherly absenteeism becomes magnified, causing his figurative invisibility to become literal.[37] In both cases, the problem is worsened by the ghost's return; it must be masochistically worked through and ultimately expelled in favor of a maternal or feminine solution. Furthermore, in *Ghost Dad*, Winston is first introduced only through his tape-recorded voice as if to preview his future ghostly state. His disembodied voice signals his absent fatherhood and links him even before his death to ghosts in *Truly, Madly, Deeply, Always, Ghost, Kiss Me Goodbye*, and other films where the ghost's voice bears the onus of revealing its presence.

The domestic agenda pursued in *Ghost Dad* pertains not just to traditionally feminine realms, but becomes linked to ghosts through a tradition of house haunting, a convention alternately spoofed or celebrated in ghost films.

Female Space/Haunted Houses

In *Ghost,* the opening scenes concern the renovation of a loft apartment. Molly and Sam are ecstatic about their new home. As they knock through a wall Molly notes the great height of the ceilings. "We can put our bedroom up there and that will leave us with all this space." Sam seems to be confused by the concept: "What?" he asks. Molly replies: "Just space!" In

Hollywood films the house/home becomes associated with the female—a domestic "space" in which the woman waits for the man. Woman is space, lack—the vessel for man's use. Yet unlike classic horror films or even gothic horror, the house is not uncanny or claustrophobic, but welcoming; in the masochistic fantasy it represents the plenitude of the maternal.

Although horror movies often pair evil spirits with big scary houses, the domestic agenda is reversed in ghost dramas and ghost comedies. Whereas in horror stories a person or family is plagued by unwanted, evil spirits who must be expelled or exorcised (*Poltergeist, House, The Changeling*), by contrast, in *Beetlejuice* the living are ghastly and frightening and the ghosts represent the classic domestic couple trying to live a wholesome, country life. The new family consists of a snotty urban sculptress, her henpecked husband (a real-estate developer), and their disaffected child, Lydia. Upon moving into the idyllic house, the husband indicates his preference for a more traditional "female" wife, as if the house itself will enable a transformation: "You're finally gonna be able to cook a decent meal!" Although the realtor gives a skeleton key to Lydia saying, "Give that to your father, that'll open any door in the house," it is not the father who will have access to the secret room where the ghosts live, but the female child.[38]

The too-late addressed in this film surrounds a purely domestic problem rather than a romantic one since the husband and wife die together. Although the couple remains intact, in the beginning of the film they have been trying hard to have a child, with no success. The realtor constantly pesters them to sell their house, implying that they do not deserve such a big house because it "really needs a family." Just before dying in a car accident, the couple decides that they should try again, but almost immediately plunge off a bridge.[39] Although the ghosts initially try to scare away the new family that moves in, they are unable to get noticed much less be scary. However, they are also unable to leave the house for fear of being eaten by a giant spectral snake with many mouths.[40]

In *Kiss Me Goodbye*, Kay's return to her old house coincides with Jolly's appearance. Kay is obsessed with moving back in with her new husband, and the opening of the film focuses heavily on her installation there. As Kay redecorates, her friend Emily remarks that since Kay has "been in limbo for three years" it is good that Kay goes back to the house, "facing up to the place" so that she can "live again." As it turns out, although Kay glorifies her relationship with Jolly, the truth about Jolly is foreshadowed in his lack of affection for the house.

Mom: And he loved this house.
Kay: He did not love this house, he hardly noticed it. Home sweet home to Jolly was room service in any town with a theater.

69

Giving Up the Ghost

Kay's return to her old house is the catalyst for Jolly's return. As with other ghosts, Jolly first makes himself known through sound: first the sound of his song and dance numbers and then—as in *Ghost Dad*—an old message on an answering machine turns itself on mysteriously as Kay passes by. The voice announces itself only to state, "I'm not home right now." Although Jolly's association with the house is suspect, revealing his absence, the house becomes the locus of resolution, providing the location for Kay and Rupert's eventual marriage.

In *Truly, Madly, Deeply,* Nina's house provides the comically disastrous backdrop to her deteriorating mental state at the beginning of the film. The cupboards will not close, the doors will not lock, the water turns brown, and rats cavort across her bed and piano. Each of the problems seems to concern something patently female. For example, the doors (front door and cupboard) will not close properly; they are too open—in the same way that Nina cannot shut herself off from Jamie at the beginning of the film, evoking the notion of female over-identification associated with melodrama. The water is another symbol often associated with the female, in this case somehow gone wrong, muddy.[41] As noted earlier, many of these qualities pertain to the abject terrors that spring from the maternal body and which the ghosts expel from the film by their very presence. The importance of re-establishing the "home" is indicative of the masochistic desire to return to the pre-Oedipal, and almost all of the films use the house or home as the mise-en-scène of the fantasized return.

Whereas in horror films the house becomes "uncanny," in ghost films the uncanny is not possible or necessary for the very reason that it is possible or necessary in horror films. As Freud understood it, the term uncanny holds within it both the terms "heimlich" which means belonging or pertaining to the home (familiar) as well as "unheimlich" which means strange and unfamiliar."[42] As we have seen in relation to the *objet a* and the abject, what is once familiar to the child later becomes strange when the child enters the Oedipal stage and achieves subjecthood. Although the object comes to be vilified as the Other, the child's former intimacy produces the almost oxymoronic sensation conveyed by the word uncanny—both strange but also uncomfortably familiar. In horror films the house becomes the symbol for what was cast away. That the house is an open vessel makes it structurally similar to the female's anatomy, triggering the uncanny response which the male purportedly first experiences in relation to the mother's body: "There is something uncanny about the female genital organs. This *unheimlich* place, however, is the entrance to the former *Heim* [home] of all human beings, to the place where each one of us lived once upon a time and in the beginning . . . the prefix '*un*' is the token of repression."[43] Because horror films dramatize and map sexual difference, the house comes to represent the many abject qualities associated with the maternal, which must be denigrated to ensure that they remain Other. In comedy ghost films where the maternal is desired, the house no longer provokes dread, but the promise of plenitude.

It is striking that the confusion experienced by members of men's groups finds expression in feelings of homelessness or a desire to find a home. "In discarding our own pasts men seemed unable to create new places of belonging. So often it was women who were used, to provide and construct these emotional homes. . . . It was a world experienced as empty and homeless."[44] Perhaps it is no accident then that at the end of *Ghost* Sam forces Oda Mae to give the embezzled money to two nuns who seek donations for the homeless.[45]

Music

The home becomes a privileged place to both stage and resolve the dilemma of the absent father, and in ghost films music becomes a primary antidote to the problem of emotional expression and communication. Many of the films equate music with the ineffable, mystical qualities of the female. This is most common in ghost films that feature love stories, where music is used as a sign of plenitude and romantic oneness.[46] Similarly, in ghost films, particularly those featuring romance, music is linked to the ineffable feminine and associated with the pre-Oedipal oneness romance tries to attain. In many of the films, the sound track plays romantic ballads or nostalgic "oldies" during scenes of romance, thus "adding" something to the scene that cannot be encompassed through the dialogue. Particularly when the characters have difficulty expressing emotion as several do in these ghost films, music compensates in order to establish the bond that will soon be broken through the death of the character.

The ubiquity of nondiegetic musical scores can be traced to early cinema where silent films were accompanied by music from an outside source. While the historical tradition of musical accompaniment is clearly a factor, a psychoanalytic understanding provides a different motivation for its use. On the one hand, synchronized (hence diegetic) sound helps anchor the voice to the body, forging coherent film subjects and film subject positions. On the other hand, non-diegetic musical scores would seem to challenge this process. By adding music that does not stem from either characters or other diegetic sources, this threatens to expose the heterogeneity of the cinematic apparatus. By implication, this fragmentation would also seem to threaten the viewer's sense of cohesion. Instead of seeing musical scoring as being threatening, however, music often provides a cohesive thread that links the various parts of the film together. "From this perspective, the nondiegetic score of the Hollywood film functions as an aural method of suturing the absences/lacks experienced by a spectator-auditor who is differently hailed by image and sound, . . . confronted with his own inadequacy, . . . or confronted by the lost object (the absent 'real' of cinema)."[47] This perspective is thus consistent with the desired oneness which is at stake in ghost films. However, while many ghost films use nondiegetic music, many also employ music as an important diegetic element, often incorporating music into the thematic or narrative core of the film.

In *Heaven Can Wait,* Joe plays the saxophone and inexplicably carries it with him when he arrives in heaven (despite the fact that he could not have been playing it when his bicycle gets hit by a car). More than anything, music is what permits Joe to overcome his difficulty in communicating his true identity after he has taken over another man's body. When his old friend and coach will not be persuaded by verbal arguments, Mr. Jordan tells Joe to "try a little music . . . it's a great persuader." Joe then plays the saxophone, thus prompting Max finally to recognize him.[48] In ghost films, where the male ghost is often invisible, voice and music become the privileged realm, signifying the importance of that which cannot be seen.

Music is also used as a tactic of persuasion or proof in *Hearts and Souls.* In the beginning of the film, Julia sings a lullaby to her son, Billy, before putting him to bed. After she dies and becomes a ghost, she is preoccupied with finding out what has happened to him. Near the end of the film she and Thomas overhear a policeman singing this same song to his daughter. It is only through the song that Julia discovers that she has found her son. Furthermore, the four ghosts are uncharacteristically musical and in early scenes teach Thomas accapella songs, which they sing together in harmony. The ghosts desert Thomas as a child by becoming invisible and inaudible, and it is not until he has grown up that they discover that Thomas is supposed to help them, entailing a reassertion of their presence. At first, Thomas is unable to perceive them. But when Milo hums their old favorite, "Walk Like a Man," Thomas finds himself singing along. Only then do the ghosts suddenly appear and become audible.

While Thomas is initially a reluctant participant, he eventually grows emotionally attached and committed to the ghosts' mission. A turning point is signaled when the ghosts spontaneously burst into a song and dance version of "Walk Like a Man" and Thomas willingly joins in, recalling their earlier "harmony" as a group. The lyrics to the song are revealing in that they express the male/female dilemma with great irony: "I'm gonna walk like a man, fast as I can. Walk like a man from you. I'll tell the world, forget about it girl, and walk like a man from you." The song articulates the way in which manliness supposedly depends on creating a disassociation from the female and the distance necessary to assert macho independence. But as with the original Frankie Valli version, the characters sing in exaggerated falsetto voices, mocking this notion of masculinity. When the song is reprised at the end of the film, it signals the awareness that the macho code has been a hoax all along.[49]

Problems with the voice or throat are common in ghost films and in this case overlap with the musical theme. Just as many male ghosts cannot make themselves heard or cannot express themselves emotionally while alive, Winthrop, in *Hearts and Souls,* is unable to sing. At the beginning of the film, he arrives at an important audition and is unable to perform—when the music starts, he opens his mouth and nothing comes out. (When the auditioner asks him what he sang last year, Winthrop admits that he did not actually sing—he was taken ill.) Just as other male characters find their "emotional" voice by the end of ghost films, Winthrop eventually does sing, overcoming his personal too-late and signaling the eventual rapprochement between the male and female romantic partners.

In *Always,* Pete is unable to tell Dorinda he loves her but teases her in the same scene about a romantic song. During the scene, Pete and Dorinda slow dance to a live band.

> Pete: You know, it's too bad we don't have a song. You know, like when couples say, "Hey, they're playing our song." You know, really it's too bad.
> Dorinda: I can't believe you forgot!
> Pete: What are you talking about? You're saying we have song?
> Dorinda: Yes, we have a song!
> Pete: You're kidding.
> Dorinda: You big lug, you're gonna break my heart.
> Pete: Hey, why don't we try that bit where, uh, that signaling to the band bit?

At this point, Pete signals the band who then plays their song, a romantic/nostalgic ballad. ("You asked me how I knew, my true love was true. . . . Smoke gets in your eyes.") Later, after Pete's death, Dorinda invites Ted to dinner while Pete watches from afar in agony. When she puts on some taped music, Pete watches helplessly as Dorinda and Ted kiss. But then suddenly, "their song" comes on and Dorinda, remembering Pete, decides to ask Ted to leave. She then dances to the song alone, wearing the frilly white dress Pete gave her in the earlier scene. Throughout the scene, Pete occasionally appears in her arms as she twirls around. The song provokes the memory of Pete for Dorinda (and visually for the audience), re-creating the union the song originally signified.

A slightly different use of music occurs in *Beetlejuice,* where the ghosts are unable to make themselves known to the family in their house despite the fact that they have used all the standard haunting techniques. Finally, they use music to communicate, forcing the music through the bodies of the dinner guests and making them dance to it. In the final scene of the film, when the ghosts become Lydia's adoptive parents (her "ghost parents") they reward Lydia's good grades by causing the music to levitate Lydia as she dances.

Other examples of diegetic music are found in *Kiss Me Goodbye,* where the ghost, Jolly, is a dancer and singer. In *Alice,* Alice's romantic liaison involves a musician, and in *Truly, Madly, Deeply,* Jamie is a cello player. Not only does Jamie conduct ghostly orchestras in Nina's living room, but he does not initially materialize in the film until Nina plays a piano piece to which Jamie's part adds the accompaniment. The music recalls their previous ineffable romantic union and finally causes Jamie to materialize to Nina.

Made in Heaven employs another elaborate use of diegetic music. In this film, the protagonist, Mike, drowns and goes to heaven, where he meets the love of his life, Anny. Eventually they both end up back on earth where Mike (reborn as "Elmo") must search for Anny (reborn as "Ally") in an effort to continue their heavenly romance. Although Mike was never musical in his former life, in heaven he inexplicably imagines a shovel, which then suddenly appears before him. Unable to explain the presence of the shovel, he asks Emmett, an angel, what it means. Emmett explains that such imagined objects often turn out to be musical instruments back on earth.

> Mike: Do you think I'll be taking it back with me?
> Emmett: Nah, probably not. Maybe the idea's in the shovel.
> Maybe it's something musical like a guitar or trumpet.

Later, when Mike is reborn into the world, he hitches a ride with a couple who turn out to be his parents from his first life. At a lunch stop they see him eyeing a trumpet in a store window and buy it for him, even though he claims not to be musical. Yet Mike (now Elmo) does turn out to be musical in this life and spends the rest of the movie writing a song titled, "We Never Danced." The phrase once again recalls the melodramatic too-late and is taken from a conversation between Mike and Anny in heaven before Anny is whisked away to be reborn on earth. In addition to focusing on this song, the film is studded with cameo appearances by rock stars, whose music slides in and out of being diegetically motivated. This "double" use of music is common in many ghost films and provides a link between the diegetic and extradiegetic, helping to smooth over the fact that musical scores usually have no source.

For example, *Ghost* features a romantic ballad that plays during two scenes of romantic union between Sam and Molly. In the first scene, the song emanates from a jukebox in Sam and Molly's living room. The old-fashioned style of the jukebox combined with the nostalgic oldies-style song supports the argument that music is used as a catalyst for accessing the maternal. (Not only is the style of song nostalgic—a crooning 1950s song, "Unchained Melody," but the words sing of returning to the sea, imagery associated with the uterine/maternal waters.) In a later scene in which Molly and Sam are briefly reunited through the help of Oda Mae, the same song plays, this time without benefit of the jukebox. As in *Made in Heaven* and *Always,* music crosses the diegetic and extradiegetic boundaries, covering over its absent source precisely through its internal nostalgic qualities, but also by its nostalgic use in the scene. In both *Ghost* and *Always,* as in *Made in Heaven,* the music is employed nostalgically because it re-creates the lost scene of union between the two lovers before the untimely death of the male. The reprise of the song thus provides both the characters and the audience with the memory of the earlier song and its association with romantic oneness played out in the earlier scenes.

The description of the maternal voice as a sonorous envelope helps explain how music can be both external to the source but also a comforting means of accessing the pre-Oedipal and the maternal.[50] Despite the fact that the voice is often associated with language and the father, the first voice that the child often experiences is the mother's. In fact, the voice may precede sight in establishing the presence of the mother to the infant. "Because her voice is identified by the child long before her body is, it remains unlocalized during a number of the most formative moments of subjectivity. The maternal voice would thus seem to be the original prototype for the disembodied voice-over in cinema."[51] The disembodied use of music thus re-creates the sonorous envelope of the mother's voice before language, mimicking the non-linguistic aspect of music as a source of sound. Whereas in horror films, the mother's voice comes to be associated with that which is rejected and vilified in sexual difference (the scream interiorized in the woman's body signaling castration), ghost films and love stories use music to re-create the way in which sound expresses the maternal voice that precedes Oedipal castration and hence sexual difference.

Birth and Rebirth

Many ghost films focus on the notion of rebirth, another important aspect of the masochistic aesthetic. Deleuze writes of the "new man," who is reborn through the glorious mother: "To become a man is to be reborn from the woman alone, to undergo a second birth."[52] Not only do ghosts represent a kind of rebirth in their very return from death, but many of the characters find peace at the end of the films through death, which itself is equated with rebirth. It is important to note that all ghosts are essentially "reborn" merely by virtue of their return to earth.

Giving Up the Ghost

In *Ghost,* Sam is not only "reborn" as a ghost, but at the end of the film the viewer is led to believe that he experiences a second rebirth. Sam proves that "you can take it with you" by continuing on into a light inhabited by the distant silhouettes of other people—a seemingly new world. More important, at the end of the film, Molly is finally able to hear Sam and he can now express the emotions he denied before—his love for her. Once the masochistic alliance has been completed, the ghosts in *Ghost, Always, Truly, Madly, Deeply,* and *Kiss Me Goodbye* all become reborn through death. Death is the true rebirth for the masochist because it represents the only means of attaining satisfaction, for "death becomes the ultimate fetish that fascinates with the promise of a mystical unity."[53] The mystical unity associated with death can also be seen in films that portray heaven as a site of pre-Oedipal bliss.

Made in Heaven is an extremely interesting variation of the ghost films discussed thus far. In films such as *Ghost, Truly, Madly, Deeply, Always,* and *Ghost Dad,* the romance is thwarted by the untimely death of one of the characters. In *Made in Heaven,* however, Mike does not meet Anny until he dies and goes to heaven. In a variation of the too-late, Anny's "birth," not her death, causes the pathos of the too-late. Instead of returning from death as a ghost to correct the problem, Mike leaves the ghostly/heaven state to be reborn again on earth to search for his beloved.

In this film, heaven is seen not as a place to die, but as the place of plenitude from whence to be born or reborn. When Mike inexplicably imagines a shovel (which then magically appears), he inadvertently creates a symbolic link between death and rebirth. Although he cannot understand why he has imagined this object, Mike later uses it to dig in the garden—symbolizing the link between death (the grave) with planting, reproduction, and birth, for he plants a garden as a kind of housewarming ceremony in honor of his wedding to Anny. He has already taken great pains to imagine the house— once again recalling that the house is symbolic of pre-Oedipal plenitude. In ghost fantasies then, the pre-Oedipal is most fully exalted in the tendency to equate its characteristics (unity, plenitude, oneness) with representations of heaven.

Made in Heaven explicitly links dying with birth, sending the dead into the pre-Oedipal realm of imaginary unity and plenitude. The similarities between heaven and the pre-Oedipal/Imaginary are striking, for in both cases boundaries are nonexistent and the child is one with its surroundings. In heaven, the characters need only think about a person or a place and they will instantaneously be there. (When Mike is told to visualize a person's face, this recalls the earliest identifications with the mother.) As in the pre-Oedipal, time and space are collapsed into a single moment that becomes synonymous with the child's presence and being. Desiring and thinking about something is to have it (as evidenced by the magically appearing shovel).[54]

Many of the other films contain scenes of birth or implicitly touch on the issue. In *Truly, Madly, Deeply,* Nina's friend gives birth to a baby girl, an event that solidifies Nina's resolve to fully reject Jamie. In *Beetlejuice,* although there is no physical birth, the childless couple conceives a daughter by appropriating her from her woefully inadequate family. *Heart Condition* ends with the revelation that Chris is pregnant with Stone's child, information that causes the reluctant Moon to reconcile himself to both of them. *Hearts and Souls* features a newborn baby who is inhabited by four returning souls. When these ghosts fulfill their missions, their souls will enter newborn babies. Even *Memoirs of an Invisible Man* concludes with a birth, with the couple pondering whether it will be an invisible baby.

Other films, including *Switch* and *Dead Again,* also involve birth. In *Switch,* a dead man inhabits the body of woman in order to atone for his sins as a womanizer. His mission is to find a woman who likes him, which proves nearly impossible due to his male chauvinism. At the end of the film however, "Amanda" (formerly Steve) gives birth to a baby girl who gazes up at her lovingly, thereby fulfilling the contract. Amanda is released at this point and ascends to heaven. *Dead Again* implicitly concerns rebirth through its story of reincarnation, as the characters Roman and Margaret are reborn as Mike and Grace in order to solve a murder mystery and resolve a karmic debt.

Comedy ghosts engage in a masochistic fantasy that seeks to re-create the hallucinatory pre-Oedipal oneness the child enjoyed before the interference of the father. The rebirth associated with the masochist not only concerns the maternal but opposes itself to sexual difference, which is then blamed on the father. In the masochistic fantasy, the male "is stripped of all virility, and reborn as a 'new, sexless man,' and the latter is invested with the phallus. . . . What is beaten in masochism is consequently not so much the male subject as the father, or the father in the male subject."[55] This explains both the ghost's rebirth (return) as well as the emphasis on absent fathers and domestic issues. While glorifying the maternal, the ghost fantasy illustrates the male's scapegoating of the father through its own suffering. The male ghost repudiates its likeness to the guilty father and instead attempts to access that which recalls the pre-Oedipal bliss with the mother.

Although the notion of rebirth through death is contained within the masochistic fantasy, comedy ghost films play out a fantasy that goes beyond mystical death and the rejection of the father. The ghost is a paradoxical device which, while appearing to concern the death and the end of the subject, in fact dramatizes a fantasy concerning the origin of the subject.

Chapter 4

Marvelous Spirits: Seeing and Speaking

Although ghosts may appear in a fantasy seemingly concerned with the end of the subject, they are in fact more concerned with the paradoxical origins of the subject. To begin to see why this is so, it is necessary to return to the relationship between fantasy and its inextricable link to the hallucinatory primal scene. Both the ghost's invisibility and its disembodied voice relate to what Freud and others call primal fantasy. Because the power of invisibility is paradoxically but inextricably related to speech (since ghosts often reveal their presence through speech), the interplay between seeing and speaking sheds insight into a dilemma concerning the precarious origin of the subject. If both seeing and speaking become contested sites of identification and subjectivity in ghost films, their manipulation must be explained as both psychoanalytic and cinematic phenomena. Thus, the effect of disembodied voices and invisible characters elicits a fantasy scenario that connects the "marvelous" qualities of the ghosts to their rise in the deployment of a primal fantasy.

Invisibility as a Primal Fantasy

Earlier, I presented a version of psychoanalytic film theory which posited that the film viewer is conceived as a male scopophilic whose power to look at the woman is part of a sadistic regime stemming from castration anxiety. In ghost films, the ghost's power of invisibility does have the potential to lend itself to this type of sadistic voyeurism. However, in these films the ghost-like quality of seeing without being seen is not necessarily sadistic but more likely to be masochistic.

In *Ghost* the tendency for male voyeurism is explicit in a scene in which Molly tries to convince the police that Oda Mae has really contacted Sam in the afterlife. One of the female detectives snidely comments, "Okay according to this psychic lady there are ghosts and spirits all over the place, watching us all the time, huh? Hell, I'm never gonna get undressed again." This is not too far from the truth, however, since in an earlier scene Molly undresses as she is watched not only by the mugger, Willy, who hides in the next room, but also by Sam (and also, of course, by the audience). In one of the earlier scenes Sam tries to tell Molly through Oda Mae that the mugger was in the apartment. Oda Mae revises Sam's words to emphasize the fact that she was seen undressing despite the fact that this element had nothing to do with the break-in, the purpose of which was to obtain a computer code.

> Sam: Yesterday when you came back from your walk with Carl you went up the stairs, you talked to Floyd, you went in and took off your clothes.
> Oda Mae [to Molly]: All right, all right, all right. When you came in yesterday from your walk with Carl. You took your clothes off, he was here—he saw everything.

In *Truly, Madly, Deeply,* the ghost is never explicitly invisible and yet the threat of being watched or sneaked up on is made obvious in several scenes in which Jamie startles Nina by suddenly appearing next to her without warning. First he pops up in Nina's bed (Nina: "Is this going to be your party trick?"). Later, he surprises her from behind the bathtub as she bathes (Nina: "Go away! . . . God, I can't even lock the door on you any more!"). Perhaps most important, he appears behind her as she converses with Mark on their first date. As she and Mark exchange personal information, Nina suddenly hears cello music and turns around guiltily, thinking she sees Jamie playing the cello in a street ensemble.

Being watched while in the process of a romantic encounter or in the process of love-making crops up in many ghost films. While *Hearts and Souls* features four ghosts who eavesdrop on Thomas's floundering romance, other films focus on more explicitly carnal scenarios. In *Ghost,* Sam secretly watches as Carl attempts to seduce Molly, unable to stop them. In *Kiss Me Goodbye,* Jolly shows up in Kay's bedroom—invisible except to Kay—just as she is in the process of making love to her fiancé. In *Always,* Pete agonizes as he watches Dorinda being courted and then kissed by Ted. In *Heart Condition,* Stone secretly watches Moon and their mutual girlfriend make love. And in *Alice,* Alice becomes invisible (through a magic potion) and witnesses several instances of love-making: first her lover and his ex-wife and later her husband and his lover. *Memoirs of an Invisible Man* also contains a scene in which the invisible protagonist watches the attempted seduction of his own girlfriend. A variation of this trend occurs in *Beetlejuice,* when Lydia mistakes the ghosts' ineffective attempts to haunt (by moaning) for the sounds of her parents making love in the next room.

Christian Metz writes, "If it is true of all desire that it depends on the infinite pursuit of its absent object, voyeuristic desire, along with certain forms of sadism, is the only desire whose principle of distance symbolically and spatially evokes this fundamental rent."[1] As we have seen, however, the distance created in the process of voyeurism need not be associated with sadism, but may instead be linked to a masochistic desire to submit to the images. Furthermore, in the process of looking, film ghosts clearly reveal their brand of voyeurism to be masochistic. Even while looking, most ghosts are unable to have any effect on the scene before them either because they cannot make their presence known and/or because they are physically impotent. As noted, *Truly, Madly, Deeply* explicitly links ineffectual ghosts to film viewers by featuring a passel of male ghosts who return to earth specifically to watch old movies. The analogy is further extended at the end of the film when the masochistic alliance is concluded from behind a glass window that separates Jamie from Nina and her new boyfriend, the blue light mimicking the earlier light from the video screen. In *Defending Your Life,* the ascent of the protagonist, Daniel Miller, through the levels of cosmic existence is delayed in a kind of way station in which he is forced to watch scenes from his life as if they were scenes in a movie.[2] Not only is Daniel unable to change the unpleasant "evidence" that appears on the screen, but he is also unsuccessful at defending his actions. He is forced to watch numerous scenes from his failed life, all of which provoke great discomfort and embarrassment. Significantly, Daniel's greatest "crime" is having been too "afraid" and essentially too "passive." His "defender," Mr. Diamond, explains the purported source of this passivity by showing a clip from Daniel's childhood in which Daniel is shown behind the bars of his playpen, looking on in tears as his parents quarrel. He is unable to prevent the fight, which involves accusations of infidelity. Throughout the course of the screenings, it becomes obvious that the father is being expelled, for the clips reveal that it is Daniel's father that creates his fear.

The scene of the child looking on helplessly re-creates the primal fantasy and illustrates the link between fantasy and masochism's desire to view from a distance. The tendency of ghosts to view carnal or romantic acts from afar is highly reminiscent of primal fantasies.[3] Such fantasies concern not just the ability to see, but also the ability to overhear. Freud discusses the case of a woman who believes that she is being photographed while in the process of an illicit love affair. She believes she hears a clicking sound coming from behind a curtain, which she believes is the shutter of a camera. Later, Freud deduces that her "fantasy" is related to an original primal scene in which the child sees and hears the parents engaged in love-making: "The sound is the noise of the parents who awaken the child; it is also the sound the child is afraid to make lest it betray her listening."[4] Kaja Silverman describes the lack of control suffered by the child in its formative stages: "Far from controlling the sound and images of parental sexuality, the child held captive within the crib is controlled—indeed, overwhelmed—by them. Adult sexuality invades him or her through the eyes and ears."[5] It is through sight and sound then that primal fantasy is both created and expressed, a fantasy which will purport to explain the origin of the subject as well as that of sexual difference.

Such fantasies may be discerned in mainstream films that employ sight and sound in the elaboration of such fantasies. The temporal structure of the melodramatic too-late describes not only a narrative pattern but is itself based on the primal fantasies of sexual desire, sexual difference, and the origin of the self. Various film genres seem to be constructed around different temporal frames, which arise in connection with these conundrums: "In contrast to pornography's meeting 'on time!' and horror's unexpected meeting 'too early!' we can identify melodrama's pathos of the 'too late!'"[6] Each of these genres rely on a fantasy scenario to address certain issues resulting from or relating to gender, sexuality, or selfhood. For example, pornography seeks a solution to the problem of sexuality through a fantasy of seduction in which the participants meet each other "on time" in a joyful orgasm. But in the horror film, the problem of sexual difference is addressed by a temporal scheme in which the (usually) teenage participants are about to have sexual relations, but are physically prevented by a violent act. Here the temporal mistiming is characterized as being "too early." Both of these genres take up a "primal fantasy," pornography a fantasy of seduction, and the horror genre a fantasy of the problem of sexual difference. Lastly, melodrama's too-late concerns the quest for the origins of the self.

> In these fantasies, the quest to return to and discover the origin of the self is manifest in the form of the child's fantasy of possessing ideal parents in the Freudian family romance, in the parental fantasy of possessing the child in maternal or paternal melodrama, and even in lovers' fantasy of possessing one another in romantic weepies. In these fantasies the quest for connection is always tinged with the melancholy of loss. Origins are already lost, the encounters always take place too late, on deathbeds or over coffins.[7]

Ghost films such as *Beetlejuice* and *Ghost Dad* conform nicely to the first two scenarios of family romance and parental fantasy, whereas many of the other films involve romantic quests. *Heart Condition* combines the two through its emphasis on romance and birth at the end of the film.

The fantasy scenarios of too-early and too-late stem in part from a certain slippage, which is the result of the fact that knowledge of origins can never be attained. The expression of fantasy is, in fact, an essentially retroactive process. In other words, since the child's pre-Oedipal state is presubjective and prior to language, the child is "too early" in relation to desire and meaning. However, after subjectivity is attained, fulfillment of desire is foreclosed upon, thus revealing that the child is now "too late." The formulation of too-early and too-late has to do not just with temporal tropes of certain film genres, but with a certain temporal disjunction inherent in the nature of fantasy itself. Here, fantasy is that primal structuring fantasy of the subject, not specific daydreams or neuroses (although daydreams and neuroses can be traced back to primal fantasies). The fantasy "originates" both before and after, but can never be pinned down. From the point of view of the subject s/he is either too early or too late and thus the temporal gap is filled by the fantasy itself. Without the gap, no fantasy would be necessary.

The difference between desire and fantasy is that desire posits an object (even though it may be hallucinatory) whereas fantasy itself becomes the scenario of this desire. That is to say, fantasy is the structure wherein the desire is expressed and fulfilled. Elizabeth Cowie elaborates on the nature of this fantasy structure: "Primal fantasy does not imply a simple causality, primacy or origin, of original content. Rather it is to be understood as originary in the instituting of a structure of fantasy, a scene of fantasized origins—the origin of the child in its parents' lovemaking; the origin of sexual difference, and its corollary castration; in the wish to take the father's place and have the mother, or usurp the mother's place and have the father—thus a parental seduction."[8] Since the primal fantasies purport to answer conundrums of origins, the problem of sexual difference is always implicated. But the castration anxiety associated with sexual difference takes on different forms as each of the different fantasy scenarios (horror, melodrama, and pornography) attempt to explain or work through sexuality. Furthermore, while horror films seem to specifically address castration anxiety, other fantasy scenarios approach the problem by disavowing difference in a return to oneness. If a masochistic interpretation of fantasy is applied, separation from the mother and sexual difference can be seen as processes ambivalently experienced and beyond the child's control. Thus, the primal fantasy of the origin of the subject concerns not the voyeuristic control the child attempts to reassert over the parents, but the lack of control made obvious through the child's distance.

The fantasy in which the child views the parents' love-making is marked by an irrecoverable distance, which is characteristic of both ghost films and film viewing. For just as film actors are no longer present, revealing by their very presence an absence, so ghosts represent the subject who is no longer "alive" or present.[9] Ghosts are thus highly reflexive expressions of filmic projections. Similarly, the slippage between the presence of the actor and his or her image is reminiscent of the slippage of time that characterizes melodrama and other genres of originary fantasies. Because the spectator and the actor are never in the same place at the same time, cinema is the story of missed encounters, of "the failure to meet of the voyeur and the exhibitionist whose approaches no longer coincide."[10] The temporal and spatial slippages that characterize the film viewing experience are thus inextricably linked to both primal fantasies and to the conundrums of subjecthood that film ghosts seem to work through in their voyeurism, invisibility, and in their ineffective attempts to communicate. The paradoxical nature of the ghost expresses the temporal and spatial slippages from which fantasy is born and which the cinematic experience re-creates. The ghost is here but not-here, dead but not-dead, late but not too-late. It returns to re-create an unsolvable problem, that of its own origins, which it masochistically works through. But although the ghost attempts to reverse the too-late, the re-creation of the original fantasy is itself—by its very nature—too-late.

Since temporal slippage is integral to the formation of fantasy, origins can never be pinned down. Although fantasy is born in this gap, the particular articulations of the fantasy scene are necessarily retroactive accounts. Again, this is so because the child is never "present" at the right time to understand his or her coming into being or into subjecthood or sexuality. Before the child is a subject, there is no self-reflection or understanding and so the fantasy (of seduction, fulfillment, etc.) is not invoked until later, when an incident reminds the child of this earlier time. Just as the fantasy must be understood as a retroactive attempt to explain origins, so must the ghost be understood as a retroactive account of the human subject. The ghost returns after the fact (after death) to repeat the original fantasy of the birth of the subject.

Because the primal viewing is beyond the child's control and because the fantasy is necessarily created retroactively, retroactive explanations are often designed to cover over the fundamentally masochistic process that is anathema to Oedipal, male subjectivity. In fact, Silverman provides such an explanation for traditional tendencies to consider voyeurism as sadistic rather than masochistic: "The spectacle of parental sexuality elicits a sense of exclusion and inadequacy. The mastering, sadistic variety of voyeurism discussed by Metz can perhaps best be understood as a psychic formation calculated to reverse the power relation of the primal scene—as a compensatory drama whereby passivity yields to activity through an instinctual 'turning around' and reversal."[11] In this meta-critique, film theory's insistent emphasis on sadism and voyeurism can be seen as a tactic designed to deny an inherent inadequacy. Such a site for "compensatory reversal" is exposed in ghost films where invisible characters might seem to be reasserting their fading subjecthood through the voice, the voice being associated with language as the entryway to the Symbolic. Yet the voice is initially associated with the mother as a pre-linguistic sonorous envelope. Furthermore, the attainment of subjecthood through the voice and language is fraught with difficulty.

Through their difficulties communicating, ghosts reveal the highly conflicted nature of the voice when it is associated with the subject coming into language. In addition, the child suffers a loss as it enters subjecthood, a loss that corresponds to the too-late of melodrama. The mistiming of communication found in melodrama and ghost comedies becomes embodied by the ghost who essentially attempts to repeat the fantasy associated with the origin of the subject and who eventually provides a utopian solution through a kind of rebirth attained in death.[12]

Disembodied Voice and the Problem of Language

The emphasis on voice, language, and communication in many ghost films leads to an analysis of the relationship among the ghost device, masochistic fantasy, and the problem of language as an expression of the Oedipal subject. While ghost films are typically Hollywood in their mythical employment of the mother as lack and father as castration, the myth of the subject's true "castration"—not by the father but by language—surfaces everywhere, exposing lack as the foundation of the subject and the paradoxical underpinning of the ghost device.

The child's first loss is associated with the loss of the mother, who is powerful and with whom the child experiences oneness in the pre-Oedipal stage. A second loss is experienced, however, when the child comes into language and the Symbolic. But the Symbolic, associated with the law of the father, is precisely what allows the fantasy of fulfillment to take its particular shape, to provide the fantasized account retroactively. In this way, the retroactive explanation is necessarily expressed through the ambivalent account of attaining subjecthood and language. Language and symbolic representation allow the subject to formulate the specifics of the fantasy, but at the same time signal the irrecoverable and irreconcilable distance of the fantasy's fulfillment. The law of the father thus becomes the scapegoat for the lack experienced by the subject: If only the father could be expelled, then rebirth through the mother could be attained. While the attainment of language is culturally linked to the father, and is necessary to the articulation of the fantasy (and in fact helps explain why many film fantasies resort to the same imagery of sexual difference), it is also vilified as the obstacle to the earlier hallucinatory oneness. The ghost is itself a retroactive account of its own life:

it acknowledges its own paradoxical underpinnings as it is caught between the too-early and the too-late, but it attempts nonetheless to articulate the process after the fact. Since it can never successfully do so, the ghost is destined to haunt, to return again and again in an attempt to dramatize and articulate an unfulfillable desire.

Language and the voice take on highly important roles in ghost films; even films that do not feature an invisible character emphasize the voice, mouth, or throat as problems or as vehicles of resolution. As we have seen in both *Ghost* and *Always,* Sam and Pete, respectively, cannot tell their girl-friends that they love them while alive, a problem dramatized masochistically by their ghostly interludes. As a ghost, Sam cannot make his voice heard except to Oda Mae, whom he must use as a "translator," and in *Always,* although Pete can make himself heard subliminally, his presence is not acknowledged and his words are twisted and used against him. Meanwhile Dorinda talks in her sleep, providing Pete with access to her feminine subconscious, to which he is now finally able to communicate his feelings. In *Truly, Madly, Deeply,* Nina's boss, Sandy, cannot communicate with his wife because he does not speak Spanish, thus necessitating that Nina become his translator. Although Jamie dies of a sore throat, his death results in his ability to communicate trivial messages to Nina in Spanish, and in fact his presence is first made known to Nina only through his disembodied voice. Meanwhile, Nina's friend Mark describes his father as being "completely silent." In *Ghost Dad,* Winston is first introduced via his tape-recorded voice, foreshadowing his stint as a ghost where his voice will go "out of sync." *Kiss Me Goodbye* introduces the ghost, Jolly, through his singing, the sound of his tap dancing, and through his voice on a message machine. *Hearts and Souls* features a would-be singer who cannot sing and romantic partners who are unable to express their emotions. In *Field of Dreams* (1989) Ray tells how he was unable to apologize to his father while alive, linking this otherwise anomalous film to other films through the problem of unexpressed emotion. The resolution to this example of the too-late is initiated through a mysterious disembodied voice, which exhorts him to "ease his pain." Later in the story, Ray's little girl almost chokes to death, compelling a ghost to step across a magic border at the edge of the field to save her. Not only does this crisis facilitate the resolution of the narrative but it somehow enables the baseball ghosts to be visible to the rest of the world.[13] In *Alice,* Alice is speechless when she first meets her lover, Joe, and later feels as if she was possessed and saying words which do not belong to her.[14] In *Beetlejuice,* the use of words is powerful enough to summon Beetlejuice from his prison, although he himself cannot say his own name and must use charades to compel Lydia to say it for him. Beetlejuice is also able to make his voice speak through other mouths and he uses this technique to force his marriage to

Lydia at the end of the film. When the couple tries to stop the marriage, he prevents them from saying his name (which would return him to his prison) by causing a closed zipper and then a metal plate to appear over the wife's mouth. He then causes the husband's teeth to fly out of his mouth. Outside of the house, the ghosts are prevented from leaving by a giant snake whose head consists of an infinite series of mouths. In *Dead Again,* the female is completely mute at the beginning of the film except for her uncontrollable screams in the middle of the night. Later an aged reporter (who will reveal key information) no longer has a voice due to throat cancer. He can communicate only through a tinny voice-box and exacerbates his condition by smoking cigarettes through a hole in his throat.[15]

Thus, although most people associate ghosts with invisibility, which suggests difficulties of seeing and being seen, it is perhaps surprising then that most ghost films focus equally on hearing, speaking, and on the mouth and voice. Among all of the films cited, the disembodied voice remains the most common factor, linking even the most disparate films to one another, and spanning the range of ghosts from visible to invisible. Because the mother in the masochistic scenario is associated with the pre-Oedipal "oral phase," in which the child finds pleasure at the mother's breast, this may explain the fixations on the voice, mouth, and throat. The most obvious arena for creating a fantasy of fulfillment stems from the child's desire for the absent breast. When the child re-creates the sucking motions in the hallucinatory recreation of original fulfillment, fantasy is created.[16] Though this moment is deemed autoerotic, the ghost displays a similar type of autoeroticism in its reflexive relation to film. The autoeroticism that creates fantasy is analogous to the self-referential quality of ghosts which, by reflecting back on themselves, seem to be self-contained fantasies.

While vision and sight are certainly important elements of primal fantasies, voice and hearing are equally important in both the creation and re-creation of fantasy scenarios. In his discussion of the cinematic apparatus, Peter Wollen notes that sound in film places the spectator in the position of being (like a ghost) an "invisible guest." While the invisible guest looks, synchronous sound and dialogue permit us to feel as if we are the third party in the conversation. Film theory has tended to privilege the role of sight in discussions of the subject formation, a bias reflected in the notion of Lacan's famous "mirror stage." Yet it must be remembered that "the scene in front of the mirror is not a silent scene, [it] is a scene in which there are the words of the mother and the crowing of the child."[17] As with music and the pre-Oedipal, psychoanalytic conceptions of the voice are conflicted, thus revealing its paradoxical nature. For while the voice of the mother is at first powerful to the child, the voice later becomes associated with language and interdiction by the father.[18]

Jean-Louis Comolli observes that "sound and speech are plebiscited as *the 'truth' which was lacking* in silent film." Thus, although the voice is often equated with a metaphysics of presence, it is primarily through language and speech that the voice takes on its ideological power in the Hollywood film.[19] In ghost films, however, the voice is exposed as the paradoxical vehicle of illusory subjecthood. As such, although ghosts problematize the voice and communication, the voice coincidentally and simultaneously becomes the necessary vehicle for accessing the maternal, expelling the father and achieving one-ness.

Invisibility and the auditory aspects of film ghosts (e.g., disembodied voice) go hand-in-hand. The disembodied voice—like the gaze—is another mark of patriarchal oppression in classical Hollywood films. Whereas women's voices are constantly associated with a female body (thereby "interiorized"), male voices are allowed a certain invulnerability due to their "exteriorization" in voice-overs and other diegetic, yet authoritative venues. According to Silverman, "[In] his most exemplary guise, classic cinema's male subject sees without been seen, and speaks from an inaccessible vantage point."[20] Although many films muddy the body/voice split, Silverman's theory directly applies to Sam in *Ghost*. Although Oda Mae can hear Sam she cannot see from whence the voice emerges. Likewise, in *Always,* the characters can "hear" Pete's disembodied voice even though they are unaware that it is originating outside of their own heads. And in *Truly, Madly, Deeply* Jamie's voice alone haunts Nina at the beginning of the film before he materializes physically.

If the male voice-over is not extremely common in mainstream films, the disembodied voice is nevertheless equated with male potency and omniscience. By exteriorizing the male voice, mainstream films map sexual difference by creating a kind of discursive hierarchy. The authority of a (male) voice becomes largely incontestable when it is situated above and beyond the diegesis. Through consistently interiorizing the female voice within the body of the female (who is also symbolically interiorized by her placement in domestic venues), mainstream films express sexual difference through a manipulation of inner and outer categories.[21] Although both Doane and Silverman discuss this kind of vocal mapping at length, neither considers a disembodied voice that can be both disembodied and interiorized within the diegesis, as is the case with many ghosts. Furthermore, the masochistic scenario undercuts the law of the father, setting forth a subject who is necessarily male (seeing but not seen), but whose voice is nevertheless thrown into question by being neither here nor there, neither fully interiorized nor fully exteriorized.

In ghost films, the disembodied male voice often speaks through a woman or other vessel of translation. As with other mainstream films, the authority of the female voice is undermined or otherwise attributed to some "other" source beyond her control.[22] This occurs in *Ghost, Always, Truly, Madly, Deeply, Kiss Me Goodbye, Beetlejuice, Switch,* and *Dead Again.* Oda Mae speaks the words Sam feeds her; Ted (the bumbling oaf whom Pete helps to achieve manhood) speaks the words Pete feeds him; and Dorinda speaks the words the "Other" would have her speak: a grocery list.[23] In *Alice,* when Alice is given a special potion to help her sort out her relationship with the mysterious stranger, she later reports that "I thought someone else was talking. The words were coming out. . . . And I was so forward, too. Completely obnoxious. But he was responsive. It was like I was possessed." In *Kiss Me Goodbye,* Kay's mother cannot help herself from insulting Kay's fiancé (the "gravedigger"), who will replace Jolly as Kay's husband.

> Mother: He's probably playing with those dead Arabs.
> Kay: Mother, that's his job.
> Mom: He's such a nerd.
> Kay: He's not a nerd. Where did you ever learn that word?
> Mom: It just came out when I met him.

Similarly, in *Beetlejuice* the title character speaks through the mouth of the girl, Lydia—both literally, through ventriloquism, but also by cajoling her to say his name through a game of charades.

Such male/female mediation is indicative of the way in which Hollywood films have traditionally robbed women of vocal authority. In ghost films, however, the male voice is undermined through its narrative context and by its masochistic bumbling. While the voice of the male represents a literal manifestation of the phallus, the male coding is a conflation of gender and language, which ghost films undermine. In *Truly, Madly, Deeply,* Nina is the typical female mediator as she helps translate languages—not only other men's words, but whole cultures of words. By splitting the voice from the body, ghost films play out the stereotypical insistence that men do the speaking, but at the same time complicate this by making their voices inaudible to other characters or incomprehensible without mediation. Although insisting on the male/female split, the films nevertheless expose the dilemma of the subject who speaks but who is also himself spoken by language. What becomes more and more apparent (and is literal in *Truly, Madly, Deeply* through the translation of languages) is that the voice speaking through the woman or other mediator is conveniently coded as male but is really the Other of language, the Other that speaks through us when we relinquish ourselves to the Symbolic. The ghost exhibits the fact that—as Lacan says—speech produces not presence, but absence. According to Silverman, "the discoursing voice is the agent of symbolic castration—that at the moment the subject enters language, he or she also undergoes a phenomenal 'fading' or 'aphanasis.'. . . [Furthermore], language preexists and coerces speech . . . it can never be anything but 'Other.'"[24] Although ghosts attempt to use their voices and language to establish their presence, they inadvertently expose the lack on which their presence is based.

Lacan theorizes that the subject is castrated or divided by coming into language, a process described as aphanasis—or the fading of the subject. Since language effectively castrates as it brings the individual into the Symbolic, the subject is caught in an uneasy paradox. To begin with, the subject has no control in his/her representation because the subject's signification is given by the Other—the subject's "subjecthood" is dependent on an Other and is not autonomous. Consequently, the subject is caught between the Other and its place in the signifying chain thus revealing the precarious and phantasmatic nature of the subject. The subject is neither signifier nor signified and so is simultaneously in and outside of language, "endlessly displaced along the signifying chain in pursuit of the (nonexistent) signifier that would fully represent it." Just as it enters language, the subject simultaneously and paradoxically fades: "the subject enters the signifying chain only to fade."[25] The precarious and phantasmatic nature of the subject is nowhere more obvious than in ghost characters who frequently fade (literally) and whose relationship to language and speech is continually called into question by the voice/body split. Lacan's theory of the subject acknowledges not only that the subject is an illusion founded on lack, but that language—itself a signifying system dependent on absence—coincides with the coming into being of the subject.

The ghost similarly mimics the subject undergoing the process of aphanasis, invisible and fading (often transparent) at the moment of the speech act. The ghost acts out this process, demonstrating through itself the phenomenal absence that occurs in speech. The ghost, while embodying a subject that coerces speech, claims on the one hand to be coincidental with language, but at the same time demonstrates the slippage between being the phallus—owning language—and the unity of the subject. When ghosts attempt to speak, they are inaudible or ignored, and when they attempt to speak through another the translation is never adequate, thus masochistically demonstrating the impossibility of the subject. Fantasy thus corresponds to the way in which all signifiers stand in for something absent while the figure of the ghost becomes, therefore, the quintessential figure to express the way in which the entire formation of the subject depends on a structure of fantasy. Just as the ghost literally represents a person who is no longer a "subject," no longer representable, so the process of entering subjecthood is also based on a lack, a fantasized object no longer there, no longer representable. In each case, there is a structuring absence, a subject that depends on an absence for its very formation.

There is something inherently masochistic about the subject since on the one hand the subject can never fully attain subjecthood (can never be the phallus—hence the fantasy of Hollywood superheroes who unrealistically claim to be), but on the other hand can never recapture the lost unity that predated entry into the symbolic. Judith Butler has analyzed the "slave morality" described by Lacanian theory—the Symbolic ushers in a law that is a "permanent impossibility" and creates a fiction of "inevitable subjection."[26] Since the subject is caught between two impossibilities, the masochistic aesthetic played out in these films seems to be an expression of the paradoxical desires for subjecthood (separate but complete) and a return to pre-Oedipal oneness (not separate, but complete).

The way in which the unrepresentable has been inflected by gender relates to the way in which ghost films employ mythical stereotyping, even while undermining or reversing it. In most films, the mapping of sexual difference serves to cover over the illusory nature of the subject and its imbrication with lack. If gender emerges as the result of the Oedipus complex and if the Oedipal interdiction is itself suspect, then the entire identificatory process of gender similarly rests on a fantasy. If the coherent subject is one of the illusions of the Symbolic, then, the coherent and fully gendered subject is an unachievable state. The child is compelled toward and averted from certain objects of desire that help determine his or her gendered identity. Yet the subject can never be a fully gendered subject: "The injunction to become sexed in the ways prescribed by the Symbolic always leads to failure and, in some cases, to the exposure of the phantasmatic nature of sexual identity itself."[27]

Ghost films dramatize the desire for an imaginary unity in the form of a masochistic fantasy, which works on a variety of levels to both produce and sustain pleasure in a fantasy of oneness. But more important, the masochistic fantasy is itself a product of the Oedipal myth—it stems directly from the myth of the repressive Oedipal regime. This is why the films insist upon the stereotypical division of gender—these sexual differences must first be mapped out as products of the Oedipus so that they can then be overcome. As Lacan aptly puts it, "when you draw a rabbit out of a hat, it's because you put it there in the first place."[28]

Thus, although the repression brought about by the Oedipal phase creates the unconscious, Oedipal repression is not solely "repressive" but also "productive" in the Foucaultian sense. For as Foucault would note, the repressed desire is the effect of the law itself: "The law is what constitutes both desire and the lack on which it is predicated."[29] What is produced then is the very myth of oneness constantly sought after but prohibited by the law of the father: "The Oedipus functions to suggest that plenitude is not innately impossible but is merely forbidden: were it not for the law of the father there could be a return to the original satisfaction associated with the mother's body. What it does is erroneously substitute paternal interdiction for the castration that is the inevitable consequence of the signifier."[30] Thus, the masochistic fantasy described in many ghost films seeks nothing if not the expulsion of the guilty father in order to return to oneness with the mother.

The problems of invisibility and the voice can be explored further in relation to viewer pleasure, for together invisibility and disembodied voices constitute the play between the fantastic qualities of the cinema and the marvelous effects of suture. Because film ghosts manipulate and comment on conventional uses of cinematic sight and sound, a more detailed description of the conventions of classical Hollywood film will help to provide a context for the physical properties of the ghosts. The tendency of film ghosts to comment comically and self-consciously on the filmic process is dependent on highly codified conventions that are best described by neoformalist theories. It may be, in part, an acknowledgment of these breaks with convention that provokes a comic response in the audience. Since ghosts seem to play with many of the systems of classical Hollywood film, they have the potential actually to subvert the system. However, ghosts do not subvert the tenacious formal conventions of mainstream films for in fact they originate within it. A neoformalist approach provides an excellent vehicle for establishing the formal and strictly physical nature of the film ghost phenomenon. It is inadequate, however, to evaluate the ideological implications of the fantasy scenario in which the ghost consistently takes part. Because the ghost is not just a formal, but also a fantasy device, it will then be necessary to return to psychoanalytic theory to relate formal systems to previous concepts of film fantasy.

Neoformalism

Neoformalist film theory describes and explains the way in which films make meaning by analyzing the formal and structural elements common to all films. The ghost is situated within one of neoformalism's most important categories of analysis, the narrative trajectory. In Hollywood films, narrative logic is the most important structuring element, with systems of space and time interlocking in subordinate roles. Together, these three systems form the irreducible core of the cinematic apparatus. Technical devices (such as dissolves, cuts, and framing) only take on meaning when understood within the context of these three systems.[31] Film ghosts are devices that operate within the three larger systems. Understanding the conventions of space, time, and narrative logic in Hollywood films is critical to this discussion because film ghosts often manipulate such conventions. For example, comedy ghosts subvert linear time by returning from the dead and causing a reversal of the too-late. (Linear time is assumed in Hollywood films, and is inextricably linked to the narrative system itself.)

Film ghosts also manipulate conventional space, which is particularly problematic. Ghosts heretically distort space both within and without the diegesis. In their seminal neoformalist work on classical Hollywood cinema, Bordwell, Staiger, and Thompson define the link between narrative and character space, revealing that the hierarchy of systems subordinates space to narrative considerations. Specifically, the techniques used to depict film space (centering, balancing, frontality, depth, sound) are almost always related to our sense of story space. "Since the classical narrative depends upon psychological causality, we can think of these strategies as aiming to personalize space. Surroundings become significant partly for their ability to dramatize individuality. Hence the importance of doors: the doorway becomes a privileged zone of human action, promising movement, encounters, confrontations and conclusions."[32] This "door-knob cinema," as André Bazin once called it, is undermined by ghosts, who often ignore doors and pop into scenes unannounced. In *Ghost,* much is made of Sam's first attempts to walk through a closed door, an ability which later becomes important to the climax of the film. In *Made in Heaven,* the characters need only think about where they want to go in order to appear there suddenly. In *Truly, Madly, Deeply,* the otherwise solid ghost appears in Nina's locked bathroom as she takes a bath. *Beetlejuice* also takes note of the importance of doorways when it has the ghost-couple draw a chalk door on the wall in order to leave their house and gain access to their cosmic "case worker" via an eternal waiting room. (Drawing the doorknob is actually the final touch, which permits the door to open.) Similarly, *Ghost Dad* acknowledges and then goes beyond door-knob cinema by having the ghost character first fall through his front door but then continue falling through the floor as well. Here, the self-conscious comment on the ghostly tactic of ignoring doors mostly serves to reinforce the importance of doors to the rest of cinematic action. Most ghosts go through doors but not floors precisely because it is necessary or convenient to the narrative. Thus the fact that ghosts have a habit of ignoring doors may have less to do with the logic of cinematic space than with narrative logic and the way in which ghosts are conceived as products of this system.[33]

Because narrative logic is the dominant system, all other elements in the film tend to be motivated by notions of cause and effect, and by the psychological imperatives of the protagonist(s). According to a classical reading, typical Hollywood cinema depends upon the characters' psychological motivations and the achievement of goals through overcoming obstacles.[34] These elements comprise what formalists call compositional motivation, and they include all the causal elements that make the story cohere—for example, psychological traits of the characters, inciting incidents, goals, and obstacles. This is not to say that other motivations do not come into play. For example, genre is one type of motivation that may override narrative causality and thus is one kind of motivation extremely pertinent to ghost films.[35] Characteristics of comic fantasy and the fantastic motivate some of the more peculiar aspects of film ghosts and help explain and situate ghosts' abnormal abilities and their violations of physical laws.

Hollywood films can also be motivated by artistic considerations, including spectacle and other aesthetic elements that exist for their own sake. Of equal interest are those elements that call attention to themselves and to the system within which they operate. Neoformalists call this "baring the device," a technique common to the comedy genre.[36] Since ghosts often "bare the device" (by walking through walls, etc.), this quality can be considered in the context of comedic spectacle and in relation to filmic reflexivity. In fact, an intriguing point about comic fantasies is the way in which humor and fantasy interact. One of the requirements of fictional fantasy is that it become a world unto itself—a world whose rules are clearly defined and highly structured. But when these rules are violated or misinterpreted, the result is often humorous: "The fact that fantasy has rules implies that misunderstandings are bound to arise."[37] The humor arising from the ghosts' interaction with the rules of the "real world" in *Ghost Dad, Beetlejuice,* and other films is a prime example of this type of comic fantasy.[38]

Despite these other types of motivations, in Hollywood films, compositional motivations of character and narrative causality tend to predominate over other systems. This analysis has been particularly concerned with compositional motivation because ghosts seem to be almost a by-product of this structure. The very existence of ghosts in film narratives must be traced to the goal-oriented protagonist and analyzed within the framework of both character and narrative structure. As has been evident in my discussion of Peter Brooks's narrative theory (which combines neoformalism with psychoanalysis) there is an inextricable interconnection between the goals of the protagonists and the structure and trajectories of the narrative. Ghosts cannot be fully analyzed as only psychologically driven "characters" or only as "plot devices," for they are clearly both.

To help further situate the ghost device within the systems of Hollywood cinema, I turn now to cinematic space as understood from a psychoanalytic perspective.[39] This will lead also to a re-examination of the voice and body, since these are both problematized by the ghost's manipulation of conventional space. In exploring the ghost as a device within larger spatial conventions, it becomes clear that devices and systems work together in intricate harmony.

Space, Bodies, and Voices

In mainstream films, screen space and synchronous sound work together to foreground a homogeneous diegetic space as well as what Mary Ann Doane calls an "organically unified" body. Although the addition of sound to the cinema carries with it the risk of exposing the "material hetero-geneity of the medium," it also becomes a primary means of creating unified characters, anchoring the body with the "presence" of a voice.[40] Just as the voice supports the body in the illusion of a unified character, it also helps anchor the body within the diegetic space. This can be seen most dramatically in the way in which the "voice-off" helps expand and unify the diegetic space, whose edges would otherwise be foreshortened and made noticeable by the frame-line of the screen. Unlike a voice over, which is often divorced from the diegesis, the voice-off is a temporarily off-screen voice. In classical cinema, the camera usually cuts or pans over to the character projecting the voice. Thus the character's presence is established beyond the frame-line and then linked to the frame's current diegetic space by means of the voice-as-bridge and by other contextual determinants. In Doane's analysis, "He/she is 'just over there,' just beyond the frameline,' in a space which 'exists' but which the camera does not choose to show. The traditional use of voice-off constitutes a denial of the frame as a limit and an affirmation of the unity and homogeneity of the depicted space."[41] In short, the combination of synchronized sound in conjunction with editing and other conventions of the cinema help create and sustain the conditions of verisimilitude as applied to space and the unified body/subject. This verisimilitude is rarely ruptured in a cinema whose project re-creates a feeling of cohesiveness and oneness in the story and hence in the viewer.[42]

For this reason (with the exception of the extradiegetic voice-over), one rarely finds a voice without a body in classical cinema, although (as Doane admits in a footnote) two kinds of cinematic voices without bodies are common: the voice of God, or the artificial voice of computers. However, she overlooks the many film ghosts who routinely provide disembodied voices as a by-product of their invisibility. Doane also asserts that for the characters in a film "there are no voices-off."[43] But here again, the device of the ghost is an exception to this rule. Many film ghosts make themselves "present" to the other characters and/or to the audience solely through their voice while remaining completely invisible. Their disembodied voices function as voice-offs for the other characters—something which is not supposed to happen according to Doane. Such occurrences are found in all ghost films that use invisibility as a device.[44]

The disassociation of the voice from the body works not so much to destroy spatial contiguity (this is maintained by the other characters' voices, common set pieces, and the audience's expectations) but more to manipulate the audience's sense of the unified subject. Whereas cinematic space in mainstream films remains mostly intact, and a key device in Hollywood cinema's hermeneutic code is entrances and exits through doors, this convention is temporarily subverted by ghosts who can go through walls and hence

94

through locked or closed doors. Many ghosts "materialize" directly into a room as if cinematically dissolving from one location to another. While providing an example of filmic reflexivity, the device also raises questions of perception.

Ghosts play on the problems of perception and subjectivity both intra- and extradiegetically, drawing the audience into the visual and aural games played out by the characters. For example, in *Heaven Can Wait,* Mr. Jordan displays many of the qualities described above—he is invisible to other characters and has the ability to walk through walls and closed doors. Nevertheless, his entry into the scene is often announced to the audience or to Joe (who can always see him) not by showing him "materialize" or walk through a wall, but by merely panning over to reveal his presence. This is a less overt or tricky way of revealing his presence and avoids calling attention to the filmic apparatus in the way that special effects would. This is one of the most common methods of linking the voice-off to the body of the off-screen character. In ghost films, however, the technique is often used as a means of showing the subjective perception of the ghost by one character at the expense of other characters who can see nothing. It also helps to implicate the audience in the problems of perspective and perception. On the one hand, the viewers may wonder whether they have previously failed to perceive the character. On the other hand, in some cases, the audience is not given the option of wondering. The camera may pan to an area of the set that was previously off-screen and thus unseen. In such cases, the perceptive qualities of the viewer's eyes seem to be synonymous with what the camera can see. In other words, a character (in this case an angel) becomes present when and only when the camera "looks" at him. The look of the camera/audience seems to call the character into existence.[45] This tactic further helps anchor the viewer's sense of contiguous diegetic space, so that it is not space itself that is thrown into question, but instead human (and filmic) subjectivity.

Ghosts' manipulation of space does not seem to disrupt the classical system itself, but works within normative conventions of space to foreground issues pertaining to the subjectivity and to the psychologically motivated narrative agent. This is, of course, consistent with traditional hierarchies of classical Hollywood films. Ghosts' tendency to ignore doors and walls usually reinforces our sense of "normal" space rather than subverting it, since such activities are confined only to ghost characters who are usually the exception rather than the rule within the diegesis. By containing such manipulations within the character of the ghost, the larger systems of space are thereby maintained. One exception to this would be *Made in Heaven,* where all of the characters subvert space and time while in heaven. The argument still applies, however, since this tendency is confined to heaven and does not affect the rest of the film or systems of space or time through which the film itself is constructed. As we have seen, however, the physical structure of the (haunted) house and the depiction of heavenly oneness in ghost films posits a conceptual use of space that opposes itself to Oedipal fantasy scenarios.

While adhering to the systems of space, time, and narrative logic, film ghosts nevertheless provide a significant variation to conventions of sound, framing, and editing, particularly when these aspects of cinema are considered psychoanalytically. From this latter perspective, the cinematic operation tries to create a sensation of cohesion and oneness in the viewer through a variety of means, most notably through synchronized sound and continuity editing (e.g., reversal angle shots). Not only does the classical Hollywood film attempt to provide a seamless, coherent storyworld, but in the process the viewer is said to be "sutured" into the imaginary fullness. But the illusion of oneness is threatened by the viewer's own exclusion from the production process.[46] Since there is usually no consistent "first person" narrator/camera in film, the diegetic character becomes the feint to cover over the invisible source of production. In her discussion of suture, Silverman thus contends that the castration crisis provoked by the "absent enunciator" is not due to woman's lack (as Mulvey contended) but due to the viewer's exclusion from the site of production. Although sound synchronization helps provide the sense of presence necessary to cover over the lack, it is nevertheless often attributed to the female in mainstream films. The female voice is consistently linked to a female body, whereas the male voice is allowed the privilege of incorporeality and the illusion of omniscience. But just as the invisible, incorporeal body of the ghost represents a fantasy scenario in which abject qualities are expelled or erased, so the corresponding disembodied voice aids in the erasure of bodily horror. Along these lines, Silverman recounts the work of Pascal Bonitzer, who "describes the embodiment of the voice in terms of aging and death, remarking that as soon as its source is revealed, it becomes 'decrepit' and 'mortal', vulnerable to stray bullets."[47] As with other expulsions of the abject in ghost films, the decrepit body is rejected by allowing the voice to be free. This not only creates a kind of hologram or simulacrum of the body but requires that the voice take on the onus of establishing the subject. Unfortunately for the ghost character, language becomes a precarious basis for its experience as an Oedipal subject. Although most ghosts employ a disembodied voice, the disconnection of the voice from the body is generally a temporary manifestation that becomes complicated by invisibility and perception.

It is difficult to characterize the male voice when it is neither attached to a body (thus interiorized, female), nor is it exteriorized (as in the male voice-over). This situation arises in the case of a ghost's voice that is detached from the body or from the simulacrum that is the ghost itself. The invisibleness of ghosts wreaks havoc on both reverse angle cutting and the voice-off, for in each case the suturing effect is ruptured. In the first case, the return of the character's look can never be sealed without someone to do the "looking." In the second case, the voice-off seems to have no referent. The ghost mimics the problem that is trying to be covered over—it enunciates the absent enunciator, presents the unrepresentable, and exposes the dilemma of the subject.

The Fantastic versus the Marvelous

If the film ghost exposes the paradox of the subject, it also problematizes subjectivity itself. Characters and viewers must question whether what they see and hear is wholly objective or subjective. The genre of the fantastic is one which by its very nature problematizes vision and language. In her analysis of fantasy, Rosemary Jackson draws a parallel between the fantastic process and the camera's "eye" in cinema, suggesting that all cinema is, in some sense, fantastic.[48] In other words, classical Hollywood cinema has the capacity to shift the viewer's focus among various "points of view"— including so-called objective ones. This constant and easy shifting creates a certain movement between "objective" and "subjective" realities. Although Jackson does not speculate on the nature of film ghosts per se, they provide a particularly pertinent case study. Film ghosts not only take part in this fantastic process of the cinema, but further problematize the notion of vision through their invisibility and through their ability to appear to some people and not to others.

Most ghost films feature a ghost who can be seen and/or heard by only one character. In *Ghost,* Sam cannot be seen by anyone (except the audience), and can be heard only by Oda Mae. In *Kiss Me Goodbye,* only Kay can see and hear Jolly. In *Heart Condition,* only Moon can see and hear the ghost, Stone. In *Alice,* only Alice can see her ex-boyfriend. In *Beetlejuice,* the ghosts can at first only be seen by the child, Lydia. *Always* complicates this process by making Pete invisible, but by making him audible to characters on a subconscious level. *Truly, Madly, Deeply* avoids the issue by simply never providing scenes in which characters other than Nina are co-present with the ghost. *Ghost Dad* permits the ghost to be seen only when the lights are out so that in bright light he is completely invisible.

Unlike traditionally scary ghost stories, most comedy ghost films do not dwell on the question of reality versus illusion, and even though most of the characters cannot see or hear the ghosts, the audience almost always can.[49] In almost every case in which the audience can see the ghost interacting with at least one character, the audience is never asked to question the reality of the ghost. Rather, the films depend on the audience's acceptance of the presence of the ghost, an effect characteristic of the "marvelous," a generic mode of the fantastic. If the fantastic depends on the uncertain reality of the ghost's presence, the marvelous depends on its acceptance.

Classical cinema permits us to see first the perspective of one character, followed the next moment by another's perspective. These shifts are usually conducted seamlessly in a process of suture produced via such filming techniques as reverse angle shots and sound bridges. Invisible ghosts complicate this, however, since the sudden shift to invisibility exposes the shift in subjectivity, making it potentially jarring. Comedy ghosts, however, do not want to dwell on the fantastic and shattering qualities of perspective and subjectivity even though they cannot ignore them. Instead they shift the fantastic response to the other characters, so that the audience finds the surprises funny rather than disturbing. Although invisible ghosts can never escape the possibility of baring the device and revealing the fragmented nature of the medium, in these films they are managed in such a way that their subversive qualities are interiorized. That is, the diegetic fantasy in which they participate provides an alibi for the disruption they cause in subjectivity, a disruption that becomes comic and thus tossed aside as threat in favor of a fantasy promoting oneness.

If the fantastic aims to disrupt, then in these films the marvelous presentation of the ghosts helps reverse this process and instead promotes a return to oneness. The audience is invited to participate in the protagonist's perceptions of the ghost, thus helping validate both the reality of the ghost as well as the subjectivity of the protagonist. Shifting the fantastic uncertainty to other characters simultaneously clinches the "reality" of the ghost as an autonomous being and deflects the fantastic away from the audience's reactions of disbelief. What is frightening and fantastic to other characters becomes marvelous and thus comic to the audience, not frightening. For example, *Ghost* provides several scenes in which characters cannot see Sam and so question their sanity. In one scene, Sam sits in a chair whose wheels allow him to easily scoot across the room, thus frightening the villain, Carl. Even though the camera suddenly and very briefly shows Carl's subjective perception—showing an empty chair rolling along—the viewer does not share Carl's fright, siding instead with Sam and laughing at Carl's confusion.

The comic response is augmented by the apparent endowment of mechanical contrivances with volitional motion (a comical notion only after its fantastic qualities have been displaced). W. H. Auden provides such an account of comedy using the example of an umbrella turning inside out in the wind: "The operation of physical laws upon inorganic objects [is] associated with a human being in such a way that it is they who appear to be acting from personal volition and their owner who appears to the passive thing. . . . The activating agent, the wind, is invisible, so the cause of the umbrella turning inside out appears to lie in the umbrella itself. It is not particularly funny if a tile falls and makes a hole in the umbrella, because the cause is visibly natural."[50] Since the invisible ghost is visible to the audience, a paradoxical rift is created between the viewer's subjectivity and that of the other characters. The films play the marvelous response of the audience off of the fantastic response of the characters—reassuring the audience that the voice is connected to the body after all. Thus, the sight of a chair moving of its own volition becomes comical, rather than threatening.

A related explanation for the comedic effect of ghosts is found in theories which posit the reverse, namely that the human body becomes comic when it resembles a machine (e.g., the Keystone Kops). For example, a comedic response may be elicited upon observing "something mechanical encrusted on the living: the attitudes, gestures, and the movements of the human body are laughable in exact proportion as that body reminds us of a mere machine."[51]

Such an example occurs when ghosts comment on the filmic apparatus by dissolving in and out of scenes, thereby calling attention to themselves as filmic "projections." In *Ghost Dad,* the "ghost in the machine" is made comically explicit by making the ghost, Winston, visible only when the lights are dimmed. Throughout the film, Winston and family fear that he will completely disappear when he occasionally "flickers" and almost "fades out." As for his voice, at one point Winston's voice becomes garbled and unnaturally slow. He is helped by a paranormal expert who explains that he is merely "out of sync" and who then uses a mechanical apparatus to correct the problem. The link between mechanically reproduced voices and ghostly disembodied voices further explains why voices without bodies tend to elicit or be associated with comedy in ghost films. Indeed, even before his death, Winston is first introduced via his disembodied voice on a tape recorder, thus linking his future ghostly state to a mechanical object. Despite this compelling link between comedy and the mechanized body, the unusual break of voice from body via the device of the ghost poses a question that goes beyond exposing the artificiality of the cinematic medium. For in many of these films, the ideological implications of the ghost more than overshadow the mere hilarity of a break with convention. The break with convention is recuperated into the diegesis precisely by creating thematic and generic motivations associated with the notion of the ghost as a continuing soul.

Another source of comedy lies in the collision of more than one ongoing series of events or one or more interpretations of a single sequence of events. This is true of both sight gags and puns where the interpretation of an action or image in the first case, or a word or phrase in the second case, carries with it the possibility of a double meaning. A similar understanding can be applied to the sight gags that often occur in ghost comedies. Here, the fact that some people (including the audience) can see the ghost while others cannot provides the possibility of two interpretations. Thus a link can be established between standard techniques of comedy and the various divergent points of view elicited by invisible ghosts.

Noel Carroll analyzes the sight gag, providing a particularly illuminating example of the phenomenon from a non-ghost film, *The Freshman* (1925), starring Harold Lloyd. The sequence begins when a man in a train accidentally drops a lighted match onto Lloyd's sweater. Lloyd, who is on the platform below, is unaware of this event as he mistakenly believes that a group of students is about to welcome him to college. When the man on the train smacks Lloyd in the back to put out the flame, Lloyd believes that he has received a hearty welcome by the dean of the college, to whom he then relays an equally overzealous slap. The dean is almost knocked over and, unfortunately for Lloyd, this unhappy misunderstanding becomes his introduction to college life. According to Carroll, the humor in this scene derives from the "interpenetration" of each character's interpretation of the same events.

> Indeed, none of the characters has the overall interpretation of the event that the audience has, for the simple reason that none of the characters is positioned in the fiction to see everything we see. Moreover, some of these event descriptions, as relativized to characters' points of view, directly conflict. Harold thinks that he is making a friend just as he is making an enemy. And it is this incongruous conflict of interpretations rooted visually in the play of points of view that gives the scene its humorous edge.[52]

When ghosts are invisible to some characters and not others, they have the potential to elicit the same type of comic reaction that traditional sight gags do when they provide conflicting points of view resulting in incongruous interpretations. The most common interpretation on the part of characters who cannot see the ghost is that they have gone mad or have drunk too much.[53] Although some of the minor characters may question their sanity, the main perceiver of the ghost ultimately rejects this interpretation, just as the audience does. This is achieved, at least in part, through initially introducing the ghost through a disembodied voice, but then "proving" the reality of the ghost's presence through its subsequent materialization.

Paranoia and (Film) Projection

Whereas the fantastic qualities of the cinema are described by its ability to show multiple points of view, synchronized sound helps anchor the subject and mitigate the sense of the fantastic. In his influential work on sound in cinema, Rick Altman asserts that sound acts as the crucial anchor for the body.[54] The disembodied voice of the ghost threatens to disrupt this process for the viewer, only to be recuperated through selective invisibility, which promotes a "marvelous" response. Just as the marvelous/fantastic use of invisibility helps reassure the viewer's sense of oneness, the marvelous helps expel the paranoiac qualities associated with hearing voices (disembodied voices) as exhibited, for example, in the woman's gothic. In comedy ghost films, a certain amount of humor stems from witnessing the reactions of characters who believe that other characters are crazy or hearing voices. Thus in *Ghost, Kiss Me Goodbye, Ghost Dad,* for example, many scenes play on the belief in the sanity of the (often) female protagonist, pitting her against the other characters who are not "in-the-know."

Paranoia is, of course, pertinent to ghosts because ghosts raise questions about whether one is being watched by an invisible presence, or about whether one is hearing voices. In gothic horror films, the woman becomes paranoid and hears voices which cannot be fully explained. According to Freud, the conviction of being watched or delusions of observation are, as Doane notes, "the most striking symptoms of paranoia."[55] In addition, paranoia is characterized by a disturbance in the ability to distinguish between subject and object, between internal and external. This is another reason why the internal space of the home becomes fraught with terror in gothic horror stories. The inability to trust fully that the interior of the home is safe from exterior evils, or—more likely—the suspicion that the surfaces of the home conceal something unseen is characteristic of paranoia in gothic horror films.[56]

Just as the abject is expelled by the presence of the ghost, revealing these films to be diametrically opposed to horror in their treatment of death, so the paranoid aspect of disembodied voices are expelled, redeeming the validity of subject/object in the mind of the viewer. The films use invisibility selectively to help align the audience with the otherwise delusional perceiver, disallowing the paranoiac interpretation and instituting a marvelous response diametrically opposite to the horror induced by gothic thrillers. The perceiving characters can be said to "project" their perceptions away from an internal subjective arena so that the ghosts are both filmic and psychic projections of what would, in other films, be a horrific neurosis.

The reflexive relation of ghosts to filmic projections is revealed again in *Ghost Dad,* where the ghost flickers like a film projection and can only be seen in dim light. (As noted, when he is having difficulty speaking, he is told that he is "out of sync.") In *Alice,* the ghost steps into a spotlight and "fades out," just as other ghosts often dissolve in and out of invisibility. In a slightly different vein, the ghost in *Maxie* is summoned through a videotape of herself appearing in an old movie, recalling other films that feature both ghosts and films as kinds of symbiotic projection systems (*Defending Your Life, Scrooged,* and *Truly, Madly, Deeply*).

Giving Up the Ghost

The concept of projection is crucial to both an understanding of ghosts as filmic devices (as self-referential projections of human beings) and also to the comedy ghost's relation to paranoia, because projection is a means of dealing with delusional paranoia. In her discussion of Freud's theories of paranoia, Doane notes that projection becomes the patient's "desperate attempt to reassert, reconstitute the opposition between subject and object which the patient lacks. As Freud points out, projection is evidence of a process of reconstruction and recovery."[57] The process is not confined to paranoiacs, however, but according to Freud, is normal and necessary in order for the subject to distinguish between ego and the external world.

If projection is a key process in separating the ego from the world, then how does it fit in with the fantasy of oneness at work in most of these ghost movies? The answer lies not only in the fact that ghosts are by nature paradoxical, but in the way in which ghosts take part in a fantasy of the origin of the subject. Just as the ghost is caught in a slippage of time (masochistically and retroactively tracing its origin) and in a slippage of space (representing an absence), so the ghost can never hope to resolve fully the dilemma of inner and outer realities, which the Oedipus has rendered separate. Ghosts embody the struggle between inner/outer, subject and object, both relying on the subject/object split but also attempting to overcome it in a fantasy of oneness. If, as Lacan argues, the confusion between internal/exterior, subject/object is, like masochism, "the foreclosure of the paternal signifier,"[58] then neither the protagonist nor the audience is asked to participate in the paranoia. Whereas the diegetic fantasies concern a desire for pre-Oedipal oneness, and whereas the ghost-characters become paradoxical representations of subjecthood, the audience is prompted to experience the hallucinatory oneness the ghost fantasy attempts to create. While horror films may play on paranoia, ghost comedies seek to recuperate the uncertainties associated with disembodied voices and invisible bodies by anchoring them in a relay system between the audience and the key perceiving character.

The ghost re-creates the coming into being of the subject, but this is also synonymous with the subject's gender, which in Freudian and Lacanian theory has been coded male. The primal fantasy in which the child witnesses the sexual act between the parents is re-created in the ghost's tendency to overhear and to oversee. But the process is exposed as masochistic and impossible, for the ghost reenacts the process of subjecthood (e.g., attempting to master the physical world), a process that proves to be impossible. This has repercussions for the way in which gender is understood, for if the fully coherent subject is, in essence, impossible, so then is gender.

Chapter 5

Gender Switching

The film ghost's efforts to return to the maternal/pre-Oedipal is part of a desire to return to the illusion of oneness. The fantasy of return is created, however, in conjunction with the coming into language, which permits the retroactive expression of the fantasy scenario. The dichotomies of gender and sexual difference employed by ghost films are thus instituted precisely because these oppositions are necessary to provide a setting for the desire of oneness. The establishment of sexual difference is thus necessary in order to frame the desire the films purport to fulfill.

Desire is born from the child's original experience of a lack or loss. Traditional psychoanalytic models associate lack with the castration anxiety that Oedipal intervention brings; theories of pre-Oedipal masochism consider this loss to stem from the child's separation from the mother (even though this loss may then be covered over through defensive strategies designed to denigrate the child/mother bond). In mainstream films, the desire to return to oneness is not confined to ghost films but is frequently expressed in terms of heterosexual romance, where romantic union becomes an attempt to re-create the hallucinatory plenitude of the pre-Oedipal.

Romance

Because many ghost films focus on romance, any analysis of gender and gender switching in ghost films must begin with a description of romantic desire and its relation to fantasy and the problem of lack. Romantic desire is integral to a discussion of gender switching because heterosexual romance depends on sexual difference, which likewise permits the possibility and perhaps even the desire to switch positions. The loss associated with female melodrama is reversed and recuperated by the ghost device and becomes instead a trope of the classical Hollywood romance, particularly the romantic comedy.

In his analysis of fairy tales Vladimir Propp concluded that narratives are characterized by the overthrow of villainy or the fulfillment of a lack.[1] The nature of lack takes on a whole new dimension when considered in light of psychoanalytic theory. By any definition, however, the formula seems pertinent to most Hollywood films. Two of the most common ways to overcome villainy or lack—triumphant battle or romantic union—typify two of the most popular Hollywood genres in the 1980s, namely action films and romantic comedies. Although action films such as *Rambo* were hugely successful in the 1980s, two romantic comedies, *Pretty Woman* and *Ghost,* were the surprise hits of 1990, financially trouncing the action films, and breaking all box-office records to date.[2]

Heterosexual romance is prevalent in most Hollywood films, even in films not specifically designated as "romances" or "romantic comedies." As Bordwell, Staiger, and Thompson point out in their study of over one hundred randomly selected films, roughly 95 percent featured or contained a romantic plot.[3] So while *Pretty Woman* might be classified as a "romance," even an action-oriented movie such as *Total Recall* is likely to contain a romantic subplot. Similarly, most of the ghost films in the last decade either feature a romance or contain a romantic component or subplot. Even *Heaven Can Wait* features a romance, despite the fact that the protagonist's initial goal is only to become a football player. Over the course of the film the romance grows in importance so that by the end of the film his desire to "get the girl" is just as important as the original goal—and in fact drives much of the plot. Similarly in *Ghost Dad,* although the father returns ostensibly to save his children from poverty, a romantic subplot complements the overall narrative. Many of these films use ghosts to unfold a fantasy of desire surrounding a return to oneness, but many also employ ghosts as vehicles for creating and expounding on scenarios of a particular type of oneness—that of heterosexual romance. All of the following ghost films contain a male ghost and feature a potential romantic relationship complicated by the too-early death of the protagonist: *Ghost, Truly Madly Deeply, Always, Kiss Me Goodbye, Heaven Can Wait, Made in Heaven, Ghost Dad, Hearts and Souls, Defending Your Life, Heart Condition,* (marginally), and *Dead Again.*

The Lacanian paradigm of subject formation demonstrates how heterosexual, romantic desire is formulated. When the child enters the Symbolic to become a speaking subject, it also necessarily takes up a gendered position. In the pre-Oedipal period the child is not gendered; entry into the Symbolic is associated with the Oedipal crisis in which the phallus signals difference, threatening the child's unity with the mother and presenting the threat of castration. The Symbolic is synonymous with the law of the father (the phallus) and simultaneously defines the male through relegating the mother/female to the status of non-male, or lack. While the Symbolic ushers in the gendered subject, in the process it also creates a lack, which becomes rechanneled into romantic and sexual desire, conceived as heterosexual if the Oedipal injunctions against incest and homosexuality are effective. In an interesting investigation into gender roles, Judith Butler notes that male and female genders are conceived in conjunction with the formation of heterosexual desire and become part of their very definition: "The heterosexualization of desire requires and institutes the production of discrete and asymmetrical oppositions between 'feminine' and 'masculine,' where these are understood as expressive attributes of 'male' and 'female.'"[4] However, the object of desire for the male (associated with the mother and the plentiful breast) is always a fantasy, the recollection of an illusory unity and satisfaction that can never be fulfilled. The lack created by the entry into the Symbolic thus opens up a space of desire for the subject. Romantic love becomes the attempt to fill that lack and restore an illusory unity with the mother. Although the classical Freudian and Lacanian paradigms assume the subject to be male, the female child should also be considered (see below).

In "From Casablanca to Pretty Woman: The Politics of Romance," Robert Lapsley and Michael Westlake provide a classical psychoanalytic account of romance in Hollywood films. Following Lacan, the authors argue that romantic love is necessarily an illusion devised to cover over the fact that the lack can never be fulfilled, for heterosexual desire is based not on a real but on a fantasmatic object. Thus, they contend that "Hollywood is the pretense that the sexual relations exist" or more precisely that Hollywood romance "does not deny that there is a lack, but it claims that it can be made good."[5] The lack is almost always associated with the feminine in Hollywood films, where women are relegated to passive positions that deny the possibility of female desire or female potency. Hollywood films consistently portray women as victims, vessels, or villains—all ways in which the lack is either embodied or vilified. What is understood by "lack," however, can radically affect the terms of the discussion. For example, although lack is often situated in or around the female in classical film, this lack could have several sources—a male perception of the female's anatomical lack, a result of the male's fear of castration—or the notion of lack can be reformulated to encompass a subject formation not driven solely by the Oedipal complex. These options are important in light of Lacan's later revisions to the theory of castration in which lack and castration do not stem (respectively) from the mother and father so much as in the myth of lack in the mother and the myth of the castrating power of the father. For the father himself is not so much the threat, but rather becomes associated with the effect of language on the subject.[6] In this view lack and castration are the necessary by-products of the subject coming into being through language—resulting in "aphanasis" or the fading of the subject.

Since the subject is necessarily divided through language, the goal of romantic union would seem to spell the end, or death, of the subject. How can films reconcile the fulfillment of a desire that leads to the annihilation of the subject who originally desired it? Most Hollywood romances simply sidestep the problem by systematically avoiding the actual sexual union. The most common method is to defer this moment to an imaginary time outside the text. Hence, the happy ending of many Hollywood romances places the reconciliation of the couple at the end of the film ("And they lived happily ever after"), allowing the actual fulfillment of desire to remain in the future. Obstacles to romance become another convenient tactic designed to cover over the impossibility of representing an impossible fulfillment. In melodrama fulfillment is denied through "if-only" strategies whereby the love is realized too late to be consummated. Lapsley and Westlake cite *Ghost* as an example of a film wherein death provides such a scenario, thus thwarting the romantic union: "Death by itself without the complication of belated self-discovery may also figure as the obstacle, as in *Love Story* (1970), *Camille, Bobby Deerfield* (1977) and, most recently, *Ghost,* where but for the fact that Sam is dead and Molly alive they would form a perfect couple."[7]

But does not the ghost subvert this too-late by returning to continue the romance? In *Ghost,* does not Sam come back precisely to provide the "belated self-discovery" by finally articulating his "undying" affection for Molly? Although the ghost device seems to reverse the trajectory of the melodrama, the fantasy figure of the ghost dramatizes the dilemma of this unfulfillable desire. It becomes both the obstacle and the solution to the romantic union. By linking fulfillment to death in a fantasy of suspension and rebirth, the comedy ghost both raises and then resolves the problem.[8] Although ghosts provide the mechanism to reverse temporarily the melodramatic tragedy, they paradoxically prolong it, demonstrating the unfulfillable fantasy nature of romantic union.

Ghost films use the Oedipal/Symbolic as an alibi to return to the pre-Oedipal, masochistically working through the impossibility of a desire created precisely at the same moment that its fulfillment is made impossible. Ghost films and other Hollywood romances institute the parameters of the diegetic fantasy's desire so as to circumscribe the viewer's desire. Although many narratives purport to fulfill this desire (the very desire they have created in the viewer) they cannot: hence the viewer's desire to work through them again and again (either through remakes or repeat viewings). Ghosts thus return again and again, mimicking the impossible but pleasurable process of re-enacting the fantasy and desire for oneness. In both cases a fantasy scenario is revisted, masochistically working through the desire for an unrealizable object of fantasy. Although at first glance the death of a character may seem to be an obstacle to fulfilling the classical romantic trajectory, it may be, simultaneously, a necessary component of the romantic comedy. If the goal of romance is the "oneness" of the couple, the goal of the romantic comedy is the deferment of that oneness. Ghosts are thus perfect narrative devices for instituting the obstacles necessary to the illusory oneness in romantic comedy, while at the same time demonstrating the masochistic nature of fantasy itself.

Gender Switching and Sexual Sameness

The desire to attain oneness in ghost films finds expression not just through a fantasy of maternal access and/or death as re-birth. In ghost films, characters change positions in an attempt to achieve sexual sameness. Just as the male ghost switches positions and becomes feminized, so does the female character assume greater power than normally expected in mainstream films. Gender switching is an important element of these diegetic scenarios and, perhaps more important, may be integral to the pleasurable identification of the film viewer.

Although Freud's original phallocentric model is a good tool in constructing a theory of masochistic pleasure, a focus on the pre-Ocdipal (which is pre-sexual and pre-Symbolic) can be used to apply the theory to both the male and female child. Even Freud—despite his preoccupation with the male—suggested that the child is initially of bisexual nature and only takes on a gendered identity in the later Oedipal stage. Scholars who stress the importance of the pre-Oedipal phase also suggest a greater flexibility in the gendering of both males and females, and revised Lacanian models open up a space not only for women as subjects but also as film spectators. Accordingly, it is possible that both men and women can vicariously assume different gendered identities while watching film.[9] Shifting identification between male and female characters can occur when the narcissistic identification the viewer experiences in the cinema is linked to his or her desire for unification with the mother.[10] The wish to overcome sexual difference is a radical re-reading of cinematic identification processes because it posits the desire for sameness instead of difference, and suggests a mode of rapprochement between two seemingly diametrically opposed genders. This is a crucial move for feminists, for it allows women to conceive of themselves as something other than object. But it also posits men as capable of taking up what would otherwise be seen as a feminized position. In a revision to her earlier work, Laura Mulvey concedes that female spectators have the capacity to identify with male characters. (They have no choice since female characters represent lack only.) However, we must conceive of the possibility of shifting identification between both genders or else be resigned to essentialist and biological notions of gender. The subject's identity may not be fixed irrevocably during childhood and, as Annette Kuhn writes, (and recalling the earlier discussion on the difficulty of speech in the male ghost): "the subject is not 'made' once and for all when language has been acquired—it is in constant flux, being formed in and through every speech act."[11]

The mechanisms of male and female subjectivity with regard to cinematic representations is not as clear-cut as many theorists had once supposed. In fact, identificatory processes are probably much more flexible than they seem on the surface. Revisions to earlier theories suggest that film viewers may have the capacity to identify across gender lines and that cinematic identification is multiple and dispersed. Significantly, it has been largely through a return to the psychoanalytic conception of fantasy that such revisions have been elaborated. Instead of supposing that male and female spectators always identify with their own gender, analyses of fantasy suggest that spectators identify with characters because of their placement in particular fantasy scenarios. Freud demonstrates the link between fantasy and shifting identifications in his account of the child's fantasy of being beaten. In this fantasy, Freud demonstrates that the child does not identify only with one of the characters in the scenario, but places him- or herself outside the fantasy as an observer so as to shift from one character to another. Whereas the fantasy begins with the notion that the child is beaten by its father, it soon becomes apparent that the child is both the observer and the observed: "Some boys are being beaten. (I am probably looking on.)"[12] Although analyses of this now infamous beating fantasy can become quite complex, the crucial point here is that the fantasizer often occupies a dual position, allowing for a fluid process of identification. This duality requires an understanding of fantasy as the setting of desire, a setting which permits the subject to take up positions of the opposite gender.[13]

The device of the ghost provides a perfect vehicle for a masochistic fantasy where active and passive positions are reversed or put into flux. Since most film ghosts share the same type of passive characteristics, ghosts can be considered narrative and filmic conventions through which opposing tendencies of passivity and activity can be worked through. Whereas a film's content might focus on the desire for the return of a loved one, as in *Truly, Madly, Deeply,* the function of the ghost as a convention of gender play would override the specifics of the particular object of desire. In her study of fantasy, Elizabeth Cowie makes a cogent point in considering this type of convention:

> Conventions are thus the means by which the structuring of desire is represented in public forms, inasmuch as, following the arguments of Laplanche and Pontalis fantasy is the mise-en-scène of desire. What is necessary for any public forms of fantasy, for their collective consumption, is not universal objects of desire, but a setting of desiring in which we find our place(s). And these places will devolve, as in the original fantasies, on positions of desire: active or passive, feminine or masculine, mother or son, father or daughter.[14]

If the opposition between active and passive is central to all fantasy then ghosts are quintessential fantasy figures by virtue of their narrative reversals and through their manipulation of active and passive gender roles. For example, in such films as *Defending Your Life* and *Made in Heaven,* which feature deceased characters in heavenly way-stations (not as invisible ghosts), not only does the male protagonist become feminized, but the female protagonist takes on qualities usually associated with male characters.

In *Made in Heaven,* gender roles become clearly reversed once the two main characters leave heaven. As with other films, the male protagonist becomes feminized through a masochistic interlude, even though he is not a ghost. After Mike dies and goes to heaven he meets Anny and falls in love. But Anny is soon born into the world as a different person. This ends the romance and creates a parallel to the too-late associated with dying in other films. Mike begs the angel Emmett to give him a chance to find her on earth. Reluctantly, Emmett makes a deal with Mike, recalling the masochistic tendency to create a contract to ensure the masochistic interlude. The deal gives Mike thirty years to find Anny (now Ally) on earth but if he is unsuccessful he will be doomed to unhappiness. Once on earth, however, the quest to find Ally does not resemble the quests of most ambitious male protagonists, for Mike (reborn as Elmo) is not consciously aware of his goal. Occasionally Elmo experiences strange flashbacks or daydreams intended to guide him toward Ally, but they instead cause him to suffer an unarticulated unhappiness. In fact, despite the clues with which his subconscious plagues him, Elmo and Ally experience a series of mistimings reminiscent of those found in the melodrama. At one point Elmo is about to bump into her at a train station when he is inexplicably waylaid by old military buddies. Later, he interrupts a kiss between Ally and a would-be suitor by blowing a sour note on a trumpet that has just been given to him. But this interruption is not sufficient to cause them to meet and merely illustrates another missed opportunity. Throughout the film, Elmo wanders aimlessly and unhappily, finding only music to provide solace.

Giving Up the Ghost

Just as Elmo takes on a feminized and ineffectual role, Anny becomes more masculine when she is born into the world as Ally—displacing the unitary oneness of the Imaginary into the individuated power of the phallus. For example, Ally's earthly husband (a film lover) ends up leaving her because he cannot compete with her. He tells her that it is too hard being with someone so successful: "You think nothing's impossible. You get an idea and you just go out and do it. Well, it's not like that for most people. It's darn hard to live with." Ally is depicted as so confident and powerful that her husband eventually leaves her after feeling emasculated. In an earlier scene, just before a missed meeting between Ally and Elmo, her husband encounters Elmo in the men's room. Before leaving, Elmo quips, "Don't forget your purse." Afterward, the husband frets about this comment and pleads with Ally to tell him whether his bag does indeed look like a purse.

Usually the male protagonist has difficulty expressing emotion; in this film the female character has the difficulty. When Ally's father dies, she bemoans the fact that she was never able to tell him how much she loved him, echoing the complaint expressed by the male characters in *Ghost* and *Always*. Finally, at the end of the film it is Ally who finds Elmo, and not the other way around, thus reversing the usual gender of active and passive narrative roles.

In *Defending Your Life,* even though Daniel is not a ghost, most of the female characters in Judgment City are powerful and the males are not. Daniel is the passive, masochistic character par excellence, and his love interest, Julia, possesses many of the qualities aspired to by men: she is brave, and saves children and animals from burning buildings. She gets what she wants, including the nicest hotel room and all the best material goods. Meanwhile, Daniel suffers in silence with his poor accommodations and makes feeble attempts to defend himself in the courtroom. His semi-incompetent defender, Mr. Diamond, refers to Daniel's prosecutor as the "Dragon Lady," and Daniel and Mr. Diamond are clearly at a disadvantage in her presence. In scene after scene, the Dragon Lady scores points at Daniel's expense, culminating in a "guilty" ruling from which he is saved only by the final plot reversal. Meanwhile in the Pavilion of Past Lives, the residents of Judgment City are invited to see who they were in a past life. Here, gender switching becomes almost de rigueur. One avuncular old man is horrified to see himself as a prissy little girl and in another booth a middle-aged woman is surprised to see herself as an enormous sumo wrestler. Julia turns out to have been Prince Valiant in a former life, while Daniel discovers that he is, once again, a somewhat emasculated male—this time a savage being pursued by a more threatening opponent.

Since the male ghost's feminization is often accompanied by the female's empowerment, the process of gender switching needs to be explored from both the male and the female point of view as an expression of the origin of the subject.

Melancholy

In ghost films, the gender roles of the ghosts and their perceivers initially seem suited to the traditional stereotypes. If most of the ghosts are male, most of the characters hearing voices or being surveilled are female.[15] The link between being the female perceiver and the feeling of being surveilled can be further explored through the psychoanalytic concept of melancholia, a topic that recalls the earlier discussion of melodrama in which a loved one is lost through death or by other means. Just as many ghosts can be seen as expressions of the paradoxical birth of the subject for the male, the female perceiver can be understood in terms of the female's earliest identifications and object choices.

Revisions to Freudian theory argue that the girl child enters the Oedipal through the symbolic castration from the mother rather than through the law of the father. As with the male child, the female child values the mother at first and she does not undergo a devaluation until the castration associated with the father's intervention. But unlike the male child, who is then exhorted to identify with the father, the female child must simultaneously devalue and identify with the mother. The result of this process is melancholy, where the child must internalize that which she also denigrates. Freud argued that melancholia is, like mourning, the result of the loss of a loved object. Whereas mourning is usually associated with an actual death, in this case, the mourning is associated with the loss of the mother as an idealized object of love.[16] The melancholy associated with the internalization of the denigrated mother thus becomes associated, not just with mourning widows, but with the female psyche itself and "does much to explain both the rigorous system of internal surveillance with which the female so frequently torments herself—her peculiar tendency to treat herself as an object to be over-seen and over-heard."[17] The association of paranoia with the female in many Hollywood films can thus be traced to the conflicted nature of the feminine psyche formed within a patriarchal regime.

In ghost films, the marvelous ghosts become the necessary projection for the woman in the recovery from paranoia. Whereas disavowal involves the refusal to recognize an unwanted quality in another (i.e., the boy disavows the female's anatomical lack), projection involves the refusal of a quality within oneself, a refusal to "be" that which is undesirable. Thus, from the female character's point of view, the ghost becomes the projection of those qualities associated with the denigrated woman—passiveness, lack of agency, the inability to be taken seriously. Freud's account of female melancholia mirrors the experience of the male ghost, who is incapable of achievement, reproaches and vilifies itself, and expects to be cast out and punished.[18] The self-punishment of the melancholic and the masochist are similar in that both are self-inflicted, despite the fact that the masochist maintains the illusion that someone else is doing the punishing. In a sense, the masochist uses the same process of projection, but in reverse, projecting the qualities of the guilty father onto the woman, thereby refusing to "be" the father but nevertheless suffering the same loss of being that the female suffers in classic melancholia. The projection of the ghost by the female character and the projection of the woman (into the rejecting role in the masochistic alliance) by the ghost both become defenses against the melancholy and paranoia suffered by the subject during the symbolic castration and the original loss of the mother.

Melancholia is suffered by the female who is asked to incorporate and identify with the denigrated mother. But the male child also experiences melancholia in that he does not immediately associate himself with the father and therefore suffers in casting off the symbiotic relationship with the mother. Kaja Silverman presents a lucid reading of this phenomenon in her study of the voice and identity in *The Acoustic Mirror:* "For the first time, the little boy apprehends woman as radically and unpleasurably other, as the site of an alien and unwanted quality. He insists upon that otherness by renouncing his Oedipal desires and identifying with the father."[19] As the boy goes through this process, however, even he is not spared the melancholy which is the female's lot. The boy's melancholy merely gets rechanneled or covered over through the disavowal of the mother and identification with the father. In short, for the male, what would be melancholic loss becomes associated instead with the prohibiting and punishing father. Judith Butler neatly connects the way in which melancholia is transmuted during the boy child's Oedipal phase: "In melancholia, the loved object is lost through a variety of means: separation, death, or the breaking of an emotional tie. In the Oedipal situation, however, the loss is dictated by a prohibition attended by a set of punishments. The melancholia of gender identification which "answers" the Oedipal dilemma must be understood, then, as the internalization of an interior moral directive which gains its structure and energy from an externally forced taboo."[20] Hence, for both the male and the female, construction of gender identities are an occasion for loss and melancholy. The male's melancholy is disguised, however, by the alibi of the punishing father and so may not recognized as such.

Just as the male ghost projects the qualities of the father onto the female, the ghost is also able to take on the qualities of the female through another process associated with melancholy—incorporation. Here, the child copes with the loss of a loved one (in this case the mother) by internalizing the qualities associated with that person. In fact, Freud himself identified melancholia as essential to ego formation. As Butler notes, "Freud suggests that the internalizing strategy of melancholia may be the only way in which the ego can survive the loss of its essential emotional ties to others."[21] Thus, while the female projects the unwanted qualities of herself onto the male ghost (projection), she also deals with the loss of the loved one by herself becoming more like him (incorporation). Similarly, the male ghost projects the unwanted qualities of his gender onto the female through the masochistic alliance (projection), while at the same time internalizing the qualities of the lost love by becoming more like her (incorporation).

This symmetrical series of reversals is part and parcel of the ghost fantasy, in which a change of positions is played out through a narrative of loss and recuperation at the level of romance. The ghost fantasy provides both projection and incorporation as devices of coping with the loss, which is necessary to subjecthood, but which is here played out as the loss of an adult romantic engagement cut short by the untimely death of the loved one. Although ghost films often concern heterosexual romances and return to the problems faced by the too-late of melodrama, this story of mourning and loss is imbricated in an original loss suffered by the child in the attainment of gendered subjectivity.

The melancholy associated with the formation of gendered identities further explains why ghosts engage in a fantasy of the origin of the subject, for the fantasy is based on a melancholic loss related to gender. Hence, while expressing the paradoxical nature of subjecthood, ghost fantasies present tactics of projection and incorporation in an effort to resolve gender problems by switching genders, and, ultimately, overcoming the separateness of gender.

Gender Switching and the Body

Several films concern gender switching much more overtly than ones previously discussed, but they do not feature ghosts in the classic definition of the word. Nevertheless, *Dead Again, Switch,* and *All of Me* all involve characters who die and whose "souls" enter another's body. All enter bodies of the opposite sex, which explicitly raises the issue of the desire to switch genders.

Dead Again uses the ideas of karma and reincarnation to promote the notion of gender fluidity and romantic oneness. In one scene, Roman gives Margaret an anklet, which is supposed to link them together for all time. "When a husband gives this to his wife, they become two halves of the same person. . . . Nothing can separate them. . . . Not even death." This idea is connected to both heterosexual romance in films such as *Made in Heaven* and a traditional gender mapping where male and female are shown to be two parts of one original whole.[22] Romance is the inevitable attractor that will lead the two halves back to their former state of bliss.

In *Dead Again,* all of the usual gender associations are played out on the bodies of Grace and Mike. Grace is a mute amnesiac who nevertheless wakes up screaming in the middle of the night. Mike is a detective and a fancy-free ladies' man. The upshot, however, is that Grace and Mike turn out to be reincarnated versions of Roman and Margaret—but oppositely gendered: Grace was previously Roman and Mike was previously Margaret.

As with many ghost films, this movie employs a kind of castration anxiety to enter into the fantasy of gender switching. Here, a child who was jealous on behalf of his mother murdered Margaret with a pair of scissors. Although the scissors are the perfect castrating symbol, they once again are merely an alibi for the return of the other half. Just as male ghosts have difficulty speaking in the earlier mentioned films, so in this film the gender switching allows us to understand that it is simultaneously Roman who is mute and amnesiac in the beginning of the film, even though he "looks" like Grace in the present. Similarly, even though Margaret was killed by the scissors in the past, that castration actually results in her "rebirth" as Mike.

The murder is itself an interesting scenario in which Roman's housekeeper's son, Frankie, kills Margaret in a jealous rage. Although the motive is purportedly jealousy on behalf of his mother, Inga (who was in love with Roman), the episode can be read slightly differently. Frankie looks to Roman as a father since he, inexplicably, does not have one. When Roman marries Margaret, who wants no part of Inga and Frankie, Frankie suffers the absent-father syndrome discussed earlier. Hence, when we later learn that Frankie's last name is Madson (mad son) we understand that he kills Margaret for causing him to lose his father. The murder weapon, scissors, becomes the highly charged, yet paradoxical symbol by which to castrate but also to attempt to gain the unattainable phallus. After the murder, we learn that Frankie's stuttering has become much worse, indicative of the price paid for not having solidified the proper patriarchal identities through the father. Just as male ghosts display difficulty speaking in fantasies that re-create the difficulties and ambivalences of subject acquisition, so Frankie also cannot quite master speech. The murder can be further unraveled when we remember that the victim Margaret is also Mike. The crime against the female is also the crime against the male (father) resulting in his repudiation as desired in the masochistic fantasy. Hence, Roman is reborn as a mute female and Margaret is reborn as a male who is identical to Roman. A certain circularity of logic prevails in that every action taken by or on one gender in the past holds ramifications for its opposite in the present.

In a flashback scene, Roman and Margaret drink champagne, a glass of which Margaret accidentally knocks over. Roman remarks: "Margaret, a woman with more beauty than grace." In the present, Mike gives the amnesiac female the name Grace, and in a scene recalling the earlier one, Mike is now the one who knocks over a cup of tea. (Notably in the second, updated scene, the actors trade places—sitting on opposite sides of the table than in the first scene.) In the former scene (set in the past), Roman playfully reads Margaret's palm, telling her, "Not much of a life-line, I'm afraid. But wait, I do see love, passionate, everlasting love." In the updated scene, Mike reads Grace's tea leaves (actually a tea bag). The difference is that here, instead of telling her future, Mike attempts to tell her past. Although Grace is amnesiac, the need to "foretell" the past is precisely the fantasy mobilized by ghosts in their dramatization of the primal fantasy. Even while the story drives forward, it does so by delving backward to explain origins.[23] Although the narrative seems to concern the solution to a murder mystery (who really killed Margaret?), Mike and Grace are unwittingly searching for their former identities—identities which reveal their oneness, and their relationship with their "other gender."

In *Switch,* the inherent oneness of gender is perhaps most apparent when Steve Brooks is murdered and goes to heaven. Although he is allowed to return to earth, it is not to avenge his murder as might be expected. Instead, he must make up for the fact that he has treated women so poorly. In heaven, God takes the form of two disembodied voices, one male and one female.

> Male Voice: Well, on the one hand you've earned enough credits
> to get you into heaven.
> Steve: Oh, thank God.
> Both Voices: You're welcome.
> Female Voice: On the other hand, you've been so consistently
> rotten to women, you deserve to go straight to hell.
> Male Voice: Perfect record. They all hate you.
> Steve: All of them?
> Both Voices: As far as I know.

Here both voices speak in unison and refer to themselves as "I." Steve—reborn in the body of a woman—eventually gives birth to a baby girl who gazes up at him/her lovingly, thus satisfying "God's" contract that Steve find at least one female who loves or likes him. At this point, Steve/Amanda ascends to heaven and a scene shows her daughter visiting her grave on earth. The headstone reads, in part: "A great guy and a very special woman." In heaven, Amanda/Steve is asked whether s/he would like to be a male or a female angel. S/he asks: "Could I think about it just a little longer?" Both voices reply: "Take your time. You have all eternity."[24]

As in *Made in Heaven, Switch* portrays heaven as a place in which genders blend and become reunited in the ultimate figure of God. And just as

God is both male and female in *Switch, Made in Heaven* presents the "manager" of heaven, Emmett, to be ambiguously gendered, almost androgynous. Emmett wears a man's suit, and yet is small and delicate of build with an almost caricatured husky voice. In *Ghost Dad,* a running gag is made of the fact that Sir Edith (who acts like an angel although he is merely a paranormal expert) has a girl's name.[25]

In *Dead Again,* the switch in gender roles demonstrates the reversal of passivity and activity in *Made in Heaven.* Here Grace turns out not to have been the original victim after all. Instead, the original female victim (Margaret) is reborn as the male investigator (Mike), thus allowing the female to switch from a passive, victimized position to a male one in which she can actively investigate her own past. Roman, the male composer, is then reborn as Grace—a mute, amnesiac female, thus allowing the male to identify with the classically female position.

When the hypnotist regresses Grace so that she can remember the trauma that has made her mute, he tells her that she will not be a participant but an observer.[26] "I want you to distance yourself from the events you're watching as if you were a witness, not an actual participant." His directions to her recall that the male ghost mimics the male film viewer in a masochistic contract in which the images may be witnessed but not participated in or controlled. Similarly, Grace (who is really Roman) must adopt the masochistically female position in an effort to learn the secret of her/his origins. The fantasy s/he views not only recalls the film screen (and in fact the audience views the flashback in black and white as if it were an old movie) but the dream screen of fantasy in which the fantasizer does not necessarily fill the shoes of one character in the fantasy but instead flits among many. Observing the scene from afar permits the switching and fluid identifications which are integral to the process of fantasy itself. As Grace/Roman begins the regressed flashback, Madson (the hypnotist, now a grown man) asks, "What was the happiest day of your life?" S/he answers, "The day we first met." Madson cautions, "Distance yourself." At this point s/he shifts to the third person: "The day Roman and Margaret first met." This tactic helps conceal from the viewer the identity of the real murderer, but also helps keep the fantasy of the past in the mode of fantasy that will permit gender switching for both the characters and the viewers. It dupes the viewer into seeing Grace as a woman, whereas she is really (or also) a man, just as it dupes the viewer into seeing Mike as a man—even though he is really (or also) a woman.

One reviewer of *Dead Again* took issue with the device of having the same characters play both the past and present characters: "As much fun as it must have been for them, it was a mistake for Branagh to cast himself and Thompson in dual roles. There is no reason why the characters from the past and the present would look alike, and it's just one of the many holes in the story that everyone becomes aware of Grace's uncanny resemblance to Margaret and no one—not even Mike—notices that he's identical to Roman."[27]

Although the writer sees the dual roles as "just one of many holes in the story," and says that there is no reason why the characters should look alike, I would argue just the reverse. In fact, the physical similarities are integral to the story and to the concept of reincarnated characters as part of a whole. Although the karmic debt referred to in the film seems to refer to avenging Margaret's death, it also involves the change of positions necessary to correct the imbalance stemming from lack of oneness. This is precisely the type of karmic debt that must be resolved in *Switch*. In both *Dead Again* and *Switch,* male characters must assume feminized positions to achieve the oneness associated with both sexes in the pre-Oedipal, pre-sexual phase. Yet both films rely on the tension between the physical, visual presence of the actors and the narrative role they must play. In *Switch,* the humor of the gender bending depends on the fact that Ellen Barkin is a woman, despite the fact that she is playing a male character.[28] In *Dead Again,* the physical and visual reality of the characters is precisely what makes the audience understand the cyclical and fluid nature of the karmic gender switch. The play of the body against the gendered position of the character is even an issue in a film such as *Ghost,* where a macho male actor plays an ineffectual role.

Although a male ghost may take up a feminine position in a narrative, this feminine position must be reconciled with the physical presence of the actor playing the role. This creates an important distinction between structural categories of gender as they appear in print fiction and those same categories as they are realized in film. A traditional understanding of gender roles assumes that "the hero must be male, regardless of the gender of the text-image, because the obstacle, whatever its personification, is morphologically female."[29] Although the narrative positions of active and passive remain gendered as male and female, the "text-image" is of great consequence in ghost films—the visual presence of the actor overlays other information regarding the character. The visual presence of gender is precisely what makes the gender switching aspect of the ghost compelling to film as opposed to a nonvisual medium. The visual presence of a male actor playing an ineffectual character establishes the incontrovertible evidence of maleness, which is necessary to establish the fantasy of reversal in the first place.

Many reviewers debated Patrick Swayze's macho presence in the role of Sam in *Ghost*. One writer noted how frustrating the role of the ghost must have been: "For Swayze, who loves to punch bad guys in the nose and eventually rip out their throats (he did that in the late, unlamented *Road House*) it must be terribly frustrating to hit air in most of the film."[30] Another reviewer noted: "It's almost touching to watch a professional hunk grappling with the problems of spiritual existence. The great thing is that he carries on being

Patrick Swayze, which really is a hopeless role-model for dead people everywhere. He swipes and kicks out and gives piggy little grunts of dismay, but to no avail. Nobody can even hear him let alone feel his fists." Later the reviewer notes, however, that although this is "that much more frustrating for him" it is nevertheless "entertaining for the audience."[31]

This is one more factor in the fluid identification and gender switching process of which ghost narratives are a part. In addition, this might help explain why there are so few women ghosts. On the one hand it may be that giving female characters the power of invisibility is too subversive since this would eliminate scopophilia aimed at women. Silverman's reading of the relation between the female voice and the cinema suggests as much: "To permit a female character to be seen without being heard would be to activate the hermeneutic and cultural codes which define woman as "enigma," inaccessible to definitive male interpretation. To allow her to be heard without being seen would be even more dangerous, since it would disrupt the specular regime upon which dominant cinema relies."[32]

This returns us, however, to a question posed at the beginning of this book, namely, "Why are all the ghosts men?" In short, few of the ghosts are female and the majority are male because the male ghost's passivity, poor communication, and ineffectuality all already belong to women under classic patriarchal structures. The dramatic value of putting a female in an ineffectual position is limited—she already fills that position.[33] The point of the ghost fantasy seems to be, at least in part, this dramatic change of gender position—played out by the characters for the viewer. This is why *Ghost* is all the more successful for putting Patrick Swayze in the role of the ghost.[34] One astute reviewer noted: "Several of Hollywood's leading players, imprudently as it has turned out, turned down the part of Sam: It does not have the robust assertiveness of the traditional male lead. But this is precisely why the film has had such an appeal."[35]

Although many film reviewers concluded that the film's marketing strategy was aimed at women, they also noted that a surprisingly large number of men watched and enjoyed the film, some repeatedly.[36] Although many men may have been moved by the love story, and may well have identified with the masochistic ineffectuality of Sam's character, *Ghost*—being a mainstream film—cleverly retains its opportunities to play it both ways. Men can easily identify with Sam, precisely because Patrick Swayze is a "man's man." Male viewers can, if they like, discount Sam's masochistic feminization because, after all, the character is dead—an obvious disadvantage for any guy. On the other hand, the ghost device provides an excellent alibi for male viewers to identify with a feminized male—a low-risk invitation precisely because the films provide an acceptable justification for such an interlude. ("Hey, he's no wimp, he's just dead!") Likewise women viewers are invited to identify with the female characters because they are played by women, but also with the male ghosts whose traumas of ineffectuality may seem familiar. In addition to being able to identify with either male or female characters, female viewers may enjoy watching macho characters undergo a certain feminization. One reviewer suggested that, as a ghost, Patrick Swayze creates a "perfect female fantasy figure."[37] Just as the device of the ghost allows male viewers to have it both ways—identifying with a man who is macho, but also sensitive—women can also fantasize a lover who is classically male, but who also has the feminine qualities which permit him to express the emotion and nurturance supposedly lacking in males, but necessary to romance. This is exactly the type of male hero who is portrayed in Harlequin romance novels, according to Janice Radway. She contends that women take pleasure in a love story in which the male hero is strong and macho, but also tender and nurturing to the heroine: "He continues to be seen as a supreme example of unchallenged, autonomous masculinity [while at the same time]. . . . The hero is permitted simply to graft tenderness onto his unaltered male character."[38]

Shortly after the release of *Ghost,* a *Time* article debated the changing roles of women and men, claiming that the image of the sensitive male was suffering a backlash in the eyes of both women and men. The article noted the "profound confusion over what it means to be a man today," and claimed that while John Wayne–types were replaced by Alan Alda–types in the 1980s, the early 1990s experienced "a new surge of tempered macho."[39] The article claimed, moreover, that "the sensitive man was overplayed," and cited Warren Farrell, author of *Why Men Are the Way They Are,* a 1986 best seller. Farrell argues that women never really wanted sensitive men and that women only liked Alan Alda because he was first and foremost a "multimillionaire superstar" who also just happened to be sensitive: "We have never worshipped the soft man. . . . If Mel Gibson were a nursery school teacher, women wouldn't want him."[40] The validity of this interpretation is not the key point to this discussion, however. The important point is that the paradoxical nature of the ghost permits a variety of interpretations for both male and female viewers but that this variety is highly controlled by the physical presence of the actor playing the ghost. The ghost device demonstrates the way in which physical surfaces of the body both play out and play with gender roles depending upon the narrative structures in which they appear. This is not to say that male and female film viewers cannot identify with a variety of characters and character positions while watching a film. It does mean that the physical body of the actor or actress provides a dimension to viewer identification that should not be discounted.

One way to understand gender is as a performance designed to fulfill the requirements of the Oedipal regime. In this view gender resides in the actions and attitudes performed by the doer. The performance becomes intimately linked over time to various surfaces of the body so that certain gestures and visual codes become naturalized in relation to certain kinds of bodies—namely, male and female ones. That is to say, the body itself becomes a kind of performance, a surface representation of what comes to be understood as an interior quality. Butler writes that "the figure of the interior soul understood as 'within' the body is signified through its inscription on the body, even though its primary mode of signification is through its very absence, its potent invisibility."[41] The body thus signifies, on its surface, those qualities we associate with innate, interior qualities. Gender and soul become linked as interior essences that can be "read" through, for example, the body of a ghost. In ghost films, the bodies of ghosts almost always retain their former characteristics—usually right down to the gender-influenced clothing.[42] Thus, even though ghosts are supposed to represent that which cannot be represented—the soul—they almost always exactly reflect the fact that the soul is written on the body—that gender is written on the body. The viewer of a ghost film cannot help but take note of the fact that they see the actor in all his glory—at least part of the time. Yet this only serves to prove the fact that a "gendered soul" is a kind of logical paradox, an argument many of the films make by suggesting that after the soul leaves a body and ascends (returns) to heaven, it has no sex. In those films where the soul is divorced from the body and then put back again (*Heaven Can Wait, Switch, Dead Again,* and *Ghost,*) the performance of gender becomes problematic.

In the 1984 film *All of Me,* gender switching similar to that found in *Switch* occurs when the soul of Edwina Cutwater enters the body of Roger Cobb after Edwina dies. Whereas in *Switch,* Steve is deposited into an anonymous female body (woman as empty vessel), in *All of Me,* Edwina takes up residence in an already inhabited male one. Roger thus exhibits characteristics of both genders as both he and Edwina vie for control of his mind and body. As with many other films involving gender switching, this film demonstrates a kind of ambivalent desire to be both sexes, while at the same time justifying Roger's displays of effeminate behavior by blaming them on a case of supernatural possession.

The film's use of mirrors is interesting in establishing the mediation of gender through the body, for although the audience usually perceives Roger struggling against an unseen female force (complete with disembodied voice), Edwina is often seen as Roger's mirror image. When Roger looks in a mirror, both he and the audience see Edwina's image. In ghost films the desire to be both sexes is played out as a fantasy of return to the pre-Oedipal phase. Death and birth become linked as a cyclical means of accessing this state of sexual duality or ambiguity. The mirror scenes in this film might be compared to the mirror phase in the Lacanian scheme, which marks the paradoxical illusion of oneness in the gaze and reflection of the mother.[43]

Several instances of literal gender switching also take place in *Ghost.* When the spiritual medium, Oda Mae, learns that she is truly psychic, she finds that she is no longer able to shut out all of the spirits who now plague her day and night. During a seance, one male spirit is too impatient to wait his turn behind all of the others wishing to make contact with their loved ones. He takes the liberty of jumping inside of Oda Mae's body and temporarily possesses her in order to talk with his wife. Oda Mae soon angrily expels him: "Get out! Get out of me you son of a bitch! Don't you *ever* do that to me again!"[44]

As in *Switch* and *All of Me,* the male voice emanating from a female body (or vice versa) is played as comically incongruous, and as with other ghostly contracts, the ghost pays a price for being allowed to communicate. After the spirit is expelled, he lies helplessly on the floor. Another spirit chides him, "Now you should know better than that. Jumping into bodies wipes you out."[45] The scene reinforces classical notions of the female as empty vessel to be entered at will by a male. But it is not until a later scene that this gender switching takes on its full meaning in the film.

In the penultimate scene of *Ghost,* Molly finally comes to believe that Sam is really present even though she cannot see him or hear him. When Sam expresses the wish to touch Molly one more time, Oda Mae reluctantly agrees to do Sam a favor and let him "use" her body.

> Oda Mae: Okay, okay. You can use me.
> Sam: Use you?
> Oda Mae: You can use my body.
> Sam: Use your body?
> Oda Mae: Just do it quick before I change by mind.

At this point, Oda Mae closes her eyes, a brief wind tussles her hair, and finally she opens her eyes and approaches Molly. The audience sees Oda Mae's hand taking Molly's, but when the camera cuts to a wide shot, Oda Mae has been replaced by Sam. The ensuing scene of romance and nostalgia is played out not between Molly and Sam-in-Oda Mae's body, but—as far as the audience can see—between Molly and Sam. The implications of this are obvious. While it is acceptable in mainstream cinema to show a female being physically possessed by a male spirit, it is unacceptable to show two female bodies in a romantic embrace. The gender switching can go only so far, in part because the possibly subversive qualities of gender switching are constantly equalized in the film by being part of the binary structure which underlies the heterosexual romance. This binary system frames the desire for a change of positions and return to oneness in the first place. While it is one thing to portray a comic fantasy in which genders reverse, this fantasy does not undo the "opposites attract" mentality on which the entire fantasy is based.[46]

Giving Up the Ghost

In *Switch,* a depiction of lesbian romance occurs between Amanda (who is "really" Steve, but in a female body) and an avowed lesbian, Sheila.[47] Steve/Amanda attempts to consummate a romantic interlude with Sheila to win an advertising account with Sheila's perfume company. However, once faced with the actual encounter, Steve/Amanda cannot go through with it. The scene is played as a flashback with Steve's male voice interpreting the actions: "Something was seriously out of sync. So I said to myself, Steve, baby, come on. You may be a gorgeous female on the outside, but you're still a hundred percent male. And Sheila here is just another rich horny broad looking to get laid. So go for it. What's the big deal here?"

But when Sheila actually attempts to seduce Steve/Amanda, the deal falls through. As Sheila leans over and attempts to kiss Steve/Amanda, the audience sees two actresses about to kiss, while the male voice continues to explain: "It got very weird. Suddenly, I felt like my pantyhose was strangling me. . . . I couldn't breathe. And then she started kissing me. And . . . and then I fainted."

The visuals show Ellen Barkin falling out of the other woman's arms, and, indeed, out of the frame itself. Later, Steve's friend Margo explains why he was unable to go through with the encounter. "She's gay. . . . And gay male or female scares the living hell out of you." Although a discussion of gay and lesbian perspectives is beyond the purview of this study, the fact remains that the fantasy of switching in the masochistic scenario derives from the heterosexual formation of the individual under the Oedipal injunctions against homosexuality and incest, one in which the male cannot be female and so must have the female to fulfill the original desire.[48]

In *Heaven Can Wait,* the possibilities of Joe taking up residence in a female body are simply obviated by the initial narrative goal. In this film, Joe's claim that he can only accept a male body are justified by his goal to become a football quarterback, an aspiration that handily excludes women. But for the mainstream audience, another reason exists—the heterosexual romantic resolution depends upon Joe being re-deposited in a male body so that he can consummate his relationship with the female love interest.

While many films engage in fantasy scenarios in which gender is switched or made temporarily ambiguous, this very desire for reversal leading to sexual oneness stems from the Oedipal and patriarchal injunctions themselves and so cannot be completely breached. The films use gendered bodies (actresses playing female characters, male actors playing male ghosts) to play out the switching processes, but these very bodies discourage certain visible scenarios from actually unfolding for the audience. It is all very well to fantasize about taking up another identity, and as suggested, viewers most likely do so across gendered lines. However, it is quite another thing for a mainstream movie to transcend the physical and visible performances of gender in the expression of a fantasy which stems from the status quo and from those very performances.

Ghost films engage in a fantasy of a return to pre-Oedipal oneness through a masochistic fantasy, which permits a change of position. This change in gendered position is integral to the desire to be both sexes and to return to the pre-Oedipal scenario where sexuality has yet to be established. The fantasy of gender switching is facilitated through the play of gender and narrative positions on the actual body of the characters. As dramatized through a physical presence, ghosts once again display their paradoxical nature. Though ghosts are intended to represent the unrepresentable (the spirit without the body), the body becomes the privileged method through which to establish the gender in order to partake in the switching fantasy. Furthermore, by casting male actors as ineffectual and feminized ghosts, the films are able to use death as an alibi for the masochistic fantasy, permitting male and female viewers to accept a feminized male without impugning the masculinity of the protagonist. The tendency to play it both ways extends to the way in which the films employ angels and the notion of cosmic destiny to enable ghosts to relinquish narrative control in the name of a higher power. Finally, the process of "giving up the ghost" is not only central to the masochistic scenario, but is also integral to the comedic aspect of ghost films.

Chapter 6

Giving Up the Ghost

In ghost films, angels and cosmic destiny perform distinct narrative functions in the creation of narrative pleasure. Unlike ghosts, angels are often overtly ambiguous in their gender. This tendency is one element in a portrayal of heaven as a site of pre-Oedipal bliss, where gender is often ambiguous precisely because the pre-Oedipal is characterized by the lack of gendered identity or by (the child's) association with both genders.[1] Although they are often similar to ghosts in their physical characteristics (invisibility, incorporeality, disembodied voice) and although the categories sometimes blur (i.e., sometimes ghosts are angels and vice versa), angels are characterized or defined by their special narrative function within the masochistic fantasy. Specifically, in comedy ghost films, angels become the heavenly representatives of narrative destiny. This allows the male ghost to partake in a masochistic fantasy that provides it (and the viewer) with an alibi for taking up a powerless, feminized position. By splitting narrative control between ghosts and angels, the films once again allow the ghost to have it both ways—the ghost gives up control only to be assured that destiny will provide the proper resolution.

Angels and Destiny in the Masochistic Fantasy

In most films angels appear as kindly representatives of heaven whose job is to help another ghost or mortal in some way. This role is distinct from that of ghosts, who are often sent back to help someone, but whose mission is often made difficult due to physical impotency or invisibility. Angels, on the other hand, help these very same ghosts and do not suffer from problems of communication and ineffectuality. On the contrary, angels are often masterful and are occasionally endowed with magical powers. In most cases, angels are representatives of a larger system (heaven, the cosmos) and thus become conduits for the expression and articulation of a higher power.

An example of such an angel can be found in *Heaven Can Wait,* in which the angel, Mr. Jordan, helps Joe find a new body when he is mistakenly killed and becomes a ghost. Mr. Jordan exhibits many of the characteristics that Joe does as a ghost (e.g., he is invisible, walks through walls), but whereas Joe has no power as a ghost, Mr. Jordan, conversely, wields a great deal. As with Mr. Jordan, Emmett, the angel in *Made in Heaven,* possesses knowledge and capabilities that make him powerful compared to the other characters. It is Emmett who allows Mike to find his true love by permitting him to return to earth to search for her. Emmett stipulates, however, that Mike must find Anny in thirty years; otherwise Mike will be doomed to unhappiness. It is often an angel who oversees and articulates (for the character and the viewer) the "contract" referred to earlier, in which the ghost is usually "allowed" to return for a specific reason, even though he must usually pay a price for this privilege. In both *Heaven Can Wait* and *Made in Heaven,* angels provide rules for the protagonist, which then take on the onus of inevitable destiny. In *Always,* Hap provides Pete with both his masochistic mission, as well as the means to move on by the end of the film. In *Switch,* the double, disembodied voices of God serve the same function, articulating the contract with Steve, who may ascend to heaven only if he succeeds in finding a woman who truly likes him. In *Mr. Destiny* (1990), Michael Caine plays an angel, Mike, who helps the protagonist, Larry, appreciate his life by providing a strange interlude reminiscent of that experienced by the protagonist in *It's a Wonderful Life* (1946). In both cases, the protagonists find themselves in alternative universes that represent what life would have been like if they had acted differently (or had never been born, as in the latter movie). The disembodied voice in *Field of Dreams* ("If you build it, they will come") provides a similar example of an anthropomorphized version of narrative destiny. In *Alice,* Alice is visited by a angel who is sent to help her with her creative writing project. (This angel is similar to the one in *Always,* who refers to spirits as "inspiration," suggesting that our creative "muses" are literally spirits or angels.)

Almost an Angel (1990) is a strange variation on the theme. In this film, the bank-robbing protagonist, Terry Dean, almost dies and receives a message from God to become a "living angel" whose mission is to help the needy. Throughout the film, the audience is led to believe that he has only hallucinated this message based on garbled signals from the television and public address system in the hospital where he has been unconscious. This interpretation is furthered by Terry's vision, which features Charlton Heston in white robes and a long beard, a fact to which Terry later makes mention.[2] Only at the end of the film does the viewer learn that Terry truly is an angel with all of the privileges attendant to that station.

Although the most common aspect among angels is their magical ability to help others, another important feature is the way in which they appear to control or have knowledge of the characters' narrative destinies. Just as many films concern "true love," which provides a kind of inevitable romantic destiny for the characters, the notion of individual and personal destiny permeates many of these films either explicitly or implicitly. Some of the films use angels to anthropomorphize the management of this destiny while in other films, the concept of narrative destiny is more amorphous. In *Dead Again,* for example, narrative destiny is not overseen by an angel or a personified God, but by a karmic system of checks and balances that mimics that of pre-Oedipal fantasy. Because fantasy scenarios provide the setting for unfulfillable desires, which are necessarily played out again and again, they therefore partake in a kind of cyclical repetition repeated structurally and thematically in ghost films through the notion of delay, suspense, and the way in which death is linked to rebirth. The cyclical nature both of masochistic fantasy, and personal and narrative destiny is nowhere more clear than in such films as *Made in Heaven, Dead Again, Heaven Can Wait,* and *Mr. Destiny,* where no matter how far afield the characters appear to stray, the road loops back to the original destination—revealing the detour to have been part of the original plan all along.

Heaven Can Wait provides one of the most striking examples of the way in which an angel becomes associated with narrative destiny. In the beginning of the film Joe has reluctantly entered the body of a greedy tycoon, Farnsworth, to woo a young woman, Betty. Although the arrangement was to have been temporary, Joe falls so much in love with Betty that he no longer wants to exchange the body of Farnsworth for that of an athlete, as originally planned. Instead, he attempts to train Farnsworth's body so that it will be fit for playing football. An angel tells him that he must leave this body because his "time is up" and he "doesn't fit." Joe feels betrayed, because in an earlier scene, Mr. Jordan had indicated that he would get a chance to play in the Superbowl:

> Joe: Hey, didn't you tell me I'd get to the Superbowl?
> Angel: All I know is that whatever you're going to do it won't be in Farnsworth's body.
> Joe: Why not?
> Angel: Because it wasn't meant to be.

Despite Joe's efforts to change his fate, Mr. Jordan impresses upon Joe that he has a destiny to fulfill, one that cannot be tampered with. In fact, the entire narrative emanates directly from a heavenly "mistake" which has derailed Joe's narrative trajectory in the first place, but which will later prove to have been part of his original destiny. (Thus, the "mistake" is part of the original plan.) The circular logic inherent in Joe's dilemma reveals that even while Joe believes he is exercising his free will, he is nevertheless only fulfilling the destiny which was his to begin with. As Joe tries to prevent being taken from Farnsworth's body, Mr. Jordan suddenly arrives on the scene to give Joe an ultimatum.

> Mr. Jordan: You must abide by what is written. There's a reason for everything. There's always a plan.
> Joe: Well, how can you expect me to give up Farnsworth now? . . . You said we were going to the Superbowl.
> Mr. Jordan: Yes, that's true. If it's meant to be.
> Joe: I'm not leaving . . . I never went back on a deal in my life but I'm doing it now, Mr. Jordan. I'm not going.
> Mr. Jordan: Your destiny is not in my hands. Please don't make it more difficult. . . . Joe, you must abide by what it written.
> Joe: She loves me, Mr. Jordan.
> Mr. Jordan: Joe, you must abide by what is written.

This scene dramatizes not only the masochistic dilemma of the ghost, but the way in which the ghost illustrates the paradox of narrative obstacles and narrative endings. Just as many ghosts embody the obstacles and delays essential to masochistic pleasure in narrative processes, so does the ghost's relationship to narrative destiny reveal the way in which obstacles and delays are bounded by a logic which facilitates the masochistic interlude through a circularity of design and intent. In other words, the character is permitted to give up his or her narrative control because "what is meant to be" is already beyond the character's purview. Similarly, consumers of narrative are invited to give up control with the understanding that the story will come to the "proper ending." An emphasis on endings (such as that found in Peter Brooks's analysis) is important but can be modified to take into account the inherent pleasure in the delays of the narrative trajectory (as opposed to delay only causing the end to be "that much sweeter").

In comedy films, the protagonist often suffers indignities and injuries that would be serious or fatal in other genres. The comedic perspective allows the audience to understand that the consequences will be mild and that the ending will be happy. A classic definition of comedy coined by W. H. Auden incorporates the tendency to avoid real suffering either for the characters or the viewers: Comedy "does not involve the spectator or hearer in suffering or pity, which in practice means that it must not involve the actor in real suffering."[3] Like ghosts, narrative film viewers relinquish their control because it is safe to do so, in the same way that many ghosts relinquish control even while being assured that no matter what they do, they will be forced to "abide by what is written." The reference to authorship ("what is written") in *Heaven Can Wait* extends the comparison, suggesting that something very powerful precedes and overrides narrative agency—something that includes the constraints of genre and—in broader terms—the various cultural formations that "speak" the character even while the character believes that s/he acts autonomously.[4]

Hearts and Souls also alludes to narrative destiny and to the audience's expectations of happy endings. In this film, the angelic figure is a bus driver whose job is to take the four ghosts back to "heaven" once they have resolved their dilemmas with the too-late. Afterward, their souls are to be reincarnated in the bodies of newborn babies. As in *Heaven Can Wait,* however, a heavenly mistake has caused the four ghosts to have been overlooked for years. Despite spending years on earth they have never been told why they have returned as ghosts—the "grand scheme," as the bus driver calls it. When he finally arrives to take them away, he bends the rules slightly to buy them some extra time. The clock is ticking, however, since their souls will soon be needed. The ghosts must hurry to accomplish their missions and the bus driver returns throughout the film, picking up each ghost in the nick of time. Again, the "mistake" is no mistake since it not only accounts for the ghosts' masochistic delay within the narrative but also provides the requisite narrative deadline.

When the last ghost, Penny, attempts to find her old boyfriend to express her love, she learns that he is many years dead. Thomas (the ghosts' corporeal helper) is furious that Penny has been cheated out of resolving her personal dilemma. He angrily confronts the bus driver who has been pressuring them to hurry.

> Thomas: It didn't work!!
> Bus Driver: What do you mean? It always works. It might seem like things are going down to the wire but they always work out.
> Thomas: The guy's been dead for seven years!
> Bus Driver: No that can't be. . . . Or, you know what? He has to be the wrong guy!

In referring to cosmic destiny and the "grand scheme" the bus driver seems also to refer to the way in which comedy films are constructed both to prolong the agony (going down to the wire), and to resolve the narrative dilemma happily. The deadline functions not only as narrative closure, but also to intensify the masochistic experience associated with obstacles to the resolution. The bus driver refuses to believe that things will not work out ("they always work out"), and he proposes an alternative, which may also have occurred to the audience sharing his disbelief. The film supplies an unexpected alternative to the happy ending, but not before making reference to the viewer's expectations about narrative closure.

While *Mr. Destiny* does not feature a "ghost," the film bears some similarity to ghost movies such as *Heaven Can Wait* and *Always,* in its angel-like character, Mike, who guides the protagonist to his destiny. As with many ghost films, *Mr. Destiny* tackles the problem of the too-late by giving the protagonist another chance. Although Larry does not "return" to his past per se, Mike allows him to experience the consequences of a changed past, as though Larry had returned to his childhood and acted differently. The film establishes the fact that Larry bitterly regrets not having hit a baseball in a big game when he was a child. His subsequent life flows from this mistake, closing off his options to wealth and romance. Naturally, it is too late to do anything about it, a concept echoed by Larry's contention that he missed the ball because he "swung too late, that's all."[5] On his forty-fifth birthday, Larry's car breaks down, and he enters a deserted bar where he meets Mike, the bartender. Mike seems to recognize him and asks if Larry was the one who lost the high school championship in 1978. This comment unleashes a flood of bitterness.

> Larry: My life is shit. Ordinary. I do the same thing every day. Boring. If I'd just hit that goddamn ball, my whole life would have turned out better.
> Mike: Some people believe that there's a reason that things are the way they are.

At this point Mike makes Larry a special drink, which he calls "The Spilt Milk." The drink recalls the trope of the too-late as well, for as Mike explains: "It's the one drink there's no use crying over. It does the job." The drink allows Larry to have another chance, reversing his destiny in the same way that ghosts return, ostensibly to reverse the tragedy caused by their untimely death. The special cocktail changes the past and thus Larry's future. Instead of a mediocre suburban life, Larry finds himself outrageously wealthy and married to another woman. As Mike explains to Larry, "You know that little incident you didn't like about your life. It's been changed. You hit the three-pitch right out of the park. When that moment changed, everything else in your life changed with it."

As with many ghost movies, however, the reversal lasts only for the duration of the film. Just as ghosts reverse the melodramatic pathos of the story, they do so only to prolong the dilemmas associated with such pathos—prolonging suffering in the classic masochistic fashion before the final resolution of death or rebirth. In *Mr. Destiny,* Larry suffers a variety of comic mishaps before realizing that he prefers his original wife, life, and destiny. In the end, Larry is permitted to return to his original life, having learned not to tamper with destiny. Larry tells Mike, "Boy you sure do know how to make a point. And listen, Mike. Whatever you've got planned for the rest of my life, it's perfect." As in *Heaven Can Wait,* the protagonist relinquishes his control to a higher power, believing that (as Alexander Pope once said): "Whatever is, is right." The circularity of such a concept is well suited for the masochistic aesthetic, which requires that the protagonist give up control—albeit in a highly controlled environment (hence the contract)—in the service of a fantasy that ends, only to be repeated.

Scrooged is another film that uses ghosts in a more angelic mode, as the vehicles for forcing a comic destiny on the protagonist. As in *Mr. Destiny,* the protagonist in *Scrooged* is not a ghost, but is put into a ghost-like, masochistic interlude by the angel-like characters. He is exposed to scenes from his life, spanning his past, present, and future.[6] As with other ghost films, the protagonist watches these scenes from a distance, unable to have any effect on them. He tries desperately to interact with the participants, but they can neither see nor hear him. The Ghost of Christmas Past (one of the three spirits who controls what he will see), explains to him that he cannot interact with any of the people before him and that he should think of these scenes instead as television reruns. As with other ghost/angel films, the protagonist experiences a masochistic interlude ultimately controlled by more powerful spirits who control his destiny.

Even ghost films that do not explicitly provide "destiny" as a narrative motivator nevertheless use a similar mechanism (through the contractual alliance) to provide an alibi for the relinquishment of control. This may be particularly important for male characters and male viewers who live in a culture that constantly demands male displays of power and control and for whom displays of passivity risk being denigrated as feminine. The device of the ghost is particularly handy as an alibi for male viewers to identify with a "feminized" male. By designating the protagonist as a ghost, the character's masculinity is in no way flawed, but is merely cast into a situation that permits—indeed, demands—ineffectuality. In fact, the masochistic condition reveals that "the masochist can always rationalize suffering as the result of external events rather than as self-generated occurrences."[7] Although the ghost embodies many characteristics of the masochistic aesthetic, in ghost films murder or untimely death may be seen as the external event par excellence, the event responsible for the character's masochistic interlude. In films such as *Heaven Can Wait, Dead Again, Mr. Destiny,* and *Made in Heaven,* which explicitly introduce the concept of destiny or fate, the masochistic alibi is revealed in obvious terms. In these cases, as Reik notes, "fate . . . has replaced the humiliating and beating partner."[8] However, the fate suffered in ghost comedies (as in all comedies) is necessarily a happy one, thus permitting the kind of double-sided pleasure in suffering that the paradoxical ghost typifies. Both the ghost and the viewer relinquish themselves to the fate "written" either by a cosmic force (for the ghost) or by the cultural and generic requirements of film comedy (for the viewer).

Cosmic Destiny Meets Comic Destiny

Since the ghost is a quintessential figure of delay and of narrative obstacle through its ineffectuality, it may be particularly suited to romantic comedies as stories of heterosexual romance, which depend on a kind of masochistic and comic ineptitude on the part of the players. Further comparisons and connections can be made between generic aspects of comedy and the way in which the masochistic fantasy of these stories depends on narrative trajectories that are simultaneously out of control for the protagonist, yet ultimately framed by a notion of comic destiny that disallows serious consequences. If comedy is broadly defined as a genre or mode in which happy endings are de rigueur, and in which unhappy consequences are funny precisely because the audience perceives no real or lasting danger, then ghosts become perfect vehicles for such comedic narratives.

The necessary absence of real death in comedy explains the presence of ghosts in the fulfillment of a comic agenda. Ghosts permit film audiences to suffer death vicariously without suffering the consequences of its finality.[9] Ghosts are thus the ultimate figure of comedic suffering dependent on a lack of seriousness and a lack of finality for humor. In an interesting essay on comedy, Wylie Sypher writes that "fate takes the guise of happy or unhappy chance, which is, of course, only a tidy arrangement of improbable possibilities."[10] Where melodramas often use mistiming as a vehicle of tragedy and pathos, comedies often exaggerate mistimings and miscommunications so that they become the absurd illustrations of comedic but benign fate. In a dramatic genre mistiming leads to tragedy because the consequences are final (it is too late to change the consequences), but in comedies, mistimings can be humorous precisely because the comedy genre assures us that there will be no final negative consequences to the mistimings—and hence, no tragedy.

The consequences of "having no final consequences" in comedy parallels the way in which ghost comedies seem to concern a kind of cyclical time associating death with rebirth. To deal with death, ghost comedies do not just bring the ghost back from death, but introduce the concept of rebirth—using death to cycle back to beginnings to create a thematic loop. Not surprisingly then, the term "comedy" derives from the term "Comus," an ancient Greek ritual celebrating fertility. The fertility god honored in such rituals was considered to be a symbol of "perpetual rebirth, eternal life."[11] In a nice turn of phrase, Christopher Fry refers to comedic characters as those who have to "unmortify themselves."[12] If comedy depends on a process of "unmortifying" oneself, then this a goal for which comedy ghosts seem to be uniquely designed. In many ghost fantasies this rebirth is intimately linked to a masochistic fantasy in which the father is expelled in a return to the maternal. While some theorists consider comedy to be a generic instance of a fantasy in which the Oedipal scenario is reversed, others read comedy as "returning to the womb, where death becomes rebirth and the grave becomes a kind of symbolic cradle."[13]

Many of the tendencies attributed to traditional comedy are remarkably similar to the fantasies associated with the masochistic scenario. In the last chapter we saw how a change in positions is integral to fantasy as understood in psychoanalytic terms. This change of positions is, furthermore, a fantasy which may underlie comedy where humor is often said to arise from the incongruities stemming from such reversals. Among the many readings of this phenomenon, Henri Bergson's is perhaps the most clearly descriptive: "Picture to yourself certain characters in a certain situation; if you reverse the situation and invert the roles, you obtain a comic scene. . . . In every case the root idea involves an inversion of roles."[14] Bergson's concept of comedic inversion describes perfectly the comic switching found in such movies as *All of Me, Switch,* and *Ghost,* as well as comic scenes in other films where the change of position is more subtle. Comedy ghosts lie at the intersection of generic fantasy (which requires and desires shifts in identification or position), masochistic fantasy (which requires a particular reversal concerning the expulsion of the father and the return to the mother), and comedy in general (which uses these tendencies as vehicles for humorous scenarios in which multiple interpretations elicit laughter).

To complicate this account, however, other perspectives note that the obstacles in comedy romance may be purely Oedipal in nature. Lucy Fischer describes this scenario: "Equal to the male youth in comedy is the patriarch—who generally poses some hindrance to the protagonist's romantic pursuits. This generational dynamic invokes another scenario—the Freudian Oedipal conflict, which is a struggle enacted between men." Fischer also rightly notes the lack of women in traditional comedy, a symptom of the Oedipal injunction to "throw mamma from the train," as Kathleen Rowe puts it.[15] The domination of male characters as ghosts, however, operates in a pre-Oedipal fantasy so that this trend is contradicted by the overall fantasized desire to access the maternal.

While the union of a heterosexual couple is usually considered Oedipal in that it perpetuates the status quo, comedy ghost films access the union by situating the female/maternal values as the "correct" ones and by positioning the male himself as the obstacle to the union. Neale and Krutnik's analysis of screwball comedy, a type of romantic comedy, also focuses on the role of obstacles in an Oedipal scenario. In screwball comedies (popular in the 1930s and 1940s), first the inherent compatibility of the couple is established and then external difficulties prevent their union. In recent ghost films, however, the couples might be incompatible due their problems of communication across gender lines; thus the obstacles are at least partly internal. But the male ghost internalizes the original incompatibility, and this then becomes externalized in the figure of the ghost (i.e., the ghost character is, himself, the problem). Neale and Krutnik explain that the earlier films achieve romantic union through a conversion of the woman: "In each case the male is situated as more on the side of 'correct values' endorsed by the narration."[16] Since the opposite conversion takes place in ghost films, the final union becomes an expression of pre-Oedipal, rather than Oedipal, fulfillment.

Many of the comic and masochistic elements of ghost films derive from the obstacles that delay the endings. The endings themselves, however, are not particularly comic except in the sense that they are guaranteed to be happy ones. In his discussion of comedy, Aristotle remarks on the connection between comedy and "Fortune," where fortune describes coincidental and beneficial destiny: "Destiny in the guise of Fortune is the fabric of comedy."[17] In other words, when destiny appears to be coincidental, contingent, and absurd, it is associated with comedy, whereas predetermined Fate often seems tragic since it cannot be reckoned with: "Tragedy is the image of Fate, as comedy is of Fortune."[18] Ghost comedies use fate as a device within a comedic framework so that even while retaining the inevitability of tragedy, fate becomes the inevitability of rebirth. Thus, while many ghost films feature somewhat serious and pontificating speeches about destiny, destiny itself is defined as benign by the genre or mode in which it appears. This strange mixture of inevitable destiny paired with a pronounced lack of control (coincidences, mistimings, miscommunications, and other comic and masochistic tropes) is perfect for the employment of a fantasy designed to let the viewer have his or her cake and eat it, too.

Romantic comedies play on the notion of true love as inevitable destiny while simultaneously focusing on the obstacles to that inevitable destiny; according to Lapsley and Westlake, "very little of such films' running time is given over to the depiction of [romantic fulfillment]. Instead, romantic narratives are almost invariably concerned with the obstacles in the way of its realization."[19] The comedy of romantic ghost comedies lies not in the resolution of romantic oneness, but in the masochistic process that prevents and delays this resolution. The fact that obstacles are often comic accounts for the coincidence of narrative obstacles to the kind of psychic obstacles that dramatize the impossibility of gendered identity and subjecthood.[20] In comically dramatizing and personifying the obstacles to both romantic plenitude as well as gendered identity, the ghost embodies both comic and masochistic obstacles. In ghost comedies, ghosts return to repeat the masochistic fantasy in which oneness of any kind will be revealed as impossible and hallucinatory.

Giving Up the Ghost

The emphasis on delay and obstacles might also help explain the repeat viewing of *Ghost* as well as many other narrative films. Audiences expect the ending to be happy, but they take pleasure in the process of reaching this inevitable conclusion as much as they do in experiencing the conclusion itself. Some scholars address this paradox by pointing to the sequence and development of narrative as inevitable masochistic elements.[21] Though some reviewers saw *Ghost* as flawed in its narrative form, and complained that the audience was way ahead of the plot, the masochistic perspective would suggest that the viewer's pleasure in watching *Ghost* might not stem solely from a hermeneutic question (what will happen; who did it) but more from experiencing the process of controlled obstacles and delay in the unfolding of the plot (how it happens).[22] The repetition associated with masochism is similar to that which Northrop Frye ascribes to repetition in comedy. Repetition in the sadistic scenario leads to an inexorable climax and resolution; so too with tragedy. Frye recalls the tragedy of Oedipus to compare the two types of repetition: "In a tragedy—*Oedipus Tyrannas* is the stock example—repetition leads logically to catastrophe. Repetition overdone or not going anywhere belongs to comedy."[23] The return of the ghost and the circular repetition of the narrative trajectories are both comedic and masochistic in their circularity, also illustrated by the way in which ghost films are often remakes of earlier films.[24]

The relationship between masochistic fantasy and comedy is complex but important to understanding ghosts as both masochistic figures and comic devices. Ghosts seem uniquely suited to fulfilling the requirements of romantic comedy, since they embody the obstacles required for the delay in the illusory fulfillment of oneness. Thus obstacles and delay to fulfillment are tropes of both comedy and masochism.[25] In returning from the dead and engaging in a masochistic scenario of rebirth through death, ghosts also demonstrate their relation to comedy's desire for lack of consequences, for new beginnings, and for an emphasis on cyclical time. As ghosts engage in a fantasy of romance, they simultaneously dramatize the dilemma of the origin of the subject in the Oedipal scenario. If this process is inherently masochistic because unachievable, it might also be potentially comic for the same reasons. The attainment of subjecthood is fraught with obstacles that can never be fully overcome except in death. Ghost comedies dramatize this process, illustrating that the paradoxical desire for wholeness can never be achieved by the subject as a subject, nor can it be achieved in romantic fulfillment. Like comedy narratives, however, masochistic ghosts refuse to see death as final or as a tragic ending to the process. Death is but the means by which to restart the process and enter into the fantasy again and again.

As with many psychoanalytic theories, theories of comedy often seem to be outside of history (comedy "is" this, comedy "expresses" that). It may be more useful to understand the way in which repetitions of stories, genres, and myths express, perpetuate, and work through the cultural values and stereotypes of the cultures in which they appear. The masochistic scenario played out in ghost films is directly connected to, and is framed by, existing patriarchal structures and stereotypes. The fact that these films appear to expel the guilty father and glorify the mother should be understood in connection with the current culture's tendency to socialize humans along specific gender lines and along a binary system that posits "man" or "not-man" (woman) as the only acceptable identities. This is the situation from which psychoanalytic theory and the Oedipal scenario derive and well describe. Even though the Oedipal scenario may be culturally specific and is itself a kind of fantasy, the stories and fantasies expressed in popular culture cannot be understood except in relation to these structures and stereotypes. Obviously, the binary system of gender is not the only way in which ghosts can be understood in the context of their immediate cultural surroundings. As vehicles of reversal and shifting identification, however, film ghosts play out a series of fantasies through gendered bodies and through narrative positions associated with gender. Western rationality is based on a notion of binary subjectivity, a subject-object split that facilitates the binary conceptions of gender, which may permit the fantasy of the ghost in the first place. The subject-object split celebrated in Cartesian philosophy creates the dichotomy of body/mind and body/spirit from which the figure of the ghost stems directly. That is, while many societies may believe in ghosts or employ ghosts in, for example, rituals and narratives, the notion of spirit as a separate entity seems to be almost the logical conclusion to the subject-object split upon which Western rationality is based. This is highly ironic, for the notion that "spirit" is separate from "body" literally "haunts" us as a kind of internal critique of rationality.

Regardless, the subject-object split is the necessary prerequisite to fantasies such as ghost stories, in which subjectivity and point of view are in question. Ghosts are structurally well suited to fantasies of reversal and gender switching precisely because the culture demands untenable yet oppositely gendered positions. As for comedy, what seems funny is certainly relative, cultural, and resides in the eye of the beholder. Previously, I suggested a link between the way in which ghosts tend to provoke crises or splits in subjectivity and the suggestion that humor may arise from the audience's perception of opposite or incongruous points of view. Yet if scholars of comedy have found a pattern of reversals (particularly Oedipal ones) in comedy, this does not necessarily suggest a universal theory of comedy.

Chapter 7

Speculating about Specters

Since there has been so little written about ghosts and angels in film, much research remains to be done. There are certainly many more interesting connections to be made about ghosts, particularly as conflicted representations of individual subjects. This study has been largely focused on gender for the sole reason that recent ghost films express a fairly coherent—as well as often explicit—concern with this issue. But gender is just one angle of pursuit, one which intersects with other types of representations in Hollywood film.

Several other avenues of research might be pursued. One particularly rich avenue of exploration, for example, may lie in the parallel construction of gender and race. At the conclusion of this chapter, I will briefly consider several ghost films for the way in which race and gender tend to be conflated. I will begin the chapter, however, by offering some analyses of ghost films from the 1940s to speculate on similarities and differences between the previous and current cycles of films. I will then conclude the book by proposing that other (non-ghost) films might be reconsidered in light of this study. Much of this chapter should be seen as speculative, as an invitation to further consideration of the rich, but up until now, "invisible" world of ghost films.

Hollywood Haunted

This study has examined only ghost films released in the last fifteen years or so; further studies could examine the earlier cycle of ghost films, beginning in the late 1930s through the late 1940s. The later cycle, this group of male-dominated ghost films, forms a coherent group in terms of narrative, visual, aural, and thematic pleasures, but it does bear similarities to several movies of the earlier cycle, in some cases as avowed remakes (*A Guy Name Joe* and *Always*) or in other cases as loose inspirations (*It's a Wonderful Life* and *Mr. Destiny*). Many of the earlier films, however, do not fit the "mold" of the later ghost films, either because they do not favor the male ghost-protagonist, or because they take part in Oedipal narratives which are at odds with those described here. For example, the original *Invisible Man* is a non-ghost film of the earlier era featuring an invisible character, while the later *Memoirs of an Invisible Man* fits the more masochistic mold. The earlier film is a horror/sci-fi hybrid in which the protagonist uses his invisibility for sadistic ends, to further his own mania for power and control. However, such a film is of interest in relation to the later cycle of ghost films for its role in the evolution of special effects in fantasy films. It might be considered for inclusion in a historical compendium of ghostly or invisible characters or examined as a product of industrial/technological processes. Thus, while this study has consisted primarily of textual analyses, future work might provide a more extensive historical context in which to understand the phenomenon—ghosts as star- or performance-based phenomena or as functions of special effects technology.

Although *The Invisible Man* is a horror movie, it inspired other non-horror films to use invisibility as a special effect. *Topper* (1937) was one such film and was also one of the first comedy ghost films in Hollywood. A variation of screwball comedy, *Topper* can be explored in the context of special effect innovations, particularly as they relate to sound film. The adoption of synchronous sound in the early 1930s coincided with the implementation of such easy tricks as rear-screen projection, and movie studios soon realized the cost-effectiveness of creating entire special effects departments to take over the manipulation of these and other trick shots.[1] The rise of special effects departments at major studios was obviously a contributing factor in the creation of film ghosts in the 1930s. The rise of screwball comedy is also related to the coming of sound in that it permitted the snappy dialogue for which the genre is famous. While *Topper* is arguably an example of a screwball comedy, the use of synchronous sound is also a necessary prerequisite to ghostly antics, which often rely on establishing the ghosts' invisible presence through the use of the voice. *Topper* is also interesting for the way in which the special effects cleverly allowed for the fulfillment of the "sex-without-the-sex" screwball dictum common to the genre, a way of satisfying the terms of the Motion Picture Production Code which prohibited sexually explicit content.[2] For example, a popular advertisement for the film referred to a scene in which the female ghost takes a shower. Almost every ad featured the phrase: "See an invisible beauty take a bath!"[3] While the special effects in the shower scene created one kind of visual spectacle, it thus cleverly averted another—that of the female ghost's naked body. The confluence of synchronized sound, special effects, and the screwball genre thus come together in *Topper*, suggesting a research angle that might combine a focus on genre with technological, industrial, and cultural analyses.

Topper is similar to recent ghost films in its comedic context and the way in which the ghosts provoke the comic "marvelous" versus "fantastic" response in the characters and viewers. It differs from the films in this study, however, in that it features a female ghost much more prominently than her male ghost companion.[4] In the original film in the *Topper* series, Constance Bennett and Cary Grant play a rich, drunken couple who die in a car accident only to return as ghosts to do a good deed. The good deed has a decidedly screwball slant, however: to promote the sexual awakening of the protagonist, Cosmo Topper. While the female's invisibility to the other characters could potentially thwart the male gaze, the audience is repeatedly treated to the display of Bennett in a variety of fashionable outfits.[5] This, coupled with the fact that Topper himself can see her, undercuts the potential to question or reverse the traditional male gaze of the female body. In terms of the issues of gender and sexuality, then, visually the film does not depart from traditional expectations. Topper's role is masochistic in the sense that he is at the mercy of the female ghost, whose antics jeopardize his standing as a respectable banker. But the trajectory of the narrative as a whole is much more Oedipal than those in this study in that the ghosts' mission is precisely to make Topper less passive and more sexually assertive. That is, Topper must overcome his mousy nature and become ultimately more masculine within his staid and conventional marriage. At the end of the film, he is celebrated for his new-found assertiveness.[6] The film's conclusion is thus at odds with the current crop of films in its celebration of sexual difference and the privileging of the male as the appropriate bearer of active desires.

A film that does feature a male spirit but also provides a slightly different view of ghost films is *The Canterville Ghost* (1944). The story's main focus is the cowardice of the men in the Canterville family, the hallmark of the "curse" that causes Sir Simon de Canterville to become a ghost in the seventeenth century. Though this situation demonstrates a masochistic position for the male ghost, the narrative goal is to "cure" this condition. Robert Young plays Caffy, a soldier who discovers that he is a descendent of the Canterville family, a relation that suggests he is also a coward in a long line of cowards. However, the curse can be lifted only if a Canterville male performs an act of heroism. Caffy succeeds and releases the ghost from his limbo at the end of the film, thereby also redeeming his own honor. The masochistic interludes of the ghost and the male lead (both of whom suffer profound ineffectuality due to their cowardice) reserve a place for this film in connection to the films studied here. However, since the male characters cannot be validated until they have proved their manhood, the film provides an essentially Oedipal scenario. In fact, it is none other than Sir Canterville's father who inflicts the ghostly curse as punishment for his cowardice. Only after the ghost pleads with his father for mercy (repeatedly screaming, "Father! Father!") is he finally released from his ghostly limbo. This film complicates the use of ghosts in comedy films by placing masochistic ghosts within a predominantly Oedipal, patriarchal narrative. This variation is not insignificant in that it mimics other non-ghost narratives in providing masochistic interludes for the male characters. However, it does not cohere as precisely to the later cycle of ghost films, again demonstrating that the ghost is a device that can be used in a variety of narratives. However, the terms of the ghostly device hinge—even in this film—on passive and active gender roles.

Divine Inspiration

Although there are exceptions, a number of ghost films from the late 1930s and 1940s bear strong similarities to more current ghost films. How similar are these films to those which followed? In addition, what is it about these earlier films that resonates with contemporary filmmakers and audiences? Although many ghost films from the earlier era are merely a response to the deaths suffered in wartime, this explanation has been inadequate to elucidate the gender issues raised by current ghost films. Both cycles of ghost films occurred in eras in which gender roles underwent (and, for the later cycle, are still undergoing) considerable scrutiny. The first group of films was made during World War II, a period that coincided with the heyday of the Hollywood studio era. Without retracing this well-known branch of film history, I would like to tender a few observations that may be pertinent to recent comedy ghost films. In no way is this discussion comprehensive, nor are these interpretations and speculations representative of a dominant reading of the films. Rather, I am merely following threads in the subtexts of the films to establish links between them and the current cycle.

As noted by analysts of film noir, the replacement of men by women in the workforce during World War II created an anxiety over gender roles upon men's return from overseas. In film noir, the femme fatale is seen as an expression of gender anxiety over women's newfound autonomy.[7] Movies concerning the war also reveal a tension regarding the place of both women and men, both on the battlefield and at home.[8] Many war films are classically male-driven stories of conquest. Films such as *Destination: Tokyo* (1943) and *This Is the Army* (1943) re-create traditional modes of Hollywood cinema.

The former demonstrates that the heterosexual couple often remains a central focus even in films concerned mainly with battles. In the latter (as with action and buddy movies of later eras) and other war films, women are a disruption to the main action, and are frequently excluded all together.[9]

But much of the anxiety generated by women's newfound power is channeled into contradictory narratives. The contradictions concern, in part, the split between the home front and the battlefield, coded as female and male respectively, but which become contested in a time of deprivation and sublimated desires. Films such as *Since You Went Away* (1944), *Pride of the Marines* (1945), and *Prisoner of Japan* (1942) all work through this tension with varying degrees of explicitness. *Pride of the Marines,* in particular, seems to offer a conflicted view of gender roles when the male protagonist goes blind and must renounce his hero status in favor of a commitment to home. This last film places its protagonist in a position highly reminiscent of that found in several ghost-related films of the era: relegated to the home front and relieved of his active narrative function.[10]

A Guy Named Joe (1944) intersects directly with both current ghost films and wartime narratives. While the remake, *Always,* used firefighting pilots to update the story, the original uses the war as a setting for a masochistic fantasy featuring a male ghost and a female protagonist. The film is notable for featuring the female character, Dorinda (Irene Dunn), as an active participant in the war, a pilot like her suitor, Pete (Spencer Tracy). As in the remake, her status as a pilot is a source of friction between the couple, the question of her femininity broached in scene after scene. In both versions, Pete gives her a beautiful dress—a reminder to him and to the audience that she is a beautiful romantic object despite her airplane flying. However, Dorinda is given the heroic mission at the end of the film—not officially, but effectively when she steals the plane of Ted, her new suitor. The mission—to blow up an enemy munitions silo—is described as extremely dangerous and difficult. It was given to Ted only because he proved himself the best pilot. Although Dorinda is guided by the ghostly Pete, this heavenly guidance is no less than what every pilot is given (male or female, including Ted), and she returns a heroine with her mission complete. As in the remake, the ghost in the earlier film is placed in a passive, feminine position of ineffectuality, and he is rebuffed by Dorinda in favor of Ted. Dorinda becomes the active narrative agent, completes a dangerous daredevil mission, and "gets the guy" at the conclusion.[11]

That Dorinda is given so much power might seem surprising in a film of this time period. But the role reversal does bear direct relation to the type of film viewer at that time. Women became part of the war effort as pilots and nurses, and also joined the workforce at home. This change in women's gender status is obvious in Hollywood films, then, in representations of characters such as Dorinda. But the celebration of this reversal, combined with the masochistic status of the male characters, is not so easily explained. If men suffered anxiety due to women's increased power, this may indeed account for representations of women as villains in films of this era. But women in ghost films are not villainized for their masculine qualities, and neither is the male denigrated for his emasculation. As noted in relation to recent films, one explanation for this phenomenon lies in the ghostly state of the character, one which justifies the masochistic interlude without impugning the concept of manhood. The specific circumstances of war, however, may provide a more specific context for the acceptance of such male characters, as well as help explain why audiences might have wanted to see such a character.

The circumstances of war include self-sacrifice as well as an unwelcome acceptance of widespread death. The reality of war-time death does account in some measure for a wish fulfillment fantasy in which war heroes do not really die. Some war films of the era use death as a vehicle to isolate the protagonist and make him that much more heroic. It might seem almost de rigueur to portray war heroes in such a manner, and certainly it fits with Hollywood stereotypes. But *A Guy Named Joe* provides a clue concerning a different facet of a soldier's conflicted position in a full-scale war.

While Pete is known as an ace pilot, he is also berated by his superiors for taking too many risks and for not following the rules. One detects a certain admiration for this "flaw," and yet his daredevil tactics are revealed to have possibly fatal consequences for the rest of the squadron. In an early scene in the film, Pete's superior criticizes his behavior: "You're trying to win the war all alone. I expect you to stay where you belong. What are you trying to do, be a hero?" Later, as a ghost, Pete witnesses a young pilot who is being reprimanded by his superior for a risky maneuver that mimicked his own flying (which cost Pete his own life). The pilot admits that he has heard of Pete's reputation and had been attempting to emulate him. Much to the ghost's chagrin, the commander then remarks that Pete's actions were not skillful but instead "might just go down as one of the luckiest incidents in the history of World War II." He has been awarded a medal, but as the young pilot is told: "Unfortunately, it came too late for him to wear. We're not training you men to die, we're training you to live and the first budding hero I catch among you will be washed out."

Before his death, Dorinda had also criticized Pete for his macho maneuvers: "You never stayed with your squadron in your whole life. You're a lone wolf in a service where men fly together. You've got hero hunger and better men than you come a dime a dozen." The context of the discussion is Pete's inability to properly commit to a relationship with Dorinda (as in *Always*). The exchange thus reveals that Pete's inability to see himself as anything but a lone wolf has serious ramifications in both his personal life and his military career. The lone hero may be a masculine ideal, but it is incompatible with couplehood and military wartime service. The first requires a relinquishing of individual autonomy to another person, while the second requires the soldier to subjugate himself to a higher command. The war effort demands that the male soldier follow orders and work within a community, a contradiction for the Hollywood hero. And yet, far from being an unusual syndrome, this dilemma may actually typify the war film as a genre: "The essential concern of the war film (until recently, at least) is to show the importance of a group working together to achieve a common goal; individuals must be welded together into a unit, a platoon, in which each works for the good of all and a clear, mutually accepted hierarchy is established."[12] This concept is articulated by the heavenly high commander in the film, whom Pete encounters when he is dead. The high commander turns out to be an air force pilot whom Pete recognizes as the greatest flyer who ever lived. As with other ghosts, Pete is given a mission he must complete back on earth. When Pete begins to boast about his ability to handle a plane, the commander sets him straight:

> Commander: You can fly fairly well and if you obey orders. . . .
> Pete: Fairly well?! Why, I can do things with a plane the designer didn't even think of!
> Commander: That's just the point, Sandidge. We work here on the general lines of trying to do things to the plane the designer *did* think of. . . . We operate on the principle of helping the other fellow.

As the conversation continues Pete learns that he will be sent back to help new flyers who need guidance. Pete comments that this system is not like the old days when he used to go up alone (a fact about which he brags several times). The commander seems shocked at this comment and explains to the equally incredulous Pete that he, like every other flyer, was "helped by every man since the beginning of time. . . . And now it's your turn to help the next man." As Pete proceeds on his mission, he is able to help his young protégé, Ted. But when Ted begins to take Pete's place with Dorinda, Pete attempts to sabotage the relationship by influencing Ted's decision making. Specifically, he tries to persuade Ted to perform the same type of daredevil stunt for which Pete had been reprimanded (and which resulted in the punishment of an unwelcome tour of duty in fogged-over Scotland). The high commander now calls him back, realizing that Pete has not fully understood the nature of the mission. As in *Always,* the mission involves relinquishing Dorinda to Ted, as well as giving up his egocentric conceptions of flying.

While air force and navy pilots would seem ideal for fantasies of solo heroism, any soldier is, in some sense, placed in a figuratively masochistic position. Soldiers are frequently deprived of an active role, and are instead often forced into a waiting mode: "In many ways, war is unlike the hunt: the soldiers are stuck in place (and so are themselves targets); they must band together in a space of noncompetition ('You'll have to watch that side!' 'I'll watch it!')."[13] As the soldiers find themselves waiting for someone to attack them, the masochistic nature of their mission becomes obvious. The fantasy of war as the setting for male heroism is thus undercut by the reality of the war setting, which often places soldiers at the mercy of violent enemy forces beyond their control.

In war films, the male finds himself at the mercy of both the enemy and his superior command. Though the superior command may be embodied by a military officer, it is ultimately the entire military machine and a patriotic, nationalist mission that must take precedence over any individual male ego. But while *A Guy Named Joe* refers to the national war effort, the highest authority becomes equated ultimately with heavenly destiny.

The Bishop's Wife (1947) makes no mention of war, but the tone of self-sacrifice is evident, merely shifted directly to a religious arena without an intervening historical referent or context.[14] The film, however, is set at Christmastime, which allows the religious aspects of the film to be tempered by a more secular fantasy of love and togetherness.[15] Though the movie does not feature a male ghost, it does provide a masochistic scenario for its male protagonist at the hands of a helping angel, Dudley. The story concerns an overworked and ineffectual bishop who is unable to raise enough money to build a new cathedral. His feelings of desperation are portrayed as the cause of tension in his marriage to Julia. While Julia pleads with him to join her in some companionship and Christmas cheer, Henry is too concerned with his work to acknowledge her, instead alternately brooding and snapping at her. He begins the narrative as an ineffectual husband and becomes even more so when Dudley arrives to help him. True to the masochistic fantasy of ghost films, the solution to his many problems is merely a pretext for resolving a rocky relationship with Julia. Before the conclusion of the film, Henry is made to suffer a number of indignities caused by the presence of Dudley himself. While Henry attempts to attend to business matters, Dudley is left to tend to Julia. As the movie progresses, Henry's place as Julia's companion is more and more supplanted by the charming angel. Much to his chagrin, Henry finds himself continually on the outside of his own marriage, magically stuck to a chair for example, while his wife cavorts with another man. When he finally regains his wife at the end of the film, a change of positions occurs. The angel is rebuffed by the wife, as if to establish a kind of equilibrium to the binary system of power and passivity created by angels and ghosts.

One component of this and other films discussed here is a "companionate" version of heterosexual romance. This model of love and marriage has repercussions for an understanding of even the later ghost films in their portrayal of male attempts at rapprochement within the "female realm." Historical accounts of the changing conceptions of love and marriage have traced marriage from an economic and highly patriarchal institution to a more companion-oriented model, where men and women are friends. Earlier notions of marriage depended on women being exchanged as property, adhering to taboos of incest and miscegenation in the advancement of the patriarchal line.[16] The newer idea of a companionate marriage has emerged and evolved over the course of this century. Whereas the earlier idea focused more on separate spheres (housewife versus breadwinner), the new model focused on "partnership and communication in the domestic sphere."[17] This newer model is at the heart of the ghost comedy thematic, as the traditional male and female spheres cause difficulties for a newer type of communication between the two genders. In Hollywood films, the companionate ideal first became foregrounded with the advent of the screwball genre, where couples were portrayed as good-natured sparring partners. This sparring is comic and lighthearted but also reveals the difficulties attendant to changing ideals. Along with the idea that couples should be friends, the screwball films helped promote the idea that couples should have fun.[18]

While not screwball comedies, *The Bishop's Wife* and *A Guy Named Joe* bear resemblance to such films by implicitly promoting the companionate ideal through the employment of the masochistic interlude.[19] While in the latter case, this ideal is submerged beneath the fighter-pilot plot, Dorinda and Pete make reference to fun as a quality that redeems their otherwise conflicted relationship. In the course of having fun, the companionate idea of friendship implies that the couple will overcome their separate spheres and participate in activities together. These two ideals are illustrated as Pete boasts that he likes to fly alone. Dorinda pleadingly suggests that they try flying together.

> Dorinda: Pete, do you realize you and I have never been up flying together?
> Pete: When I fly for fun I like to fly alone. You know how I feel about women in the air. Promise to get a desk job and I'll take you up.
> Dorinda: Wrong gal, Pete. Wrong place, wrong time, too. Pete, why don't you be a good guy and marry me? I wonder what kind of kids we'd have. . . . Cute! Not a brain in their heads but they'd have fun!

By the end of the film, the heavenly commander persuades Pete that flying alone was just an illusion to begin with. He and Dorinda do end up flying together at the end of the film, and Pete relinquishes his lone wolf attitude for

144

the newer model of coupledom, albeit one that the new suitor will enjoy instead of him. Again, it is possible to interpret Dorinda's heroic accomplishment as belonging to Pete since he "helps" her from the back of the plane, thus undercutting her role as a strong female character and diffusing the ideal of a more equal couple. However, Pete's help is not reserved for Dorinda but is the assistance all pilots (male and female) receive. So while Dorinda accomplishes as much as any other fighter pilot, the flight together at the end also fulfills the companionate model of togetherness. If the war film is one in which the characters "must all hang together or hang separately,"[20] then this sentiment refers to both the lesson learned by soldiers in wartime and the male's discovery that his loner attitude must be overcome in his personal life.

In *The Bishop's Wife,* the companionate model becomes the goal for Henry and Julia, but it is initially thwarted by his preoccupation with job-related troubles. Dudley first appears in answer to the bishop's prayers regarding the cathedral. But as the story progresses, Henry is frustrated that Dudley does not seem very helpful in actually assisting with this goal. Instead, Dudley takes Julia ice skating and out to lunch. As Julia begins to ignore the bishop in favor of Dudley, he jealously confronts Dudley. Although he believes the angel has been sent to help him build the cathedral, at the end of the film Dudley reveals that this was not his mission. Instead, he was sent to answer his prayers and to give guidance, revealing that what Henry really needed and wanted (without realizing it) was a marriage in which both partners have a role and in which fun keeps the flame alive. Henry never does succeed in fulfilling his original goal. The cathedral is never built, as Henry realizes that his family is more important than his original hubristic goal.[21]

It's a Wonderful Life makes explicit reference to World War II and bears a direct link to both these and more recent films. While it is has been examined to a much greater extent than most of the other films in this study, I include a brief assessment of it because it fits the masochistic model and returns us to difficulties in gender created by a binary model. For despite the companionate model of romance, gendered expectations create a contradictory mode of compatibility. As in the other films, the dilemmas of male ambition versus domesticity are played out against the backdrop of wartime sacrifice and heroism. The gender-imbued dichotomies worked through here are similar to, and prefigure, many of the ghost films of the 1980s and 1990s.

The main character, George Bailey, resembles other Hollywood protagonists in his pursuit of classically male ambition. While his soon-to-be-wife, Mary, yearns for a home and family, George's ambition is to travel the world and to escape the clutches of domestic life. Despite the protagonist's masculine aspirations, the narrative trajectory is decidedly masochistic in its thwarting of his desire. As in *The Bishop's Wife,* George never does succeed with his original goal, which does nothing to detract from the film's happy ending. George's inability to go off to war is but a long line of obstacles to his dream, and one which explicitly dramatizes gendered dilemmas caused by shifting roles during wartime. His inability to enlist as a soldier relegates him to the domestic sphere from which he has been trying to escape and becomes all the more excruciating when his brother, Harry, returns as the hero George had hoped to be. George is disqualified from military service, of course, because of an ear injury suffered when saving this same brother from a watery death.

Symbolically, we might say that Harry is rescued from the maternal waters, enabling his unfettered achievement of masculine pursuits. The water motif occurs elsewhere in the film, for example when George and Mary plunge into a swimming pool at the high school dance. In the Oedipal scheme, the male naturally fears being re-engulfed by the maternal waters, a fear ostensibly played out in this film. Yet from a masochistic perspective, this engulfment is in no way unequivocal or undesirable. George and Mary's descent into the water marks an early turning point and prefigures the domestic bliss attained at the end of the film, one which is clearly celebrated. The film asks the question: How can a man be a father and a husband and still be a man? While the protagonist's personal ambition is classically masculine, the film ultimately uses a masochistic scenario in an attempt to resolve a dilemma posed by oppositely coded genders.

As with other masochistic fantasies, the film throws into question the role of the authoritative father. The difficulty of fatherhood begins early in the film when, as a child, George turns to his father for help. George is prompted by a sign on the wall that states,"Ask DAD, he'll know." And yet dad does not know, and is unable to help. Later his father dies, further abandoning him as a father figure, and thus recalling the trope of the absent father discussed in relation to current ghost films. On the other hand, a maternal bond is suggested when his mother seems to know better than he does what it is he really wants, namely Mary. This is portrayed in a comic light, when, despite his protestations, George ends up at Mary's house upon her return from college. Mother smiles knowingly. Soon after, George expresses his dilemma: embrace Mary and become one with her in marriage, or reject her as seems to be necessary to fulfill the Oedipal/Symbolic split. Although he violently protests that he'll "Never marry. Never! I want to do what I want to do," George says these words while passionately kissing Mary. George both desires Mary but at the same time fears the powerful dependency associated with the female. This tension can never be truly resolved because the male identity attempts to define itself precisely by its independence and difference from women. But something happens that allows George to resolve to return happily to Mary in the end.

When George tries to commit suicide, an angel, Clarence, is sent down to delay his "improper death." After having saved George by making George save him (Clarence) from drowning (itself a curiously gendered conundrum in which a somewhat asexual angel accomplishes his goal by making himself the passive victim), Clarence becomes the vehicle whereby George "returns" in a ghostly state. Although the audience is struck by the film noir decrepitude of Bedford Falls, George's anguish stems at least as much from the fact that he is not "recognized" by anyone, even his own mother. Although he is not invisible, like a ghost he cannot be acknowledged and has no identity. The ghostly episode acts as a kind of therapeutic interlude in which George will recover from the impossible conflicting desires of wanting to admit his dependency but not being able to. Upon contemplating the house that he and Mary will eventually live in, George remarks disdainfully that he "wouldn't live in [it] as a ghost." However, it is his "ghostly" episode that causes him finally to appreciate the house as the site of domestic harmony. Clarence allows him to "regress" to a kind of pre-preOedipal state (he is "un-born") in which the Oedipal trajectory is played out to its logical, nightmare conclusion: He is so independent from others that his mother does not even recognize him. Only by acknowledging that his identity is entirely dependent on others (and on the mother) and not completely independent can George "cure" himself and allow himself the dependency necessary to his family life.

The film thus acknowledges the way in which identity is dependent on recognition of others and in particular that the male identity depends also on the female to constitute it as active subject. (Thus, the female is not just "not-male" as proposed by the Oedipal interpretation. Here, the male is not-female.)[22] As with ghost scenarios, the film operates within binary categories and can only throw them into flux through a process of reversal. But the constructed nature of the binary categories is hinted, when Mary announces that she is pregnant. When George asks whether it is a boy or a girl, Mary answers "yes," as if to imply the as-yet ungendered possibilities of the baby. Although the categories themselves are not overturned, the ghostly interlude provides the male protagonist with a kind of gender reversal that permits a rapprochement, a kind of solution, to an unsolvable dilemma.[23]

In addition, the interlude George experiences is a timeless delay and a repetition (the repetition of his life in parallel), which permits the kind of transformation Todorov and others deem as the work of narratives. The function of the ghostly interlude is to provide a delayed space in which both the character and the viewer can suspend traditional gender roles and experience the crux of the narrative's otherwise unresolvable thematic. In the final analysis, even though the endings of narratives are crucial, this does not deny the play of experience that occurs during the delays and repetitions preceding the end. The kind of "feminine" delay in these films is a crucial narrative and cinematic device that leads to the protagonist's eventual transformation.

Finally, *The Ghost and Mrs. Muir* (1947) features a male ghost but it does not adhere to the current cycle of ghost films in portraying a masochistic male protagonist. For example, the male ghost is much more powerful than any in the present cycle. The dead sea captain effectively scares away those he does not want inhabiting his house (thus resembling a classic horror film house-haunting), and he is able to do so by manipulating his voice as well as material objects. Although the nature of the ghost and the thrust of the narrative are thus different from more current comedy ghost films, the ghost is nevertheless similarly employed as a device that mobilizes gendered stereotypes within the context of active and passive positions.

In this film, Mrs. Muir (Lucy) moves to the seaside to escape her dead husband's domineering mother and sister. She rents a cottage with her maid and young daughter, despite the fact that the house seems to be haunted by a sea captain who has driven all the previous tenants away. When Captain Gregg fails to frighten her off, he decides to let her stay in "his house" and they strike up a romantic, if conflicted, relationship. When Lucy runs out of money for the rent, Captain Gregg suggests she make money by helping him write his biography and have it published. Although the book is a success, Lucy meets and falls in love with a man, Miles Farley. Realizing that he cannot compete with those from the land-of-the-living, Captain Gregg gives up his haunting and temporarily disappears, causing Lucy to forget about him and believe that she has only dreamed him. Unfortunately, Farley has been married to another woman all along. Lucy is left lonely and forlorn until her death at the film's conclusion when Captain Gregg reappears and they are finally reunited as ghosts.

On one level, *The Ghost and Mrs. Muir* presents a view of Lucy as a liberated woman in a turn-of-the-century, patriarchal society. Lucy spends a good deal of the film attempting to assert her independence and lead a life of her own choosing. In the very first scene of the film, she explains to her sister and mother-in-law why she must leave them: "I've never had a life of my own. It's been Edwin's life and yours and Eva's. Never my own." Although her independence remains a constant point of contention throughout the film—even up until her death when her last words are for the maid to "stop bossing" her—this portrait of an emancipated woman is complicated by her relationship with the male ghost.

Captain Gregg may be a spirit, but unlike many more recent ghosts, he possesses many bodily and earthly attributes. He is able to control his physical surroundings in very tangible ways. At one point, he (invisibly) grabs Lucy's in-laws and literally drags them out the front door against their will. And unlike other ghosts who have no choice about whom they haunt, Captain Gregg tells Lucy that nobody can see or hear him unless, as he says, "I choose that they should."

The title of the film may be a tip-off to Lucy's relationship to the ghost. Although widowed, Lucy is still haunted by her former association with her husband through her last name, and the ghost in this film represents a return of the absent husband. But because she has described her husband as being somewhat ineffectual, Captain Gregg is also representative of an unfulfilled desire for a more ideally masculine husband. It would seem to be an impossible romance, of course, because Captain Gregg embodies both the masculine subject and the impossibility of its attainment due to his ghostliness.

The title of the film not only refers to Lucy's gendered place within society but also to the Captain's contradictory role within the narrative. As an objectified, unnamed "ghost" the Captain is implicitly less a character than a product of Lucy's subconscious, hence the fact that he tells her he is able to appear to anyone, but instead chooses only to "haunt" Lucy. The ghost then may be an objectification of Lucy's, as well as the audience's, conflicting desires. The difficulty in deciding whether the ghost is a subject in his own right or an object of Lucy's fantasy foregrounds the contradictory quality of the ghost as a narrative device. In this film, the ghost represents a kind of repressed excess that disturbs the otherwise static and binary oppositions. This disruption stems from the pre-Oedipal stage in which gender roles are not fixed, a stage "we cannot remember, but disrupts our speech and haunts our dreams."[24] The ghost represents such a disturbance—literally haunting Lucy and reminding her of repressed desires and identifications. It disrupts her speech in two important ways. To begin with, Lucy's otherwise pretty language becomes peppered with crusty, sailor language. Although she at first cannot bring herself to type a particularly vulgar word that the Captain dictates to her (when writing the book), she finds herself blurting out unladylike phrases throughout the film.

The disruption of speech is also made literal by the way in which the Captain is able to separate his audible voice from his (invisible) body and cause Lucy to appear to be speaking when she is not. When Gregg frightens a man out of their train compartment, the man apparently sees only Lucy. But he hears a man's voice say, "Clear off you blasted mud-turtle! There's no room!" The gentleman can only conclude that Lucy has said this and leaves in horror, replying to Lucy (not the Captain), "I beg your pardon, madam!" Several other times during the film, Gregg speaks, but the other characters believe that it is Lucy who is speaking. A similar mediating tactic is used in *Ghost,* for example, but its function here is different in that the ghost is not subject to his ghostly state but instead uses it to control the situation. That is, the male ghost does not require a female to mediate his wishes or to communicate, as in *Ghost.* However, the effect of his voice appearing to come from her mouth provides a variation of the gender switching found in later films, endowing Lucy with some of the macho qualities associated with the sea captain's off-color speech. (The effect is mitigated somewhat, however, since the audience is aware of the Captain's presence.)

The Captain's ability to communicate is further mediated by Lucy in a different but significant way. Specifically, Captain Gregg literally "ghost writes" the book that Lucy writes in order to make enough money to support herself. The book, titled "Blood and Swash," is published under the pseudonym "Captain X." As with later ghosts, this mediation may allow for a double interpretation. In the first case the audience may assume that Lucy is incapable of writing such a book and is "authorized" to be a writer and support herself only through the help of a man. In the second case the audience may accept Lucy as the real author, imbued with both the vocabulary and authorial autonomy of the male character. The latter interpretation refers back to the ghost as figment of Lucy's imagination and redeems Lucy as the narrative agent of her own story. However, the ghost remains representative of the unassailable presence of patriarchal authority, subconscious or not, and is thus reminiscent of the gendered stereotypes that subtend the main characters.

Either reading is possible, and yet the contradictory status of the ghost allows the categories to be worked through in a fantasy setting. As a figment of Lucy's imagination, the ghost is the embodiment of the heterosexual injunction to identify with one sex, and thereby desire the Other. Thus Lucy must both desire the Other (the man) who defines her as woman, but also merge at some level with the Other since this fantasy stems from her own unconscious.[25] Lucy has no role models for becoming the kind of woman who creates her own destiny, so she hallucinates a role model with whom she can identify through impossible desire. Lucy needs the fantasy figure because the Other is seen as necessary in the very process of formulating the identity. Since Lucy is alone for the first time, bereft of the husband who previously defined her, she creates an Other with and through whom her conflicting needs may be addressed.

At one point in the film (before writing the book), Lucy despairs that she has never done anything useful with her life: "I feel so useless. Here I am nearly halfway through life and what have I done?" The maid reminds her of her daughter, Anna, saying, "I suppose you call Miss Anna nothing?" Lucy completely dismisses this idea: "Oh heavens. I can't take any credit for her. She just happened." Lucy does not consider the maternal ideal as a possible locus of identity.[26] To be an individual, Lucy feels she must reject the notions associated with femininity and instead embrace more masculine ones.

As with other characters in recent ghost films, Lucy is unable to escape the gendered tautology she inhabits and which constitutes her identity, but which erupts as a haunting in her writing and speech. The only way for

Lucy to take charge of her life is to find an "other" who can constitute her as the subject instead of the object. But the only way to do this is to reaffirm the initial gender split and assume the values inherent in this system.[27] Thus initially Lucy affirms an absent Other while denying that she herself is capable of writing. The only way for Lucy to be an individual is to be as "male" as she can since the individual is by cultural definition a male. Lucy must both identify with the male and objectify him as her Other (as man does to woman) so that she can become properly positioned as the writing subject.

Romance and Sex

The device of the ghost is indeed an ideal vehicle for staging fantasies of gender flux in the context of a culture that operates along binary gender lines. The changing conception of romantic love may have influenced the use of ghosts in fantasies in which gender plays a role. While the companionate model continues to operate today, its portrayal in films has been further complicated by several factors. Specifically, as romantic love is seen more as a friendship than an economic union, the historic evolution of such a relationship surfaces in Hollywood films as nostalgic, but also increasingly sexual. On the one hand, the romantic couple is characterized by psychological and spiritual compatibility. This "meeting of the minds" is portrayed in ghost movies and other romances as proof that there is one and only one "right" mate. Thus the companionate model can be seen as the expression of a higher destiny, a trajectory played out in the movies described here.

On the other hand, the increasingly overt sexualization of both men and women in the postwar era (a trend perhaps perpetuated during World War II and that continued into the 1970s and beyond)[28] may represent a detour in the portrayal of purely romantic love, as sex became divorced from love in the popular imagination, and became merely the expression of individuality (usually male). Films of the 1950s and 1960s focused less on romance, and the sexual revolution helped shift the emphasis toward an ideal of uncommitted sexual freedom.[29] The postwar years also saw a much more gritty version of reality portrayed on the screen, a trend which perhaps added to an atmosphere in which ghost fantasies might not have thrived.[30] In the early 1980s, as the United States began to come to grips with the AIDS virus, the perceived dangers of unbridled sex may have caused the spiritual component of the companionate model to re-emerge. The link between sex and spirituality is, in fact, part of the original notion of companionate marriage, where sex is the medium to express love, "a true union of souls, not merely a physical function."[31] Though the lack of many ghost fantasies in the 1950s and 1960s—and their reemergence in the late 1970s and 1980s—may be attributed to a number of factors, it seems likely that the above changes bear relation to the trend.

Crises as Catalysts

The reasons for the prevalence of current fantasy films are several (for example, the stresses of modern-day life, such as AIDS and changing gender roles) and they demonstrate a connection to the earlier era. Both eras confront the specter of death in epidemic proportions, and both suffer from changes in gender expectations. The specter of war muddies the comparison a bit, however. Although World War II provides a landmark by which to locate the gender anxiety in the earlier era, the war experiences in Korea and Vietnam were somewhat different. As a national effort on a worldwide scale, 1940s public and official responses to the war were mobilized in a much more monolithic fashion. Neither the Korean nor the Vietnam War inspired the same type of national support, and the latter was so contested and despised that Hollywood did not even attempt to portray the conflict until well after it was over.[32]

Though the aftermath of war was markedly different in each period, the 1970s was nevertheless a period in which the United States suffered a "legitimacy crisis" on a grand scale. This crisis was only partly in response to a failed war experience; it was also due to a troubled economy and revelations of wrongdoings by corporations and government officials, Watergate being the most egregious example. Race riots and assassinations in the 1960s had also set the stage for a new sense of public reality in which authority figures suddenly seemed vulnerable.[33]

If the mid-1970s suffered such widespread crisis in authority, the resurgence of film noir movies in this period may not be a coincidence.[34] This crisis in confidence pushed the country to the political right by the end of the seventies, paving the way for the Reagan era of conservatism and a corresponding shift in the ideological content of Hollywood films.[35] The renewed confluence of film noir narratives and ghost comedies in both eras seems striking. If a crisis in confidence prompts an emergence of film noir, both eras' noir films are nevertheless "answered" by what Valenti aptly termed "film blanc." The comparative label suggests a connection between the two genres beyond an emphasis on opposing tone and visual style, including a reworking of gender roles, albeit from different perspectives. In both the 1940s and the 1970s a crisis of authority surfaced in films as a crisis of male power. In response, the dominant project of contemporary Hollywood cinema has been the correction of gender imbalance through a reassertion of patriarchy. This mission is discernible in all sorts of films, and perhaps most overtly in horror films, where violence against women has been described as "more gruesome, more violent, more disgusting, and perhaps more confused, than ever before in history."[36] The depiction of violence against women is one manifestation, but the trend is also integral to fantasy films such as *Star Wars,* which is an outright Oedipal fantasy. Though the ghost films discussed here seem anathema to the trend, their appearance in two eras of gender-anxiety can surely be no coincidence.

Race and Gender

The ghost films in this study have raised questions about the narrative, visual, and aural presentation of characters as players in fantasy scenarios of gender flux. The binary categories activated by these scenarios are complicated by a consideration of race, which itself has often been expressed as a binary concept. One of the most deeply embedded social dualities has long been between the racial categories of black and white. As with gender, the categories have been "useful" more as rhetorical strategies than as accurate descriptions of real people, with the terms "white" and "black" being symbolic rather than descriptive. The very notion of race is problematic. My use of the term denotes socially and culturally constructed, not natural, categories.[37] Although the categories of black and white have often set the terms of racial debate, a number of other racial categories are commonly used as a way of distinguishing one set of people from another.[38] Even when considering a variety of races or ethnicities, racial descriptors are frequently applied to every group but white people. Thus "white" becomes a kind of "non-racially" coded norm, and everybody who is "not-white" is seen to be part of a racial group.[39] This recalls the way in which men have traditionally been considered the norm for individuals, while women, or ambiguously sexed individuals, are preemptively stigmatized as not-male. The insistence on considering white-male as one category and everybody else as Other thus provides a clear, if over-simplified, point on which to begin a comparison of race and gender.

Although most of the films in this study do not explicitly concern themselves with race (as either a point of contention or of pride), several of the films do make overt reference to it either through the strategic placement of "non-white" actors or through dialogue and narrative content. Clearly, movies dominated by white actors that do not approach race thematically or narratively are as susceptible to an examination of race as those that foreground the issue. As with many Hollywood films, the presence of "whiteness" often serves to make race an "invisible" issue (at least for white audiences).[40]

Ralph Ellison's famous novel, *The Invisible Man,* leads to an obvious comparison between blacks' place in society and the masochistic place of ghosts in current films.[41] Blacks and racial issues have clearly been "invisible" to much of the mainstream Hollywood industry for years. The place of race might be best described as a structured absence, which nevertheless tends to haunt Hollywood cinema. This is particularly true of certain genres such as Westerns, where racial annihilation undergirds even those narratives that do not specifically pit "cowboys" against "Indians." As with women, when blacks and other non-whites are considered by Hollywood, they tend to be either revered or vilified along racially stereotyped lines. In *Ghost,* we find both of these tactics, but the latter is particularly interesting in the context of the ghost fantasy.

In this film the murderer is a shifty-looking Puerto Rican from a bad neighborhood, a classic example of a character whose evilness stems implicitly from his ethnicity while simultaneously being coded by the narrative as simply non-white. As Judith Mayne notes, the film operates in a "near-infantile" way in its conception of white and black as good evil.[42] But while Willy's evilness is coded black, Oda Mae's blackness is coded as feminine and—not coincidentally—celebrated in the masochistic fantasy. Interestingly, the character of Oda Mae departs little from previous stereotypes of the black female. As the mammy figure, she serves as a spiritual aide to the white couple, and her motherly status combined with her comic antics are consistent with the portrayal of blacks as kindly helpers and buffoons.[43] It is also no coincidence that the one person able to access the supernatural is both black and a woman. Many of the qualities earlier described as feminine and maternal are also often associated with black characters in Hollywood films. Two of the most striking are spirituality and musicality. In *Framing Blackness,* Ed Guerrero notes the prevalence of music in Hollywood films that feature black "stories," particularly stories concerning black slaves: "During Hollywood's classic period (1930–1945), there was hardly a plantation film made that did not contain some sort of sentimentalized musical interlude performed by the devoted slaves on the plantation or the black servants of the postbellum years."[44] While the history of black Americans does include an incredibly rich history of music, I want to address only the narrative and thematic contexts of the music in these films.[45] The equation of music with a heightened sense of spirituality, an insistence on "soul," finds expression not only in relation to black characters, but in ghost fantasies. These fantasy narratives are all the more interesting then, for by conflating music and supernaturalism, they also become emblematic of racial formulations in the culture at large.

In Hollywood movies the threat of the Other may be exaggerated in narratives of miscegenation or ghetto-ridden crime, while in other cases the threat (and the guilt generated by this prejudice) becomes smoothed over by representations of black people as musicians and performers, or as kindly spiritual advisors. The equation of blacks with "soul" is manifested in ghost films that access the spiritual realm through black characters and/or equate music with soul, creating a kind of thematic transference that overlaps with gender as a realm that is "Other" and therefore difficult for the white male to access. (Thus, in ghost films we can discern a circular conflation: black = music = soul = spirit(ual) = ineffable, irrational = women = not-white/male = Other = black.) Richard Dyer's observations on the invisibility of whiteness as a cultural category has provided an important basis for this discussion. But his remarks about *The Night of the Living Dead* provide a further point of interest in that they recall my contention that comedy ghost films operate to expel or deny the abject associated with the corpse in horror films. The zombies in this movie are equated with the "dead" qualities of white people, in contrast to the soulfulness of black culture. Just as the male characters in ghost films must access the feminine/maternal, ghostly states provide an antidote to white characters' purported lack of soul. Thus in ghost films, characters coded as "having" a race may be considered abject and thus expelled (Willy). More commonly, however, such characters oppose the abject and are portrayed (pre-Oedipally) as having musical and spiritual qualities to which the white characters desire access (Oda Mae).[46]

A white male ghost provides another avenue by which to explore the gender/race relationship. bell hooks notes that "white men seeking alternatives to a patriarchal masculinity [have] turned to black men, particularly black musicians,"[47] thus echoing a desire mobilized in ghost films. But this desire is complicated by conceptions of race and gender as expressions of social inequality. In particular, hooks discusses the way in which black liberation has often been described in gendered language. That is, historically, the "freedom from racial domination was expressed in terms of redeeming black masculinity."[48] If racial discrimination is considered tantamount to emasculation and racial freedom is equated with manhood, then the repercussion of a fantasy in which male characters are emasculated bears investigating as a metaphor for racial power relations.

Heart Condition refers directly to the relationship between the ghostly state and racial inequalities. Much is made of the fact that the protagonist, Moon, is a racist, which makes his heart transplant highly ironic in that the heart that saves his life belonged to a black man, Stone. Much to Moon's chagrin, he is unable to ignore the ghost of Stone, who haunts him relentlessly to obtain help in solving his murder. When Moon at first refuses to acknowledge Stone's presence, Stone provides an analysis of the situation: "Personally I think that this racism, this refusal to acknowledge me stems from feelings of inadequacy. I mean you look at me, you see someone college educated, damn good looking, hung like a Shetland pony, and you feel threatened. Am I hitting a nerve? Oh, I see you can talk to the cat but you can't talk to me. . . . Racial prejudice I can understand, but ghost prejudice is an entirely new concept."

Giving Up the Ghost

Stone's comparison of Moon's racial prejudice and his refusal to acknowledge Stone as a ghost provides an explicit reference to the historical place of black men in society, revealing the symbolic importance of his situation. In *Ghost Dad,* however, this comparison is submerged beneath the ghostly alibi. When Bill Cosby's character, Winston, first emerges from the car wreck that "kills" him, he approaches a white (male) state trooper. Despite Winston's gesticulations, the trooper ignores him. Winston does not understand why he is being ignored, not realizing that he is actually a ghost and thus invisible to the other man. And yet, this black male ghost does not articulate an otherwise obvious interpretation. The scene concludes with the policeman urinating on Winston, a harsh insult if read metaphorically, but here treated comically. Whereas *Ghost Dad* places the protagonist in a compromised position in which he must struggle to prove himself in an all-white, good-old-boys office, the relationship between his ghostly status and racial prejudice is never suggested.[49]

Instead of characterizing Winston's ghostly state in racial terms, *Ghost Dad* focuses on jokes about Winston's manhood. When Winston first encounters his children as a ghost, he is unable to speak and uses charades to communicate. When Winston begins the charade, he makes a hand signal which prompts the eldest daughter to guess, "You've got a very small. . . . ?!! Huh? No!" Winston is making the well-known charades gesture for "little word" but it is read by the audience as a joke about penis size. Winston then pantomimes something that prompts the youngest daughter to guess, "You're a big sissy!" On the third try, the children finally guess the truth, creating a series of equivalencies: small penis (emasculation), big sissy (emasculation), ghost (emasculation). Furthermore, when Winston tries to explain to his girlfriend that he will not be able to keep a date with her (due to all the ghostly complications) she misunderstands him. When he says he "can't" she takes this to mean that he cannot perform sexually. (In fact, she later complains that he has fallen right through the bed.) As in other ghost films where the original inability of male communication becomes full blown in the ghostly state, in *Ghost Dad,* the original difficulty might be extended to include an implied, racially inflected emasculation that the ghostly states magnifies or makes obvious.[50]

In *Heart Condition,* Stone's manhood (before death) is equated with his blackness. Upon awaking from his operation Moon is horrified to see a giant black penis stuck between his legs, a joke played on him by his white (male) police buddies. Throughout the film, several other jokes allude to the fact that Moon's new black heart will somehow endow him with unexpected sexual potency, another black stereotype.[51] While black men are often characterized as being sexual (and even rapacious) studs, their social placement undercuts their masculinity, a contradictory position embodied by the ghost.

Stone is deprived of his manhood by being made a ghost, but his masculinity is transferred to Moon, thus capturing both aspects of the black man's dilemma as Stone is both masculinized and then emasculated. If white society has often perceived black male sexuality as a threat, it is here mitigated by making Stone a ghost. The scenario is unusual, however, in that it portrays Stone as the lover of a white woman, the same woman that Moon loves. In fact, it is Stone's baby, not Moon's, that Chris gives birth to at the end of the film. Again, the device of the ghost provides the potential for at least two readings. The first emasculates Stone and undercuts a reading of him as a contender for an interracial romance. The other features a black actor, Denzel Washington, as the romantic partner of a white female and the father of a mixed-race baby, a rare Hollywood representation.[52]

Truly, Madly, Deeply provides a less "black and white" consideration of racial and ethnic otherness, transcendental—in part—by virtue of internationalism. As an interpreter in a translation agency, Nina makes friends with several characters from other countries. While Maura tells Nina that in Chile she made documentary films, in London she has been relegated to housekeeping work. Another acquaintance, Roberto, had been a doctor in his native El Salvador but now works as a waiter. In the middle of the busy restaurant, his boss erupts in a racist diatribe, accusing Roberto of stealing money from the till. Nina is sympathetic to their plight and uses her language skills to help. They are unable to take control of their lives because they have entered a culture that refuses to acknowledge them. Like ghosts, these characters occupy marginal positions and are unable to communicate properly.

It is risky to overstate the analogies drawn from these films, since the similarities between race and gender can break down when pursued further. Nevertheless, the fantasy scenarios portrayed in ghost films mobilize cultural representations on more than one level. Since the categories of active and passive already operate in the culture in terms of both gender and race, and since many audience members may easily identify with "victimized" characters, the commonalities bear further exploration. Furthermore, if it is possible for white male viewers to identify with masochistic (feminized) ghosts, what are the implications of this when racial identifications are mobilized?[53] This discussion is preliminary, but it is intended to show that the masochistic fantasy invoked by ghost films should be further examined for its operation on multiple levels of cultural representation.

Rereading Hollywood

Before concluding, I will briefly consider several other mainstream films for their possible similarities to those in this study. The masochistic aesthetic, so explicitly dramatized in comedy ghost films, may be applicable

to a wider variety of films than first imagined. For example, a more masochistic perspective might be applied to action or horror films that have traditionally been considered sadistic. Even a film such as Hitchcock's *Rear Window* (1954), which is often referred to as an allegory of sadistic film
spectatorship, might be re-examined in light of a masochistic scenario. For
example, we might consider the protagonist of *Rear Window,* Jefferies, to be
"castrated" (his leg is broken) and immobilized at his window, watching his
neighbors as if he were watching a film from a seat in a theater. According
to the sadistic model of spectatorship, his girlfriend, Lisa, is presented as
a spectacle for his (and our) gaze. Only after she is sadistically observed in
a victimized position through the telephoto lens of his camera is Jefferies's
desire awakened for Lisa. Robin Wood sees Jefferies's use of the telephoto
device as a substitution for the phallus: "It is the fear of castration and the
drive to reaffirm 'potency' with which the male spectator is invited to identify. Jefferies attempts to assert his 'possession of the phallus' through the
power of the look."[54] This entire scenario should be more closely examined
in the context of the narrative in which it actually appears. In this light, the
protagonist's ordeal appears to be extremely similar to that found in ghost
fantasies. To begin with, Jefferies is established as having been a photo-
grapher before his accident, and thus wielded "the look" long before his
"castration" at the window. What is significant is not that he looks, but the
way in which he looks and the realm of experience at which he looks. Before
the accident, Jefferies was a roving journalist who took pictures of worldly
("manly") adventures. The broken leg, however, suddenly puts him in a passive position and encourages him to examine a sphere of reality previously
unimportant to him—the domestic. Each of the scenarios Jefferies witnesses
from his window provides alter egos for him and Lisa, providing possible
permutations of domestic relations.[55]

As in *Ghost,* then, we might consider the way in which the murder
mystery becomes the vehicle that forces a solution to the male/female rift established at the beginning of the film. Lisa wants to get married; Jefferies
cannot allow himself to be pinned down. The alter egos across the courtyard
clearly comment on the problem, with the murderer's wife epitomizing the
nagging domesticity Jefferies fears. Thus the murdering husband is a travel-
ing salesman, and the soon-to-be-murdered wife is so mired in her domestic
space that she is literally housebound due to some unarticulated infirmity.
The various domestic scenarios Jefferies views through his telephoto lens
provide him with a realm of experience which—as a man—he fears he cannot control and to which he has not been permitted access in real life. As
noted, the patriarchal system exhorts men to take no interest in, or to denigrate, issues traditionally related to the female. Instead, they must flaunt their
worldliness and independence to appear properly masculine. Jefferies finds

158

himself in a masochistic mode of experiencing the primal fears and identification with the female and her accompanying domestic sphere. Like a ghost, Jefferies watches from a distance and is completely unable to control what he sees. Furthermore, it is not Jefferies but Lisa who is mobile—who takes action, who penetrates space, thus reversing the traditional gender roles. Jefferies's masochistic interlude and the reversal of gender roles permit him to reconcile his commitment to Lisa with his role as an independent traveler. Just as the masochistic fantasies described in this study provide a means by which the protagonists can switch gendered positions, so does this film (the so-called quintessentially sadistic film) permit the same type of masochistic interlude in which active and passive gender roles are in flux. Just as male ghosts must access the feminine, in this film Jefferies experiences a masochistic interlude that acts as an antidote to his inability to interact successfully with Lisa, thus re-solving (if not solving) the inherent contradictions instituted by a culture of mutually exclusive, binary gender roles.

This is not to suggest that all mainstream films should be reread as masochistic. However, although most films may not be monolithically masochistic or sadistic, they can potentially provide multiple types of pleasures. Carol Clover discusses this phenomenon with regard to recent slasher films. Even though the "final girl" of such films is masculinized at the end, she must suffer during the course of the film before she can emerge victorious. Her role in the feminized/victim function takes up the greater part of the film viewer's experience, and it is she who suffers the longest (unlike the other characters who are more quickly dispatched). Indeed, Clover seems to suggest that this "suffering" is necessary if (at least) the male audience is to accept her victory at the end.

Although I would not venture to argue that a violent, action-adventure film such as *Total Recall* (1990) is a masochistic fantasy in the same manner as comedy ghost films, the protagonist of this film nevertheless experiences an extended interlude in which he loses narrative control and even loses his identity. At the beginning of the movie he expresses an ambition to go to Mars. He tells his wife: "I want to be someone!" In a reversal of classic gender roles, she responds: "You *are* someone. You're the man I love!" He is soon rebuffed by her (she is not his real wife) and is rebuffed again by his real wife during the early part of the film. In fact, he is chastised for not having "come home" and for not having gotten word to Melina ("not calling"). But these insensitive traits are not characteristics of the new Quaid, a softhearted hero who chucks child mutants under the chin and fights for their liberty. Like Clover, Yvonne Tasker has provided a compelling argument concerning the masochistic elements common to male-oriented action films. Both arguments concern a different type of film in which the body is the site of masochistic suffering, and both temper their reference to masochism through the identification of the sadistic, heroic component on which the movies depend. Yet these studies suggest that the landscape of Hollywood cinema is layered with moments of masochistic "pleasure" tied to gender anxiety.

In *Die Hard* (1988), the hero, McClain, spends most of the movie undergoing the most grueling punishment, unable to reveal himself to his punishers (and hence fight them "man-to-man"). He is not only at their mercy, but he relies on the mediating tactics of a (notably) black policeman to save himself. A conflict between McClain and his wife, Holly, is expressed in terms of his inability to cope with her career success. Her accomplishments at the office (complete with the presentation of a gold watch) bring him to the scene of the crime in the first place. McClain is particularly dismayed to find that Holly has been using her maiden name, Gennaro, a discovery that leads to a spat at the film's beginning. Their marital difficulties constitute a subplot that is only provisionally solved at the end of film, overshadowed by McClain's heroic efforts. But a compromise of sorts is tendered: he refers to her as Holly Gennaro, she counters with Holly McClain. Clearly, the masochistic moments of this movie take part in a macho male fantasy quite different from those of ghost films. But as Tasker notes, the "tension between power and powerlessness" undergirds this and other action pictures, subjecting the hero to a punishing narrative trajectory before the final triumph.[56]

Regarding Henry (1991) is a different kind of film, but it is interesting for casting an "action star" in a non-action role. While Harrison Ford may be best known for his swashbuckling characters, here he plays Henry, a ruthless prosecutor who suffers a critical injury in a random robbery. Before the injury, Henry is portrayed as a workaholic with no time for his wife and daughter. When he scolds his young daughter for spilling juice, he begins by trying to apologize (at the wife's behest) but ends up giving her a stern lecture. As the daughter watches in silence he concludes by offering a Latin phrase, which he translates as "He who is silent is understood to consent."[57] The words are ironic, of course, as Henry becomes the silent one after suffering brain damage from the shooting. Though he initially loses his memory and the ability to speak and move, he gradually regains some memory and relearns these skills. But his memory is so damaged that he no longer recognizes his family or his former life. In his disoriented state he wanders around the house, finally pleading with the maid to tell him what he actually "did" before the accident. She replies that all he did was work. In a different scene, his daughter explains to him that before the accident he used to lecture her about the work ethic instilled in him by his father. Upon considering the ideas, Henry concludes that they make no sense. Henry's masochistic interlude causes him to reject his father's advice and instead focus on his domestic life. He rekindles his romance with his wife and creates a new rapport with his daughter, who teaches him how to tie his shoelaces and make cookies. When he reveals that he cannot remember how to read, his daughter teaches him this as well. (Notably, the first line he reads aloud is, "Are you my mother?") At the end of the film, both parents rescue the daughter from a snobby boarding school, and the three are reunited thanks to Henry's hard-won conversion. As with Patrick Swayze in *Ghost,* the casting of an actor usually associated with more macho roles may help to intensify the masochistic interlude, rather than detract from it.

Finally, the problem of gender undertaken by this study might also be investigated in with relation to business practices in the film industry. The large number of male ghosts is not only indicative of a masochistic fantasy but is implicated in a long-term trend that has tended to exclude women from leading roles. Contemporary actresses often bemoan the dearth of leading roles for women, a situation apparently based on the industry's opinion that women are not capable of drawing as much money at the box office. The opinion becomes a circular argument and a self-fulfilling prophesy, since fewer women are given a chance to prove it wrong, and fewer dollars are provided to finance "women's films" adequately.[58] This returns us to the earlier observation that Hollywood protagonists are not just coded as male, but usually are male. Perhaps this is the same problem dramatized in the ghost films themselves, namely that the (male-dominated) industry has difficulty dealing with so-called feminine topics: "The problem is less the number of roles available to women than the film industry's discomfort with projects involving relationships, *feelings* and *communication*—the kind of things women are more likely to go into than men" (emphasis mine).[59] However, the success of such films as *Ghost* may indicate that the industry has underestimated the way in which both male and female viewers find pleasure in fantasies that specifically invite fluid identifications across gender stereotypes—the same stereotypes that permeate the film industry and perhaps contribute to the cultural need for masochistic ghost fantasies in the first place.

With further inspection, we might find that most Hollywood films provide and facilitate complicated narrative pleasure and that film theory has not always accounted for such complexity. The fantasy scenario suggested by the films in this study should be understood, not as aberrations, but as one type of common fantasy scenario provided by mainstream films.

Conclusion

In the preceding pages I have attempted to reveal the striking similarities among a variety of current films, all of which feature ghosts and/or angels. Although ghost films are nostalgic fantasies, the type of nostalgia revealed in current films is a very specific one. The nostalgic fantasy hinges not only on magically resuscitating a dead character, as has been widely suggested, but also on dramatizing a masochistic dilemma surrounding gender reversal and the origin of the subject.

The similarity between ghosts and film viewers in the engagement of the masochistic scenario is an important one. Both ghosts and film viewers submit to images that cannot be controlled and may take pleasure in the distance and delays inherent to narrative. While all narratives contain both delays and conclusions and may provide multiple sites of masochistic and sadistic pleasure, the specific scenarios played out in these films provide a masochistic mise-en-scène for the articulation of a fantasy in which a change of positions is ultimately played out for the viewer's enjoyment. While characters enact various gendered and narrative roles, taking part in the literal realization of the masochistic fantasy, the viewer is invited to identify not just with the actual characters, but with the shifts that occur across gender roles.

Aspects of the masochistic process can occur even in films that do not contain angels or ghosts. Although ghosts have proven to be explicit devices of narrative delay, they fulfill an existing narrative function, albeit in a fairly novel manner. Too much attention has been given to artificial "happy endings" and not enough to the experience at the centers of narrative. The end and the delay depend on each other to make narrative work. This is precisely the tension at issue in movies such as *Ghost* and *It's a Wonderful Life,* where the feminine and the masculine conflict, and where the protagonist's identity depends on his repressed feminine half, although he cannot "recognize" it (à la George Bailey) until after his ghostly interlude.

Although the masochistic aesthetic described in this study is made quite explicit by the fantasy scenarios attendant to ghosts, the implications of this study go beyond the interpretation of this handful of ghost films. Given the fact that the films in this study are not experimental (to the contrary, they are usually criticized for being conservative and formulaic), this analysis is further proof of recent claims that mainstream films may facilitate a variety of pleasurable fantasies and cross-gender identifications heretofore overlooked. Furthermore, this analysis suggests that theories of both classical Hollywood film and of cinematic pleasure have tended to overlook the way in which all protagonists have the potential to engage in masochistic interludes within the body of a given narrative. This is seen most clearly by comparing the role of the masochistic ghost to the comically inept protagonists in popular comedy genres. In the preceding chapters I drew connections between the masochistic ghost and the origin of the subject, noting that the formation of masculine identity under patriarchal law is by nature impossible to achieve. There is clearly a connection between comic male protagonists as "perpetual bumblers" and the difficulties of gendered identity. If narratives are designed to address some type of lack (from whence the goal originates), then the male protagonist is necessarily put in positions that compromise his narrative agency and hence his masculinity. Although some might deem this process sadistic in its drive toward mastery, the effect of mastery would be to extinguish narrative whereas, in fact, narratives are repeatedly regenerated. Narratives are clearly not generated from the mastery associated with the sadistic impulse. On the contrary, it is precisely because mastery is impossible that narratives regenerate themselves, dramatizing a repetition of an inherently masochistic process. Furthermore, the process of being made ineffectual is extremely important for the male protagonist and the male viewer because this process facilitates a suspension of passive and active categories and an engagement of varied identificatory positions. In a culture that endlessly exhorts the attainment of an unattainable identity based on mutually exclusive binary ideals, mainstream narratives may provide cathartic venues for dramatizing and working through this difficult process. Thus, it may be the culture's constant exhortation to an impossible mastery, rather than the sadistic impulse itself, which makes the masochistic interlude necessary.

NOTES

Chapter 1

1. See for example Dan Fainaru, "Lifeless *Ghost,*" *Jerusalem Post,* Oct 16, 1990; Desson Howe, "Death Takes a Holiday: Why Are We Just Dying to See Movies about the Afterlife?" *Washington Post,* August 26, 1990, sec. C, 3; Jack Mathews, "Hollywood's Feel-Good Fantasies," *Los Angeles Times,* August 5, 1990, 4; Janet Maslin, "It's Tough for Movies to Get Real," *New York Times,* August 5, 1990, 9; Dana Parsons, "Ghost Film Taps into Some Spooky Regions of Us All," *Los Angeles Times,* October 21, 1990, sec. B, 1; James Ryan, "Hollywood Hunts for What's Hot," *BPI Entertainment News Wire,* October 2, 1990.
2. "Ghost," *Wall Street Journal,* December 12, 1990, 84; Larry Rohter, "Top Movie of the Year a Sleeper: It's 'Ghost,'" *New York Times,* November 3, 1990, 13. David Ellis, "A Ghost With Legs," *Time Magazine,* November 5, 1990, 25.
3. Ellis, "A Ghost With Legs," 25.
4. Herman Feifel, quoted by Howe, "Death Takes a Holiday," sec. C, 3.
5. Peter L. Valenti, "The 'Film Blanc': Suggestions for a Variety of Fantasy, 1940–45," *Journal of Popular Film* 6, no. 4 (winter 1978): 295. A similar analysis is made by John Lyttle in a more recent article on ghost films, "Raising the Spirits of the Age: Films about Ghosts Are Suddenly in Fashion," *The Independent,* October 4, 1990, 17.
6. With the exception of Rosemary Jackson (who deals mostly with horror and who tends to conflate the terms "fantastic" and "fantasy"—see below), most popular and scholarly literature is in agreement on this point. See, for example, Richard Corliss, "Giving Up the Ghost: Two Movies Trivialize Matters of Life and Death," *Time,* July 16, 1990, 86; Tom Genelli and Lyn Davis Genelli, "Between Two Worlds: Some Thoughts Beyond the 'Film Blanc,'" *Journal of Popular Film and Television* 12, no. 3 (fall 1984): 100–111; W. R. Irwin, *The Game of the Impossible: A Rhetoric of Fantasy* (Urbana: University of Illinois Press, 1976); Leonard Klady, "The Hopeful Dead," *American Film,* March 1990, 16–18; Clayton Koelb, *The Incredulous Reader: Literature and the Function of Disbelief* (Ithaca: Cornell University Press, 1984); Andrew Sarris, "The Afterlife, Hollywood-Style," *American Film* 4, no. 6 (April 1979): 25; Valenti, "The 'Film

Blanc,'" 295–303; Diana Waggoner, *The Hills of Faraway: A Guide to Fantasy* (New York: Atheneum, 1978).

7. See Michael Ryan and Douglas Kellner, *Camera Politica: The Politics and Ideology of Contemporary Hollywood Film* (Bloomington: Indiana University Press, 1988).

8. Genelli and Genelli, "Between Two Worlds," 105.

9. Klady, "The Hopeful Dead," 18.

10. Rosemary Jackson, *Fantasy: The Literature of Subversion* (New York: Methuen, 1981), 6.

11. Laplanche and Pontalis, quoted in Peter Brooks, *Reading for the Plot: Design and Intention in Narrative* (New York: Vintage Books, 1984), 55. For Freud's account of desire and the death drive refer to his discussion in *Beyond the Pleasure Principle,* trans. and ed. James Strachey (New York: W. W. Norton, 1961).

12. Brooks, *Reading for the Plot,* 98.

13. Ibid., 104.

14. Laura Mulvey, "Visual Pleasure and Narrative Cinema," in *Narrative, Apparatus, Ideology: A Film Theory Reader,* ed. Philip Rosen (New York: Columbia University Press, 1986), 205. See also Teresa de Lauretis, *Alice Doesn't: Feminism, Semiotics, Cinema* (Bloomington: Indiana University Press, 1984), 103.

15. De Lauretis, *Alice Doesn't,* chap. 5. Also refer to Vladimir Propp, *Morphology of the Folktale* (Austin: University of Texas Press, 1968); Jurij M. Lotman, "The Origin of Plot in the Light of Typology," trans. Julian Graffy, *Poetics Today* 1, nos. 1, 2 (autumn 1979): 161–84; Annette Kuhn, *Women's Pictures: Feminism and Cinema* (New York: Routledge and Kegan Paul, 1986). See Carol Clover's *Men, Women, and Chain Saws: Gender in the Modern Horror Film* (Princeton: Princeton University Press, 1992) for a more complicated account of this process.

16. De Lauretis, *Alice Doesn't,* 120. Also see Roland Barthes, *The Pleasure of the Text,* trans. Richard Miller (New York: Farrar, Strauss and Giroux, 1973) in which narrative pleasure is described as Oedipal in nature.

17. I am not using the terms male and female to designate any innate biological qualities, but merely as a way of describing culturally coded narrative positions.

18. Mulvey, "Visual Pleasure and Narrative Cinema," 198–209. Also see, in particular, Christian Metz, "The Imaginary Signifier" (excerpts), in *Narrative, Apparatus, Ideology: A Film Theory Reader,* ed. Philip Rosen (New York: Columbia University Press, 1986), 260–69.

19. De Lauretis, *Alice Doesn't,* 119.

20. See in particular, Mary Ann Doane, *The Desire to Desire: The Woman's Film of the 1940s* (Bloomington: Indiana University Press, 1987).

21. For an insightful analysis of occult horror films see Clover, *Men, Women, and Chain Saws.*

22. Peter Wollen refers to film spectators as "invisible guests." "Discussion," in *The Cinematic Apparatus,* ed. Teresa de Lauretis and Stephen Heath (London: Macmillan, 1985), 59.

23. See chapter 7 for a further discussion. The subversive potential goes largely unfulfilled, but the female ghost remains a fascinating character.

24. Maxie is the name of the title character, a female ghost who returns to revive her career as a film actress. *Beetlejuice* features a man and wife couple. An even later film, *Hearts and Souls* (1992) features four ghosts: two white men, one black woman and one white woman. *Maxie* remains the only film, however, featuring a single female protagonist.

25. Kristine Brunovska Karnick and Henry Jenkins, "Acting Funny," in *Classical Hollywood Comedy*, ed. Kristine Brunovska Karnick and Henry Jenkins (New York: Routledge, 1995), 161. They describe this as a post-1960s phenomenon, part of a larger trend. Interestingly, the examples provided include *Switch* and *Memoirs of an Invisible Man,* which they describe as "odd wish fulfilling fantas[ies]" in which the characters desire a change in race, gender, or age in order to restabilize their identity and "resolve personality defects" (161). Also see Steve Neale and Frank Krutnik, *Popular Film and Television Comedy* (New York: Routledge, 1990), 17–18, in which the authors note that comedy seems especially suited to hybridization.

26. Karnick and Jenkins follow this model in their consideration of comedy. See also Alistair Fowler, *Kinds of Literature: An Introduction to the Theories of Genres and Modes,* whose work they draw on. Fowler draws on Wittgenstein's notion of family resemblance.

27. Karnick and Jenkins, "Acting Funny." See also Vivian Sobchack's use of genre in *Screening Space: The American Science Fiction Film* (New York: Ungar Publishing Co., 1987). Here she compares the science fiction to the horror genre, placing films on a kind of continuum. Also see Robin Wood's essay, "Ideology, Genre, Auteur," in *Film Genre Reader,* ed. Barry Keith Grant (reprint; Austin: University of Texas Press, 1977), which calls for a comparison of thematic and ideological patterns *across* generic boundaries as a way of showing the overlapping connections between seemingly different types of films.

28. Peter G. Beidler, *Ghosts, Demons, and Henry James* (Columbia. University of Missouri Press, 1989); Margaret L. Carter, *Specter or Delusion? The Supernatural in Gothic Fiction* (Ann Arbor: UMI Research Press, 1987).

29. See Peter Penzoldt, *The Supernatural in Fiction* (London: Peter Nevill, 1952), 4–8, 53, 57; John R. Reed, "The Occult in Victorian Literature," in *Literature of the Occult: A Collection of Critical Essays,* ed. Peter B. Messent (Englewood Cliffs, N.J.: Prentice-Hall, 1981) 100, 103; S. L. Varnado, *Haunted Presence: The Numinous in Gothic Fiction* (Tuscaloosa: University of Alabama Press, 1987), 83; Diana Waggoner, *The Hills of Faraway: A Guide to Fantasy* (New York: Atheneum, 1978), 9; Dorothy Scarborough, "Modern Ghosts," in *Literature of the Occult: A Collection of Critical Essays,* ed. Peter B. Messent (Englewood Cliffs, N.J.: Prentice-Hall, 1981), 105–16.

30. For a discussion of traditional ghost literature, see Penzoldt, *The Supernatural in Fiction;* Scarborough, "Modern Ghosts"; Beidler, *Ghosts, Demons, and Henry James;* Carter, *Specter or Delusion;* Howard Kerr, John W. Crowley, and Charles L. Crow, eds., *The Haunted Dusk: American Supernatural Fiction* (Athens: University of Georgia Press, 1983).

31. Penzoldt, *The Supernatural in Fiction,* 11, 16, 34; Waggoner, *The Hills of Faraway,* 11.

32. Tzvetan Todorov, *The Fantastic: A Structural Approach to a Literary Genre,* trans. Richard Howard (Cleveland: The Press of Case Western Reserve University, 1973), 46.

33. Ibid., 25.

34. Ibid., 47.

35. Irwin, *Game of the Impossible,* 55.

36. Waggoner, *The Hills of Faraway,* 101.

37. Waggoner defines nostalgic fantasy as being "the other face of comic fantasy, expressing the fulfillment of the heart's desire through tenderness and melancholy rather than through humor. . . . Events are not important in nostalgic fantasy; character and emotion are" (*The Hills of Faraway,* 56).

38. As Northrop Frye notes, "Comedy usually moves toward a happy ending." *Anatomy of Criticism: Four Essays* (Princeton: Princeton University Press, 1957), 167. For general theories of comedy see Robert W. Corrigan, *Comedy: Meaning and Form* (San Francisco: Chandler Publishing, 1965). For more specific applications of comedy to film see Andrew S. Horton, ed., *Comedy/Cinema/Theory* (Berkeley: University of California Press, 1991) and Neale and Krutnik, *Popular Film and Television Comedy.*

39. In *Made in Heaven* the lead character dies and goes to heaven but the cutting short of romance is inverted by having the participants fall in love in heaven. The romance is cut short not by the death of one of the characters, but by the birth of one who must leave heaven and be born on earth. This will tie in later as I explain how this scenario has less to do with death than with the origins of the subject.

40. Doane, *The Desire to Desire,* 91. Doane draws on the work of Franco Moretti, *Signs Taken for Wonders: Essays in the Sociology of Literary Forms,* trans. Susan Fischer, David Forgacs, and David Miller (London: New Left Books, 1983); Jean Laplanche and J. B. Pontalis, *The Language of Psychoanalysis,* trans. Donald Nicholson-Smith (New York: W. W. Norton, 1973); Jean Laplanche, *Life and Death in Psycho-analysis,* trans. Jeffrey Mehlman (Baltimore: Johns Hopkins University Press, 1976).

41. Ibid.

Chapter 2

1. Studlar bases much of her theory on Gilles Deleuze's *Masochism: An Interpretation of Coldness and Cruelty* (New York: Zone Books, 1989). While Studlar's account of masochism has been the most influential to my thinking, see also Kaja Silverman's work, *Male Subjectivity at the Margins* (New York: Routledge, 1992) and works by Carol Clover, *Men, Women, and Chain Saws;* D. N. Rodowick, *The Difficulty of Difference* (New York: Routledge, 1991); Yvonne Tasker, *Spectacular Bodies: Gender, Genre and the Action Cinema* (New York: Routledge, 1993); Linda Williams, "Film Bodies: Gender, Genre, and Excess," *Film Quarterly* 44, no. 4 (summer 1991): 2. Freud's account of masochism can be found in the following selections: "Three Essays on the Theory of Sexuality," 239; "Instincts and Their Vicissitudes," in *The Freud Reader,* ed. Peter Gay (New York: W. W. Norton, 1989), 562; "A Child Is Being Beaten," 107; "The Economic Problem in

Masochism," in *Sexuality and the Psychology of Love,* ed. Philip Rieff (New York: Macmillan/Collier Books, 1963), 190.

2. Gaylyn Studlar, "Masochism and the Perverse Pleasures of the Cinema," in *Movies and Methods: Volume II,* ed. Bill Nichols (Berkeley: University of California Press, 1985), 612. Freud discusses the fort/da concept in *Beyond the Pleasure Principle.*

3. Brooks, *Reading for the Plot,* 108.

4. Ibid., 97 (my emphasis).

5. Studlar, "Masochism and the Perverse Pleasures of the Cinema," 605.

6. Tania Modleski, "The Search for Tomorrow in Today's Soap Operas," *Film Quarterly* 33, no. 1 (fall 1979): 12.

7. Ibid.

8. Jean Laplanche and J.-B. Pontalis, *The Language of Psycho-Analysis,* trans. Donald Nicholson-Smith (New York: Norton, 1973), 244. Because Freud believed that such a perversion was similar to that of the female in the Oedipal structure, masochism is often referred to as feminine masochism, and for these same reasons it supposedly cannot be applied to females but only to males. Therefore, what is seen as a perversion in males is seen as "normal" in females.

9. Gaylyn Studlar, *In the Realm of Pleasure: Von Sternberg, Dietrich, and the Masochistic Aesthetic* (Urbana: University of Illinois Press), 1988, 23.

10. Deleuze, *Masochism,* 20.

11. The character's name is Moony, but he is repeatedly referred to as "Moon," an apt reference to a femininely charged symbol.

12. The little girl, Lydia, is the only one to see and hear the ghosts at the beginning of the film. This exception will be discussed in the next chapter where I discuss the maternal and the domestic.

13. Maslin, "It's Tough for Movies to Get Real," 9.

14. Caryn James, "Ghosts Must Catch the Spirit of the Time," *New York Times,* July 29, 1990, 17.

15. I will address the viewer's stake in the reality of the ghosts in my discussion of the fantastic and paranoiac in chapter 4.

16. Clover, *Men, Women, and Chain Saws,* 70. Also see Laura Mulvey, "After thoughts on 'Visual Pleasure and Narrative Cinema' inspired by *Duel in the Sun,*" in *Psychoanalysis and Cinema,* ed. E. Anne Kaplan (New York: Routledge, 1990), 24–35.

17. Janet Maslin, "Looking to the Dead for Mirth and Inspiration," *New York Times,* July 13, 1990, 8 (emphasis mine).

18. Deleuze, *Masochism,* 68, 76.

19. Thus in many films, we see a conflation between the maternal and the feminine, the one being associated with the other.

20. Deleuze, *Masochism,* 18.

21. Ibid., 75.

22. Ibid., 16, emphasis mine.

23. I will elaborate on this notion later. The male's inability to express his emotions and to commit to a relationship are stereotypes that are well represented in Hollywood films. The difficulties of communication between men and women has been

addressed in such best-sellers as Deborah Tannen's *You Just Don't Understand: Women and Men in Conversation* (New York: Ballantine, 1990) and John Gray's *Men Are from Mars, Women Are from Venus* (New York: Harper Collins, 1992).

24. Deleuze, *Masochism*, 18.

25. Ibid., 34.

26. Ibid., 71.

27. Studlar, *In the Realm of Pleasure*, 181.

28. Pat H. Broeske, "Outtakes: 'Ghost': Why It's Still Scaring Up Repeat Business," *Los Angeles Times*, November 18, 1990, 32; John Hartl, "Summer's Golden 'Ghost'—Fantasy Romance Makes Hearts Beat, Cash Registers Ring," *Seattle Times*, August 30, 1990, sec. F, 5; Dave Kehr, "Three Balanced Performances Spark 'Ghost,'" *Chicago Tribune*, July 13, 1990, sec. D.

29. Maslin, "Looking to the Dead for Mirth and Inspiration," sec. C, 8. Similar views are expressed by James, "Ghosts Must Catch the Spirit of the Time," 17; Corliss, "Giving Up the Ghost," 86; Terry Kelleher, "'Ghost': Patrick Swayze as a Dead Hero," *Newsday*, July 13, 1990, 15.

30. Kehr, "Three Balanced Performances Spark 'Ghost,'" sec. D.

31. Parsons, "Ghost Film Taps into Some Spooky Regions of Us All," sec. B, 1.

32. This trend gained popularity in the field of literary studies with "reader-response" types of theories but has seen many variations, particularly as applied to cinema studies. David Bordwell provides one of the most accessible ways of thinking about this by suggesting that film narratives "cue" the viewer in the construction of meaning. This process includes an activation of generic expectations as noted above. See in particular *Narration in the Fiction Film* (Madison: University of Wisconsin Press, 1985); David Bordwell and Kristin Thompson, *Film Art* (Madison: University of Wisconsin Press, 1993).

33. Metz, "The Imaginary Signifier," 244–78.

34. Nick's character is, of course, different from many of the ghosts discussed in that he is neither dead, nor incorporeal. Furthermore, he is he able to manipulate the physical world.

35. Note also that as with Jamie's constant sneezing and coldness, handkerchiefs and tears are common motifs in the masochistic fantasy as defined by Deleuze. In the stories of Masoch, the characters frequently wear fur for the purpose of avoiding colds: "it is worn less for the sake of modesty than from fear of catching cold . . . Masoch's heroine's frequently sneeze. Everything is suggestive of coldness" (*Masochism*, 53). Jamie's physical coldness becomes a running gag as Nina turns up the heat to ninety degrees and buys him hot water bottles. Jamie sneezes constantly and tells Nina: "I've gotta be careful. Because you know I'm prone to colds, and you imagine, I get a cold now it could last forever." Nina laughs. Jamie: "I'm not joking. I'm serious." The cause of Jamie's death turns out to have been none other than a sore throat. Although in Masoch's works it is the woman who is cold, in these films the ghost character often embodies the masochistic qualities itself and, just as the ghost can be seen as the embodiment of the masochistic contract in and of itself, here the ghost similarly takes on the characteristics which are integral to the masochistic scenario. (Coincidentally, in *Heart Condition*, the ghost also has a sneezing problem. He attributes it to a cat allergy.)

36. Studlar, "Masochism and the Perverse Pleasures of the Cinema," 613.
37. Also see the discussion of *Dead Again* in chapter 5 and *Scrooged* in chapter 6.
38. In this case the dual narrative is complicated by the multiple ghosts. As explained in the next chapter, however, the emphasis on the male is balanced by a fantasy that attempts to correct a male/female imbalance.

Chapter 3

1. Jean Laplanche and J.-B. Pontalis, "Fantasy and the Origins of Sexuality," in *Formations of Fantasy,* ed. Victor Burgin, James Donald, and Cora Kaplan (London: Routledge, 1986), 24.
2. Ibid., 43.
3. Quoted in Studlar, *In the Realm of Pleasure,* 26.
4. Rodowick, *The Difficulty of Difference,* 84.
5. The most common example of the fetish is described by Freud when the child understands the mother's lack and then, by way of denial, transfers the missing power onto an object last associated with the mother (the breast, a piece of clothing, etc.). As I have noted, however, fetishism is usually associated with a scenario in which the woman's inherent lack is disavowed. My use of the term disavowal hinges on the fact that a lack is covered over, but not that the lack resides in the female. In the masochistic scenario what is disavowed is the mother's separateness. In the next chapter, I will complicate this explanation somewhat, but the process of disavowal remains the same in any case.
6. Deleuze, *Masochism,* 32–33.
7. Howe, "Death Takes a Holiday," sec. C., 3.
8. Doane, *The Desire to Desire,* esp. chapter 3; Williams, "Film Bodies," 2.
9. Also see *Ghost* and *Always* for notable scenes of so-called excessive tears. Reviewers typically treated such scenes with obvious disdain. See, for example Ralph Novak, "Picks and Pans," *People,* July 23, 1990, 8, and Sheila Benson, "An Afterlife Love Story," *Los Angeles Times,* July 13, 1990, sec. F, 1.
10. Both Doane and Williams draw on the work of Moretti here. See Moretti, *Signs Taken for Wonders.*
11. See Julia Kristeva as well as Barbara Creed who employs Kristeva's conception of the abject. Kristeva, *The Kristeva Reader,* ed. Toril Moi (New York: Columbia University Press, 1986), and Creed, "Horror and the Monstrous Feminine: An Imaginary Abjection," *Screen* 27 (1986): 44–70.
12. The "a" refers to "autre" meaning "other." The "petit" is meant to distinguish this use of "other" from the "Other" of the Symbolic, while nevertheless pointing out the connection between the two. See Jacques Lacan, "Translator's note," in *Ecrits: A Selection,* trans. Alan Sheridan (New York: W. W. Norton, 1977), xi.
13. Psychoanalytic theory uses the male child as its model of the subject, which reveals the bias in Freud's thinking but also reveals a common bias in traditional conceptions of gender and human agency. I will continue to discuss psychoanalytic theory from the male child's perspective in part because it has great significance for male ghosts. In chapter 5 I will discuss the female's perspective.
14. Creed, "Horror and the Monstrous Feminine," 47.

15. Ibid.
16. In this film the ghost, Jamie, is not incorporeal or immaterial. He remains solid and touchable for Nina, even though he can show up behind locked doors as can most other ghosts. His body remains cold, however, as a mark of its difference from living bodies.
17. Creed, "Horror and the Monstrous Feminine," 48.
18. Kristeva, quoted in ibid.
19. See chapter 5.
20. Jonathan Rutherford, *Men's Silences: Predicaments in Masculinity* (London: Routledge, 1992), 6. Barbara Ehrenreich's book *The Hearts of Men: American Dreams and the Flight from Commitment* (New York: Anchor Books, 1983) traces the male "flight from commitment" over the last forty years or so. She asserts that "the male (breadwinner) role was 'instrumental'—rational and task-oriented—and the female role was 'expressive'—emotional, attuned to the feelings of others" (34), employing Talcott Parson's use of the words "instrumental" and "expressive."
21. Nancy J. Chodorow, *Feminism and Psychoanalytic Theory* (New Haven: Yale University Press, 1989), 109.
22. Jessica Benjamin, *The Bonds of Love: Psychoanalysis, Feminism, and the Problem of Domination* (New York: Pantheon Books, 1988), 170. This inability to "assume the other's position" is the very problem the ghost fantasy seeks to redress.
23. Roger Horrocks echoes this with anecdotes from his clinical practice: "This is the constant threnody I hear from those men who come to see me in therapy: to become the man I was supposed to be, I had to destroy my most valuable side, my sensitivity, my femininity." Horrocks, *Masculinity in Crisis* (New York: St. Martin's Press, 1994), 25.
24. Rutherford, *Men's Silences,* 7. An article in *Time* questions the changing conception of manhood. In a sleight of hand, the author turns Freud's question on femininity into a problem of male mystique, concluding that the strong silent type is a result of male "marginalization": "Freud, like everyone else, forgot to ask the second question: What do men really want? His omission may reflect the male fascination with the enigma of woman over the mystery of man. She owns the center of his imagination, while the fate of man works the margins. Perhaps this is why so many men have taken the Mafia oath of silence about their hopes and fears. Strong and silent remain de rigueur." Sam Allis, "What Do Men Really Want?" *Time,* October 1, 1990, Special Issue, 80.
25. Clover, *Men, Women, and Chain Saws,* 82. Benjamin notes how the male has come to be associated with rational science and the female with nature. "Beginning with Bacon, modern science adopted the metaphor of subduing nature and wresting her secrets from her" (*The Bonds of Love,* 189). Thus while occult horror films seem to desire access to the ineffable feminine, it is only to re-appropriate it to the rational, visual (male) world.
26. Clover, *Men, Women, and Chain Saws,* 112.
27. Mary Ann Doane, "Ideology and the Practice of Sound Editing and Mixing," in *The Cinematic Apparatus,* ed. Teresa de Lauretis and Stephen Heath (London:

Macmillan, 1985), 50. Benjamin also explores these cultural oppositions in depth. See especially "Gender and Domination," in *The Bonds of Love.*

28. I have resisted the temptation of calling attention to the way in which the English language insistently resorts to visual metaphors to express cognition, perception, and understanding. Particularly when speaking of film ghosts, phrases such as "speculation," "it appears," etc., can take on multiple and sometimes ironic meanings. I have purposely employed this awkward mixed metaphor to call attention to the visual, which is privileged as the bearer of truth in the Oedipal scenario. In ghost films, however, the voice and language are equally important and become the proof of presence for the invisible ghost. Furthermore, by equating the visible with the rational, Oedipal and patriarchal epistemologies do create a kind of blind spot with regard to the expression of the non-visible, hence emotion, spirituality, etc.

29. Chodorow, *Feminism and Psychoanalytic Theory,* 69.

30. Ibid. Horrocks notes: "Working as a psychotherapist I hear this complaint so often: my father was so remote, I never knew him" (*Masculinity in Crisis,* 27).

31. Rutherford describes men's ambivalence for the father and the implicit reliance on the mother. "Men needed women to speak that part of themselves that was excluded from representations of masculinity: love, fear, need and intimacy. . . . Mothers had provided a mediating role within the family, their conflict management often protecting the son from his father (*Men's Silences,* 16, 20). Horrocks concurs, quoting Mary Ingham: "If financially my mother had always depended on my father, emotionally my father had always existed through her" (*Masculinity in Crisis,* 27).

32. Doane, *The Desire to Desire,* 179.

33. In *The Bonds of Love,* Benjamin discusses the "public rationality" that promotes the divisions of public and private spheres along sexual lines. In particular, she notes that "this public rationality necessitates that woman's different voice be split off and institutionalized in the private sphere" (197).

34. Moon asks her why she has to keep snapping pictures constantly. Chris tells him it is for self-defense and asks him why he carries a gun. Moon replies, "I'm a cop." Chris nods, "Yeah, well I'm not."

35. As the daughter, Diane, prompts him to remember her name, she seems to be expressing her subconscious desire for revenge: "Di(e), Di(e). . ."

36. There is an alternate ending to some versions of *Ghost Dad,* in which this last speech is deleted and the closing credits roll.

37. Chodorow remarks: "The father, because his work takes him outside of the home most of the time, and because his active presence in the family has progressively decreased, has become an 'invisible father'" (*Feminism and Psychoanalytic Theory,* 51). Here and above, Chodorow draws on the work of the psychoanalyst and social theorist Alexander Mitscherlich. The ineffectuality suffered by the ghost's invisibility dramatizes this difficulty as integral to male subjecthood, which will be addressed in the following chapter.

38. Doane (*The Desire to Desire,* 134) notes how gothic horror films often feature a secret room from which the woman is barred access. In *Beetlejuice* this is reversed since the female child is the only one to gain access. Also note that in

Hearts and Souls, Thomas gives Anne the keys to his house at the end of the film, a symbol of their romantic union.

39. In *Ghost Dad, Beetlejuice, Made in Heaven,* and *Switch* the characters all meet death in the water, a decidedly feminine resting place. Of these, all but *Switch* also involve automobiles, traditionally phallic objects which are then exchanged for a plunge into maternal waters. See note 40 below.

40. As will become apparent, the mouths here can be associated with the pre-Oedipal, oral phase of the child. See in particular page 86 of this book.

41. The association of water to the maternal as a powerful engulfing force has been frequently noted by psychoanalytic theorists including Freud, who made pejorative analogies between the two: "Merging was a dangerous form of undifferentiation, a sinking back into a sea of oneness—the 'oceanic feeling' that Freud told Romain Rolland he frankly couldn't relate to." Benjamin, *The Bonds of Love,* 47. Chodorow speaks of common folk tales in which the dread of the mother's power is translated into "poems and ballads [which] talk about fears of engulfment by whirlpools and allurement by sirens" (*Feminism and Psychoanalytic Theory,* 35). Many have also noted the obvious similarity between the French word for mother and sea—"mère" and "mer."

42. Recounted in Doane, *The Desire to Desire,* 139.

43. Ibid.

44. Rutherford, *Men's Silences,* 8–9.

45. One reviewer noted that many of the spirits in *Ghost* seemed to be wandering the streets of New York with no place to go. He referred to them aptly as a "population of discontented ghosts—the ectoplasmic homeless." Jay Carr, "A Romantic 'Ghost' to Believe In," *Boston Globe,* July 13, 1990, 29. An interesting aside concerns the use of "home" in another film by the screenwriter of *Ghost,* Joel Rubin. He also wrote *Jacob's Ladder,* supernatural/horror film released in 1990. Maslin notes that the director Adrian Lyne was particularly clever in commercializing the supernatural elements of the film: "When Adrian Lyne, a director of cleverly commercial tastes, took on this project, he blue-penciled the demons and added a sweet-looking, deceased child of Jacob's who, in the end, would help lead his father home. One of Mr. Lyne's most inspired touches was the idea of making Jacob's idea of heaven the apartment he once shared with his wife and children." Janet Maslin, "Spiritual Rewards," *New York Times,* November 19, 1990, sec. 2, 15.

46. In her discussion of love stories, Doane writes, "Symptomatic of this apparent overreliance on unbounded affect is the exaggerated role of music in the love story . . . its function is no less than that of representing that which is unrepresentable: the ineffable" (*The Desire to Desire,* 97).

47. Steve Wurtzler, "She Sang Live, But the Microphone Was Turned Off: The Live, the Recorded, and the *Subject* of Representation," in *Sound Theory, Sound Practice,* ed. Rick Altman (New York: Routledge, 1992), 100.

48. Doane writes, "Music marks a deficiency in the axis of vision. Because emotion is the realm in which the visible is insufficient as a guaranteed, the supplementary meaning proffered by music is absolutely necessary. . . . The incessant recourse to music . . . and its heightening effect suggest that the rationality of the image is a disadvantage" (*The Desire to Desire,* 85).

49. Here the nostalgic 1950s-style music is linked to the ghosts who die in 1959 and remain dressed in 1950s-style clothing throughout the film. To the 1990s audience they resemble nothing more than a retro-style singing group. The irony of the song, however, causes the music to play a slightly different role than that described for *Ghost* and other films.

50. The maternal voice as a sonorous envelope is described by Guy Rosolato in "La voix: entre corps et langage," *Revue française de psychanalyse* 37, no. 1 (1974): 81; Doane, "The Voice in the Cinema: The Articulation of Body and Space," in *Narrative, Apparatus, and Ideology: A Film Theory Reader,* ed. Philip Rosen (New York: Columbia University Press, 1986): 335–48; Silverman, *The Acoustic Mirror: The Female Voice in Psychoanalysis and Cinema* (Bloomington: Indiana University Press, 1988).

51. Silverman, *The Acoustic Mirror,* 76.

52. Deleuze, *Masochsim,* 100.

53. Studlar, *In the Realm of Pleasure,* 123.

54. In one strange scene Anny's father points to a book he is reading and motions to Anny's mother. "Here, I want to show you something," he says. We now see their reflections from behind as they sit in front of a mirror. The wife/mother replies, "Oh, I already know that," once again indicating a simultaneity with knowledge and being. Their reflections might suggest preliminary knowledge of difference as described in Lacan's mirror stage. However, it is a double image, connoting both genders.

55. Silverman, *Male Subjectivity at the Margins,* 211.

Chapter 4

1. Metz, "The Imaginary Signifier," 262.

2. Also see discussion of *Dead Again* in chapter 5.

3. I refer here to primal fantasy as described by Freud and elaborated upon at length by Laplanche and Pontalis in "Fantasy and the Origins of Sexuality," in *Formations of Fantasy,* ed. Victor Burgin and Cora Kaplan (London: Routledge, 1986), 5–34.

4. See ibid., 18.

5. Silverman, *Male Subjectivity at the Margins,* 164–5.

6. Williams, "Film Bodies," 11.

7. Ibid.

8. Elizabeth Cowie, "Fantasia," in *The Woman in Question,* ed. Parveen Adams (Cambridge, Mass.: MIT Press, 1990), 160.

9. See Metz, "The Imaginary Signifier," in *Narrative, Apparatus, Ideology: A Film Theory Reader,* ed. Philip Rosen (New York: Columbia University Press, 1986), 259–64.

10. Silverman, *The Acoustic Mirror,* 3.

11. Silverman, *Male Subjectivity at the Margins,* 165.

12. The ghost films at hand seem to lie somewhere in between the horror and the melodrama, thus partaking of the indeterminate temporal schemata marking the origins of fantasy itself. Neither on time nor too early, but not too late either, since

this is the trajectory that is reversed. Most literally, we can trace the time scale to the course of the subject's life: in the horror/slasher film (see Clover, *Men, Women, and Chain Saws*) the subjects are usually prepubescent teenagers and thus "too-young." In the pornographic film, adults engage in sex as representatives of fully sexual beings. In the melodrama as in the ghost films, the specter of death might equate the "too-late" to the "too old" so that the life cycle of the subject corresponds to the primal fantasies of subject formation and sexual identity. Not by coincidence, many of the ghost films not only reverse the too-old by bringing back the subject as a ghost, but also focus explicitly on birth, creating a full circle. Such films include *Truly, Madly, Deeply, Switch, Beetlejuice,* and *Heaven Can Wait.*

13. Although I would argue that *Field of Dreams* partakes in a similar fantasy to other ghost films in that it tries to resolve a problem of communication and return to a nostalgic past, the way in which the ghosts function is quite different. In this film, the "ghosts" are more like memories in that they appear as younger versions of themselves, not as apparitions of themselves after death. Furthermore, the film uses nostalgia for baseball to celebrate an Oedipal dilemma between father and son, not a desire to glorify the mother. The problems of subjecthood and the difficulties of expression by the Oedipal subject make this film similar to other ghost films in its use of ghosts as paradoxical expressions of Oedipal oneness. As with *The Invisible Man,* the fact that ghosts can be used as devices in both Oedipal and pre-Oedipal fantasies makes it all the more fascinating that this film is the exception, rather than the rule.

14. *Alice* provides some interesting variations on the use of invisibility. Although her ex-boyfriend returns as a ghost to give her advice, Alice becomes a kind of ghost when she is given a potion that makes her invisible.

15. In *Scrooged,* a little boy (the Tiny Tim equivalent) has been mute since the death of his father. He regains his voice as the end of the movie.

16. See Laplanche and Pontalis, "Fantasy and the Origins of Sexuality," 23–26.

17. Wollen, "Discussion," 59–60.

18. Doane, "The Voice in the Cinema," 346.

19. Jean-Louis Comolli, "Machines of the Visible," in *The Cinematic Apparatus,* ed. Teresa de Lauretis and Stephen Heath (London: Macmillan, 1985), 132.

20. Silverman, *The Acoustic Mirror,* 51.

21. Ibid., 164. Also see Doane, *The Desire to Desire,* esp. chapter 5.

22. According to Silverman, "Woman's words are shown to be even less her own than are her 'looks.' They are scripted for her, extracted from her by an external agency, or uttered by her in a trancelike state. . . . Even when she speaks without apparent coercion, she is always spoken from the place of the sexual other" (*The Acoustic Mirror,* 31).

23. Lacan writes, "the unconscious of the subject is the discourse of the other." Jacques Lacan, "The Function and Field of Speech and Language," in *Ecrits: A Selection,* trans. Allen Sheridan (New York: W. W. Norton, 1977), 55.

24. Silverman, *The Acoustic Mirror,* 43–44.

25. Robert Lapsley and Michael Westlake, "From *Casablanca* to *Pretty Woman:* The Politics of Romance," *Screen* 33, no. 1 (spring 1992): 31.

26. Judith Butler, *Gender Trouble: Feminism and the Subversion of Identity* (New York: Routledge, 1990), 57.
27. Ibid., 56.
28. Jacques Lacan, "The Circuit," in *The Seminar of Jacques Lacan: Book II,* ed. Jacques-Alain Miller, trans. Sylvana Tomasell (New York: W. W. Norton, 1988), 81.
29. Michel Foucault, *The History of Sexuality, Vol. I,* trans. Robert Hurley (New York: Vintage Books, 1990), 81.
30. Lapsley and Westlake, "From *Casablanca* to *Pretty Woman*," 44–45.
31. David Bordwell, Janet Staiger, and Kristin Thompson, *The Classical Hollywood Cinema* (New York: Columbia University Press, 1985), 6. Except where noted, my discussion of neoformalism derives from this influential work.
32. Ibid., 54.
33. The tendency to pass through walls and doors recalls Tom and Lyn Davis Genelli's discussion of "transit," which they see as a common motif in spiritual fantasy movies of the 1980s ("Between Two Worlds," 101). Transit is a term used to indicate spiritual and psychological transcendence or transformation. Transit (in fact, "mass transit") is a recurring motif in many of the films, many of which feature vehicles of transportation as metaphors for the ghostly interlude. *Heaven Can Wait* provides an airplane to take souls to heaven, *Hearts and Souls* employs a city bus (often seen entering or exiting a tunnel), *Defending Your Life* features special trolley cars, and in *Ghost* Sam finds the solution to his communication problems in the New York subway.
34. Bordwell et al., *The Classical Hollywood Cinema,* 13.
35. Using a different type of example, when a character bursts into song in a musical it is often motivated more by the generic requirements than by narrative demands. According to Bordwell, genre is a type of "intertextual" motivation that may manifest itself in any number of ways. Another type of intertextual motivation concerns a star's persona. For example, we expect Katharine Hepburn's characters to be feisty and independent because we have seen her play such characters in many other films. For a more relevant example see the discussion of Patrick Swayze's screen persona in relation to his character in the film *Ghost* in chapter 5.
36. Bordwell et al., *The Classical Hollywood Cinema,* 22.
37. Waggoner, *The Foothills of Faraway,* 51–52.
38. As described in this section, the audience's understanding of cinematic reality is constructed by numerous conventions, many of which routinely override verisimilitude or resemblance to actual physical reality.
39. Although Peter Brooks and many others combine psychoanalytic concepts with neoformalism, I am well aware that this strategy is not followed by Bordwell and Thompson, whose *Classical Hollywood Cinema* I have relied on in explaining neoformalism in cinema.
40. Doane, "The Voice in the Cinema," 336.
41. Ibid., 338.
42. Ibid., 345. Also see Silverman, *The Acoustic Mirror.*
43. Doane, "The Voice in the Cinema," 339.
44. Even films that do not feature invisible ghosts nevertheless use the voice-off to introduce or focus on the ghostly character. For example in *Truly, Madly, Deeply* the

ghost Jamie is first made present only through his voice. Only later does he emerge as a solid, visible ghost. Another example occurs in *All of Me* where the female voice of the dead character, Rowena, often emerges from the lips of the male character played by Steve Martin. After her death, we occasionally see her body-image in mirror reflections.

45. In *The Address of the Eye,* Vivian Sobchack provides a phenomenological account of cinema that provides an interesting "perspective" on this process. Her discussion of figure and ground in relation to intentional perception and the incontrovertible link between the camera's and the film viewer's perception would suggest that the camera does, in a sense, call the ghost or angel into existence for the viewer merely by panning over to it (i.e., attending to it).

46. Silverman, *The Acoustic Mirror,* 13.

47. Ibid., 49.

48. Jackson notes, "The fantastic problematizes vision (is it possible to trust the seeing eye?) and language (is it possible to trust the recording, speaking 'I'?)" (*Fantasy,* 30).

49. Despite their "fantastic" nature, even fantasy films depend on or are informed by an element of realism, another type of motivation common to mainstream films. Realistic motivations concern the extent to which story, setting, character behavior, etc., will appear lifelike. Although films often seem to present entirely realistic representations of the world, even realistic motivation is usually subordinated to compositional requirements. Although ghosts are not usually considered "real," they do conform to or subvert notions of reality and verisimilitude. "In Hollywood cinema, verisimilitude usually supports compositional motivation by making the chain of causality seem plausible. Realism, writes one scenarist's manual, 'exists in the photoplay merely as an auxiliary to significance—not as an object in itself.' Frances Marion claims that the strongest illusion of reality comes from tight causal motivation." Bordwell et al., *The Classical Hollywood Cinema,* 19.

50. W. H. Auden, "Notes on the Comic," in *Comedy: Meaning and Form,* ed. Robert Corrigan (San Francisco: Chandler Publishing, 1965), 62.

51. Henri Bergson quoted in J. L. Styan, "Types of Comedy," in *Comedy: Meaning and Form,* ed. Robert Corrigan (San Francisco: Chandler Publishing, 1965), 232.

52. Noel Carroll, "Notes on the Sight Gag," in *Comedy/Cinema/Theory,* ed. Andrew S. Horton (Berkeley: University of California Press, 1991), 29.

53. The scenario in which a character attributes his or her perceptions to alcoholic delusions is extremely common and can be found even in one of the earliest ghost comedies, *Topper* (in which the ghosts themselves are heavy drinkers). The link between ghosts and liquor as an alcoholic "spirit" is thus made literal. Such scenes also occur in *Ghost Dad, Kiss Me Goodbye, Mr. Destiny, Alice, Almost an Angel, Maxie, All of Me,* and *Heart Condition.*

54. "Indeed, if we take the risk of flying about at all, it is certainly in large part because we know that our bodies are anchored by sound, and by the single, continuous experience that it offers. It is thus the sound track that provides a base for visual identification, that authorizes vision and makes it possible. The identity of Hollywood spectators begins with their ability to be auditors." "Sound Space," in *Sound Theory, Sound Practice,* ed. Rick Altman (New York: Routledge, 1992), 62.

55. Doane, *The Desire to Desire,* 126.
56. Ibid.
57. Ibid., 130.
58. Lacan, *Ecrits,* 16–17.

Chapter 5

1. Propp, *Morphology of the Folktale.*
2. Geraldine Fabrikant, "The Media Business: Advertising Campaign Helps Sleeper Become a Hit," *New York Times,* Sept. 19, 1990, sec. D, 24; Hartl, "Summer's Golden 'Ghost,'" sec. F, 5; Steve Pond, "The Women's Movement," *Washington Post,* September 21, 1990, sec. B, 7.
3. According to Bordwell et al., "Of the one hundred films . . . ninety-five involved romance in at least one line of action, while eighty-five made that the principal line of action" (*The Classical Hollywood Cinema,* 16).
4. Butler, *Gender Trouble,* 17.
5. Lapsley and Westlake, "From *Casablanca* to *Pretty Woman*," 28.
6. Ibid., 32.
7. Ibid., 43–44.
8. I am fundamentally in agreement with the way in which Lapsley and Westlake argue that romance functions in Hollywood film. The difference between us lies not in whether ghosts subvert the project of the Hollywood romance (they do not), but more precisely lies in determining the way in which the fantasy of union is specifically deployed and facilitated through ghosts as returning, masochistic characters.
9. See, for example, Studlar, "Masochism and the Perverse Pleasures of the Cinema" and *In the Realm of Pleasure;* Kuhn, *Women's Pictures;* Silverman, *Male Subjectivity at the Margins;* Cowie, "Fantasia"; Clover, *Men, Women, and Chain Saws;* Rodowick, *Difficulty of Difference.*
10. Studlar, "Masochism and the Perverse Pleasures of the Cinema," 615.
11. Kuhn, *Women's Pictures,* 47.
12. Silverman notes that setting off text in brackets indicates Freud's "interpolations, or additions made by the patient at his prompting" (*Male Subjectivity at the Margins,* 201).
13. In his discussion of the aforementioned fantasy, Rodowick notes as much, writing that "Freud demonstrates that phantasy life unfolds across positions of sexual difference" (*Difficulty of Difference,* 70).
14. Cowie, "Fantasia," 167.
15. For example, Kay in *Kiss Me Goodbye,* Oda Mae in *Ghost,* Dorinda in *Always,* Nina in *Truly, Madly, Deeply,* the kids (associated with the feminine and domestic) in *Ghost Dad,* Alice in *Alice,* and the female child in *Beetlejuice.*
16. Silverman, *The Acoustic Mirror,* 156.
17. Ibid., 157.
18. Ibid., 155.
19. Ibid., 17.
20. Butler, *Gender Trouble,* 64.

21. Ibid., 57–58.

22. See Francette Pacteau's discussion of myths from Aristophenes to Plato to nineteenth-century fables, all of which adhere to the notion that human's original state was one of androgyny. "The Impossible Referent," in *Formations of Fantasy,* ed. Victor Burgin, James Donald, and Cora Kaplan (London: Routledge, 1986), 62–84. Also see *The Butcher's Wife,* a film starring Demi Moore that was released in 1991, soon after *Ghost.* In this film, Moore's character depicts the myth that men and women were once part of the same being, and that "true love" occurs when the two halves find one another.

23. See Brooks, *Reading for the Plot.* Despite arguing for an Oedipal, sadistic mode, Brooks claims that all narratives are an attempt to uncover origins.

24. Notably, the theme song to this film is Judy Collins's "Both Sides Now," in which she sings, "I've looked at love from both sides now, and still somehow . . . it's love's illusions I recall." An apt song, indeed, especially in light of the earlier discussion on the inherent illusory nature of romantic oneness.

25. Many of the other angels are, at the very least, highly un-macho. Many of them speak with English accents which might be understood as more refined and thus more feminine: James Mason, Michael Caine, Audrey Hepburn, etc.

26. See Raymond Bellour for an analogy between hypnotism and the fascination of looking in cinema: "The subject of hypnosis gives up his/her look under the domination of the double movement which grips it tightly: regression, idealization. The subject-spectator is submitted to a similar domination in that light form of hypnosis which belongs to the spectator: the hypnosis of cinema." "Believing in Cinema," in *Psychoanalysis in Cinema,* ed. E. Anne Kaplan (New York: Routledge, 1990), 107.

27. Jack Mathews, "A Trip Back in Time Again," *Newsday,* August 23, 1991, 17.

28. Similarly, in *All of Me,* Steve Martin's maleness is in constant battle with Lily Tomlin's exaggerated femaleness.

29. De Lauretis, *Alice Doesn't,* 103.

30. Fainaru, "Lifeless *Ghost,*" entertainment page.

31. Johnstone, "Haunted By a Lightweight Lover," features page.

32. Silverman, *The Acoustic Mirror,* 164.

33. The 1985 film *Maxie* is the exception to the recent spate of male ghosts in films. Here, a female film actress briefly returns as a ghost but then immediately inhabits the body of another woman, Jan. Whereas Jan is staid and mousy, Maxie is an over-sexed lush who uses Jan's body to pursue Jan's husband as well as fame as a film star. The result of the possession is that Jan's husband is permitted to enjoy his otherwise mousy wife as if she were a sexually charged, "other woman." As with many ghost films, this movie lets the male character have things both ways: his beautiful but dutiful wife (she works for a bishop) is permitted to display and act out her desire for career and sex (desires usually denied to women), but all under the auspices of a supernatural possession. At one point Jan buys a sexy dress and then claims, "I don't know what possessed me to buy it. You know it really isn't me." Near the end of the film, she remarks of Maxie, "I never dreamed anyone could *want* anything so badly. I almost envy her."

34. The use of Swayze in this role might be seen as a case of intertextual motivation played "against the grain." For a more in-depth discussion of the way in which the

star persona cuts across textual fields see Richard Dyer, *Stars* (London: British Film Institute, 1979); Dyer, *Heavenly Bodies: Film Stars and Society* (New York: St. Martin's Press, 1986).

35. Johnstone, "Haunted by a Lightweight Lover." Cf. other male actors in classic melodrama. Doane notes that many female melodramas and love stories of the 1940s featured male leads who were less than macho: "The genre does seem to require that the male character undergo a process of feminization by his mere presence within a love story. The male stars who tend to play the romantic leads in these films—Charles Boyer, John Boles, Louis Jourdan, Paul Henreid, Leslie Howard—were clearly not chosen for their overly 'masculine' qualities" (*The Desire to Desire,* 116).

36. Joel Rubin, the screenwriter, was reportedly "gratified by how other men have reacted to the film," quoted in Susan Wloszczyna, "'Ghost' Writer Presses All the Right Weep Buttons," *USA Today,* July 17, 1990, sec. D, 2. Similar observations were made by Mathews, "Hollywood's Feel-Good Fantasies," 4, and Broeske, "Outtakes," 32. Broeske also provides reactions from male audience members who loved the film and saw it repeatedly. One reviewer noted that appealing to women can be a lucrative marketing ploy. Women make up large percentage of any potential audience, but "Adult females normally bring along adult males." Pond, "The Women's Movement," sec. B, 7.

37. Johnstone, "Haunted by a Lightweight Lover."

38. Janice A. Radway, *Reading the Romance: Women, Patriarchy, and Popular Literature* (Chapel Hill: University of North Carolina Press, 1984), 148.

39. Allis, "What Do Men Really Want?" 80.

40. Ibid. Note the release a year or so later of the film *Kindergarten Cop,* which featured the macho hunk, Arnold Swarzenegger, playing a kindergarten teacher.

41. Butler, *Gender Trouble,* 135. See also Michel Foucault, *Discipline and Punish: The Birth of the Prison,* trans. Alan Sheridan (New York: Vintage Books, 1979), 29–30.

42. Many review articles noted the designer clothes sported by Patrick Swayze in *Ghost.* (Also see chapter 7. Promotional materials and reviews of the 1937 film *Topper* revealed a focus on the swanky, sexy clothes worn by the ghosts.)

43. As Lucy Fischer writes of this film, "In envisioning a female doppelganger in the mirror, the male comic hero reveals a wish to return to a time of maternal union when 'all of him' was 'all of her.'" Fischer, "Sometimes I Feel Like a Motherless Child," in *Comedy/Cinema/Theory,* ed. Andrew Horton (Berkeley: University of California Press, 1991), 69.

44. The analogy between this unwanted physical penetration and rape is obvious.

45. Once again, the possession is compared to sexual intercourse: the result of physical penetration causes the male to be "spent."

46. As in the earlier example, Sam must pay the price for being allowed to communicate to Molly. When the bad guys arrive, Sam jumps out of Oda Mae's body, but is now rendered completely ineffectual.

47. Note the obvious attention given to their names: A-"man"-da, and "She"-ila.

48. Gay and lesbian scholarship has recently created a new and often distinct approach to film analysis. Much of it concerns the re-reading of "straight" films

from a gay perspective, and the celebration of a "camp" aesthetic. See for example, Alex Doty's essay, "Queerness, Comedy and *The Women,*" in *Classical Hollywood Comedy,* ed. Kristine Brunovska Karnick and Henry Jenkins (New York: Routledge, 1995), 332–47, in which he also describes queer theory's revalorization of an auteur approach, which (although employed differently here) had previously fallen out of favor with many film scholars. While such approaches can clearly add much to this discussion, this study attempts to interpret "straight" films within the framework of a mainstream, heterosexual paradigm. Since the thrust of this argument is that all people are bisexual in the pre-Oedipal stage, I am alluding to a type of homosexual identification and pleasure. However, the gender switching in these films operates with reference to a dynamic in which opposites attract, despite the suggestion that viewer identification can shift back and forth.

Chapter 6

1. Note that this presupposes only two genders. While it might be possible to conceive of more than two genders, current cultural norms and psychoanalytic theory are formulated on a two-gender hypothesis. See the discussion at the end of this chapter.
2. A priest asks Terry whether he received a sign from God: "God spoke to you?" Terry replies, "I believe he did. Hey, don't you reckon he looks just like Charlton Heston!"
3. Auden, "Notes on the Comic," 61.
4. Some recent theories of film authorship understand the concept of auteurism as an anthropomorphized term that refers less to a single person than to numerous influences in a film's style and content. The author is seen more as the signature of a particular style rather than a person with conscious intent. If the "author is dead," then here the author is beyond death.
5. In his alternate destiny, Larry discovers to his horror that his actions as an evil CEO have driven his best friend Cliff (now a lowly office worker) to the verge of suicide. Larry tries to prevent him from jumping: "If there's something wrong maybe I can help." Cliff replies, "It's a little late for that."
6. Note that this recalls the tendency of ghost films to collapse time.
7. Theodor Reik, quoted in Studlar, *In the Realm of Pleasure,* 228.
8. Ibid., 118.
9. Robert Corrigan writes that in comedy, "death is never taken seriously or even considered as a serious threat" (*Comedy, Meaning and Form,* 6).
10. Wylie Sypher, "The Meanings of Comedy," in *Comedy: Meaning and Form,* ed. Robert Corrigan (San Francisco: Chandler Publishing, 1965), 29.
11. Susanne Langer, "The Comic Rhythm," in ibid., 124.
12. Christopher Fry, "Comedy," in ibid., 17.
13. See for example, Corrigan, *Meaning and Form;* Ludwig Jekels, "On the Psychology of Comedy," in ibid.; Martin Grotjahn, "Beyond Laughter: A Summing Up," in ibid.; Fischer, "Sometimes I Feel Like a Motherless Child," in *Comedy/Cinema/*

Theory, 60–77, for a discussion of comedy as a reversal of the Oedipal scenario. Frye and Grotjahn both remark on comedy's return to the womb. See Frye, *Anatomy of Criticism,* 186, and Grotjahn, "Beyond Laughter," 273. Mikhail Bakhtin's makes reference to the relationship between the crib and the grave in his discussion of the carnivalesque, in *Rabelais and His World,* trans. Helene Iswolsky (Bloomington: Indiana University Press, 1984), 21.

14. Quoted in Jekels, "On the Psychology of Comedy," 264.
15. Fischer, "Sometimes I Feel Like a Motherless Child," 61. Kathleen Rowe notes that the romantic comedy "may show Oedipus to be a fool, but it still places him at the heart of the story." "Comedy, Melodrama and Gender: Theorizing the Genres of Laughter," in *Classical Hollywood Comedy,* 45. Also see Corrigan, *Comedy: Meaning and Form,* 3, and Frye, "The Mythos of Spring: Comedy," in ibid., who refers to this as Greek New Comedy: "What normally happens is that a young man wants a young woman, that his desire is resisted by some opposition, usually paternal, and that near the end of the play some twist in the plot enables the hero to have his will" (141).
16. Neale and Krutnik, *Popular Film and Television Comedy,* 144.
17. Langer, "The Comic Rhythm," 123.
18. Ibid., 126.
19. Lapsley and Westlake, "From *Casablanca* to *Pretty Woman,*" 38.
20. Judith Butler writes, "Hence there is a necessary or presuppositional impossibility to any effort to occupy the positions of 'having' the Phallus, with the consequence that both positions of 'having' and 'being' are, in Lacan's terms, finally to be understood as *comedic failures that are nevertheless compelled to articulate and enact these repeated impossibilities"* (*Gender Trouble,* 46, emphasis mine).
21. Studlar writes that "masochistic suspense is paradoxical. Frequently it does not depend on the question of what will happen but on when and how" (*In the Realm of Pleasure,* 120).
22. Maslin, "Looking to the Dead for Mirth and Inspiration," sec. C, 8. See also note 29 in chapter 2 for other similar views.
23. Frye, "Mythos of Spring," 145.
24. Among those that are either explicit or implicit remakes: *Ghost, Always, Scrooged, Heaven Can Wait, Kiss Me Goodbye,* and *Mr. Destiny.*
25. As Frye notes, "The obstacles to the hero's desire, then, form the action of the comedy, and the overcoming of them the comic resolution" ("Mythos of Spring," 142).

Chapter 7

1. John Brosnan writes that "the introduction of sound hastened the spread of special effects departments and by the early 1930s all but one of the major studios maintained such a unit." *Movie Magic: The Story of Special Effects in the Cinema* (New York: New American Library, 1974), 44. The 1938 sequel, *Topper Takes a Trip,* was nominated for an Academy Award for its special effects. This was the first year such an award was given. According to Linwood G. Dunn and George Turner, most major films of the 1930s utilized special effects to some extent. Lin-

wood G. Dunn and George E. Turner, *The ASC Treasury of Visual Effects* (Hollywood: American Society of Cinematographers, 1983), 49.

2. See Molly Haskell, *From Reverence to Rape: The Treatment of Women in the Movies* (New York: Penguin Books, 1974); Sarris, "The Afterlife"; Ed Sikov, *Screwball: Hollywood's Madcap Romantic Comedies* (New York: Crown, 1989), 20. The Production Code prohibited nudity and explicit references to sexual activities. The screwball comedies' verbal innuendoes and slapstick physical comedy may have been an unintended, yet "productive" effect of the Code's censorship.

3. Press booklets for *Topper*, Billy Rose Theater Collection, New York Public Library at Lincoln Center, New York.

4. The male ghost is featured at the beginning of the film, but as the movie progresses, the female ghost takes center stage. The male ghost "disappears" until the end.

5. The spectacle of Constance Bennett as both a ghost and a fashion plate provides yet another avenue of analysis. The link between standards of feminine beauty and consumerism is unavoidable. See Louise Banner, *American Beauty* (Chicago: University of Chicago Press, 1983) for a discussion of changing modes of beauty in the early part of the century. While Banner tends to gloss over the role of cinema, Virginia Wright Wexman discusses at some length the creation of female movie stars in connection with consumer culture. Wexman, *Creating the Couple: Love, Marriage, and Hollywood Performance* (Princeton: Princeton University Press, 1993), 133–59. Their construction as beauties depended, in part, on cosmetics and fashionable clothes. While the average female viewer could attempt to emulate this through her own purchases, the female movie star's beauty was most often portrayed as a natural, innate quality. In *Topper*, Constance Bennett is portrayed as a fashionable ghost, just as she was in life. Her beauty and star appeal is thus expressed as an inner quality that transcends mortal boundaries.

6. *Blithe Spirit* (1945) is another film that features a female ghost. She returns from death when she discovers that her husband has remarried. The film won an Oscar for special effects.

7. See, for example Thomas Schatz, *Hollywood Genres: Formulas, Filmmaking and the Studio System* (New York: Random House, 1981); Wexman, *Creating the Couple;* Doane, *The Desire to Desire;* Haskell, *From Reverence to Rape;* Kuhn, *Women's Pictures;* Linda Williams, "Feminist Film Theory: Mildred Pierce and the Second World War," in *Female Spectators: Looking at Film and Spectators,* ed. E. Deidre Pribram (New York: Verso, 1988), 1–30.

8. *The Canterville Ghost* employs a wartime setting to illustrate the protagonist's heroism. In an extended and insightful analysis of this era Dana Polan describes the war period as a "contradictory moment," the symptoms of which surface continually in war movies of the era. He writes, "probably no subject is as much a site for discursive representation . . . as the role of women in the war effort." *Power and Paranoia: History, Narrative, and the American Cinema, 1940–1950* (New York: Columbia University Press, 1986), 79.

9. Polan, *Power and Paranoia,* 139. *The Canterville Ghost* features only a little girl but no heterosexual romantic possibilities. The little girl, "Lady Canterville,"

clearly has a crush on Caffy, however, and is one of the motivators of his heroism. At the end of the movie, she tells Caffy that sometimes one has to wait a long time to get something one really wants. She then tells him that she is about to turn seven, suggesting maybe he will wait for her. As noted, the emphasis on waiting (the ghost waits three hundred years to be released, Caffy waits until the last minute to overcome his cowardice) is a common attribute of ghost fantasies.

10. Silverman discusses the masochistic qualities of this film in *Male Subjectivity at the Margins.* Polan discusses the film at length in *Power and Paranoia.*

11. Dorinda had earlier rebuffed Ted, but then decides to take him back after completing the mission. Earlier in the film, Ted almost announces (rather than asking) that he will marry her. She initially accepts, but remarks that he has been rather presumptuous in expecting her to say yes.

12. Barry Keith Grant, "Experience and Meaning in Genre Films," in *Film Genre Reader* (Austin: University of Texas Press, 1986), 118. This dilemma is found in other genres as well. For example, the Western exhibits this same dichotomy, yet works through the problem as an expression of savage lawlessness vs. domestic civilization. Robert Ray also notes the emphasis on teamwork in war movies. He notes, however, that the 1939 film *Only Angels Have Wings* nonetheless focused on individual heroism. He deems this film the archetypal source for later war movies, saying that all of the major combat films which followed were basically remakes. Ray, *A Certain Tendency in Hollywood Cinema: 1930–1960* (Princeton: Princeton University Press, 1985), 120.

13. Polan, *Power and Paranoia,* 89.

14. A remake of this film, *The Preacher's Wife,* is being released as I write this. See the discussion of race at the end of this chapter. The combination of an all-black cast with a religious, musical setting is relevant to the ghostly theme.

15. See also *It's a Wonderful Life* and the various versions of Dickens's *A Christmas Carol* in this era, including *Scrooged.*

16. See Tina Olsin Lent, "Romantic Love and Friendship: The Redefinition of Gender Relations in Screwball Comedy," in *Classical Hollywood Comedy,* ed. Karnick and Jenkins; Steven Seidman, *Romantic Longings: Love in America, 1830–1980* (New York: Routledge, 1991); Wexman, *Creating the Couple.* Wexman draws primarily on Levi-Strauss and Engels. See also Frank Krutnik, "The Faint Aroma of Performing Seals: The 'Nervous' Romance and the Comedy of the Sexes," *The Velvet Light Trap* no. 26 (fall 1990): 57–72.

17. Wexman, *Creating the Couple,* 13.

18. For example, in *Topper,* much of the ghosts' good deed is accomplished by attempting to make Cosmo have fun. Though the film accomplishes this differently than other films in this study, it nevertheless provides a complementary example.

19. The problems of generic classification surface here, as elsewhere. Both films clearly have comedic elements and their stars are associated with comic or screwball roles: Spencer Tracy and Irene Dunn in *A Guy Named Joe;* Cary Grant and David Niven in *The Bishop's Wife.* Loretta Young, in the latter, appeared in both comic and dramatic roles.

20. Thomas Sobchack, "Genre Film: A Classical Experience," reprinted in *Film Genre Reader,* ed. Barry Keith Grant (Austin: University of Texas Press, 1986), 110.

21. As the angel complicates his life and steals his wife, Henry finally capitulates to the wealthy donor Mrs. Hamilton, who wants the cathedral built in her husband's honor. This is a low point for Henry, who has been at the mercy of Mrs. Hamilton, a shrewish and powerful woman who has told him how ineffectual she thinks he is. She now tells him she wants a large stained glass window of St. George and the Dragon and stipulates that St. George must resemble her dead husband. Henry then coyly asks her who the dragon will resemble.

22. Notably, the father remains dead and absent from George's "un-born" scenario.

23. Ray notes that the "goal of *It's a Wonderful Life* was to liberate George, and the audience, from the frustrations caused by this desire, which the film identified as mistaken" (*A Certain Tendency,* 187).

24. Judith Butler, "Gender Trouble, Feminist Theory, and Psychoanalytic Discourse," in *Feminism/Postmodernism,* ed. Linda J. Nicholson (New York: Routledge, 1990), 330.

25. Butler writes that "the tenuousness of all identity is exposed through the proliferation of fantasies that exceed and contest the 'identity' that forms the conscious sense of self. But are identity and fantasy as mutually exclusive as the previous explanation suggests? Consider the claim, integral to much psychoanalytic theory, that identifications and, hence, identity, are fact *constituted* by fantasy" ("Gender Trouble," 333).

26. Benjamin writes, "the female difficulty in differentiation can be described almost as the mirror image of the male's: not the denial of the other, but the denial of the self" (*The Bonds of Love,* 78).

27. To the male subject, motherhood represents dependency, and as Benjamin notes, "the denial of dependency is central to the bourgeois ideal of individual freedom" (Ibid., 187).

28. Although the trend began earlier (see Tina Lent's discussion of the Flapper female as an example, in "Romantic Love and Friendship,"), Polan notes that the problem of sexually transmitted disease had to be confronted, en masse, during wartime. This was one step in facilitating a more frank approach to sexuality (*Power and Paranoia,* 127). See also Ehrenreich's account of the 1950s male "rebellion" in *The Hearts of Men.*

29. The shift in films from fun and romance to films portraying a more sexual type of relationship (or lack thereof) is described by Krutnik in "The Faint Aroma of Performing Seals," 59–61. Haskell also documents this shift in *From Reverence to Rape,* 323–71. Most films depicted sexual freedom as a male prerogative.

30. Films such as *The Man with the Golden Arm* (1955) and *Marty* (1955) broached social problems and depressing storylines with unusual frankness. In the 1960s, the trend toward explicit violence appeared in such films as *Bonnie and Clyde* (1968). The breakup of the Studio System in 1948 was responsible, in part, for the cinematic landscape in the postwar era. An influx of foreign and independent films, television, and the waning of Production Code strictures also influenced the range and the explicitness of American cinema.

31. Margaret Sanger, quoted in Seidman, *Romantic Longings,* 90. Wexman (*Creating the Couple,* 167–70) notes that the companionate concept of marriage received much attention after the war. As times changed, the dominant youth culture and

freer visions of sexuality changed the focus of the companionate ideal to incorporate sexual pleasure.

32. Both war experiences are relevant to issues of race, which may have some bearing on ghosts, gender, and race (see chapter 7). Particularly during World War II, black men found themselves in a different social configuration than that of peace time. See Thomas Cripps's account of these changes in relation to cinema in *Making Movies Black: The Hollywood Message Movie from World War II to the Civil Rights Era* (New York: Oxford University Press, 1993), esp. chapter 4, "The Making of the Negro Soldier."

33. Ryan and Kellner, *Camera Politica,* 9. Robin Wood also speaks of the "breakdown of ideological confidence that characterizes American culture throughout the Vietnam war period and becomes a major defining factor of Hollywood cinema in the late 60s and 70s." *Hollywood from Vietnam to Reagan* (New York: Columbia University Press, 1986), 23. Ray discusses the effects of the major events of the 1960s in *A Certain Tendency,* 250.

34. Examples of movies might include: *Farewell My Lovely* (1975); *The Postman Always Rings Twice* (1981)—both remakes. *Fatal Attraction* (1980) and *Body Heat* (1981) were considered film noir-ish in theme and style.

35. Ryan and Kellner, 10, 84. The connection between ghost fantasies and conservatism breaks down if one agrees with the authors that conservatism wanes in the late 1980s. This rightward shift, reoccurs, however in the early 1990s as evidenced by both political and social trends.

36. Wood, *Hollywood from Vietnam to Reagan,* 70 (see 172–74 for a discussion of the reassertion of "The Father"). Ryan and Kellner concur with this assessment (*Camera Politica,* 65).

37. As David A. Hollinger remarks, only "tiny fractions of a person's genetic inheritance . . . is taken into account by such a mode of classification." Many scholars agree that there really is no such thing as race. Hollinger, *Postethnic America: Beyond Multiculturalism* (New York: Basic Books, 1995), 34. Also see Ella Shohat and Robert Stam, who argue that: "Racial categories are not natural but constructs, not absolutes but relative, situational, even narrative categories, engendered by historical process of differentiation." *Unthinking Eurocentrism: Multiculturalism and the Media* (London: Routledge, 1994), 9. Their reference to narrative categories is particularly relevant to this discussion.

38. Hollinger refers to the "ethno-racial pentagon" that divides people in the United States into one of five categories: Euro-American or white; Asian American, African American; Hispanic or Latino; and Indigenous or Native American (*Postethnic America,* 23). Hollinger debates the usefulness of these categories, while acknowledging that many groups have adopted them as a strategy for gaining official redress for past prejudices.

39. See, in particular, Richard Dyer's influential essay, "White," *Screen* 29, no. 4 (Autumn 1988): 44–64.

40. See Dyer, "White," for an insightful discussion of this tendency.

41. The pejorative term "spook" to refer to black people also suggests a rather obvious comparison.

42. Judith Mayne, *Cinema and Spectatorship* (New York: Routledge), 152. Mayne devotes a chapter to a comparison of racial stereotypes in *Ghost* and *Field of Dreams.*

43. Ibid., 142. For discussions of the black mammy stereotype see Donald Bogle, *Toms, Coons, Mulattos, Mammies and Bucks* (New York: Viking, 1973); K. Sue Jewell, *From Mammy to Miss America and Beyond* (New York: Routledge, 1993); Ed Guerrero, *Framing Blackness: The African American Image in Film* (Philadelphia: Temple University Press, 1993).

44. Guerrero, *Framing Blackness,* 20.

45. For a comprehensive history of the role of music in African American culture, see Lawrence W. Levine, *Black Culture and Black Consciousness: Afro-American Folk Thought from Slavery to Freedom* (New York: Oxford University Press, 1977).

46. bell hooks, among others, notes the ambivalent desire of white culture to possess black qualities. Shohat and Stam note that Hollywood films have appropriated black and Latino music without referencing their cultural roots. They note, however, that several recent films do feature music of other cultures in much more explicit ways: "Recent nostalgia films like *Dirty Dancing* and *Hairspray* . . . enthusiastically foreground the black and Latino influence on 'White' popular culture, projecting communal utopias in which Euro-American characters are viscerally 'possessed' or 'entranced' by the very Afro-American or Latin cultures repressed in antecedent cinema" (*Unthinking Eurocentrism,* 235). (In *Beetlejuice,* the characters are physically "possessed" by Caribbean music.)

47. bell hooks, *Black Looks: Race and Representation* (Boston: South End Press, 1992), 95.

48. bell hooks, *Yearning: Race, Gender and Cultural Politics* (Boston: South End Press, 1990), 58.

49. As Mayne points out in *Cinema and Spectatorship,* his colleagues salute him for potentially being the youngest executive to rise to his level. No mention is made that he is the only black male among an entirely white office (and he does not look particularly young either) (152).

50. Tasker notes that a "totally passive hero is a contradiction in terms, whilst an aggressively active black hero seems to provoke altogether too much anxiety for Hollywood to deal with" (*Spectacular Bodies,* 40).

51. See, for example Guerrero, *Framing Blackness;* hooks, *Black Looks, Yearning;* James Snead, *White Screens Black Images: Hollywood from the Dark Side* (New York: Routledge, 1994); Tasker, *Spectacular Bodies.*

52. According to hooks, many black audience members found the film offensive and racist (*Black Looks,* 32). However, at least this interracial relationship is consummated, albeit offscreen. Compare this to the *Pelican Brief,* which places Denzel Washington in a potentially romantic lead role with Julia Roberts, but then never follows through. Wexman discusses how the birth of American cinema was formulated in D. W. Griffith's romantic storylines, which played on the fear of miscegenation (*Creating the Couple,* 43–54).

53. Despite its obvious tendency to activate all the usual stereotypes, *Heart Condition* might offer the opportunity for an alternative reading through offering a potentially doubled interpretation of Stone's position.

54. Robin Wood, *Hitchcock's Films Revisited* (New York: Columbia University Press, 1989), 378. Jeanne Allen also provides an insightful account of this film in "Looking Through *Rear Window*," in *Female Spectators.*

55. For example, one window scene entails a domestic dispute, and another a failed romance.

56. Tasker, *Spectacular Bodies,* 150.

57. A more appropriate rendition might be: "*She* who is silent is understood to consent."

58. See for example, Elaine Dutka, "Women and Hollywood; It's Still a Lousy Relationship," *Los Angeles Times,* November 11, 1990, 8; Suzanna Andrews, "The Great Divide: The Sexes at the Box Office," *New York Times,* May 23, 1993, 15.

59. Dutka, "Women and Hollywood," 8.

BIBLIOGRAPHY

Allen, Jeanne. "Looking through *Rear Window*." In *Female Spectators,* ed. E. Deidre Pribram. New York: Verso, 1988.

Allis, Sam. "What Do Men Really Want?" *Time,* October 1, 1990, Special Issue.

Altman, Rick. "Sound Space." In *Sound Theory, Sound Practice,* ed. Rick Altman. New York: Routledge, 1992.

Andrews, Suzanna. "The Great Divide: The Sexes at the Box Office." *New York Times,* May 23, 1993.

Ansen, David, "Immaterial Affections." *Newsweek,* July 16, 1990, 61.

Auden, W. H. "Notes on the Comic." In *Comedy: Meaning and Form,* ed. Robert Corrigan. San Francisco: Chandler Publishing, 1965.

Beidler, Peter G. *Ghosts, Demons, and Henry James.* Columbia: University of Missouri Press, 1989.

Bellour, Raymond. "Believing in Cinema." In *Psychoanalysis in Cinema,* ed. E. Anne Kaplan. New York: Routledge, 1990.

Benjamin, Jessica. *The Bonds of Love: Psychoanalysis, Feminism, and the Problem of Domination.* New York: Pantheon Books, 1988.

Benson, Sheila. "An Afterlife Love Story." *Los Angeles Times,* July 13, 1990.

Bordwell, David. *Narration in the Fiction Film.* Madison: University of Wisconsin Press, 1985.

Bordwell, David, Janet Staiger, and Kristin Thompson. *The Classical Hollywood Cinema.* New York: Columbia University Press, 1985.

Broeske, Pat H. "Outtakes: 'Ghost': Why It's Still Scaring Up Repeat Business." *Los Angeles Times,* November 18, 1990.

Brooks, Peter. *Reading for the Plot: Design and Intention in Narrative.* New York: Vintage Books, 1984.

Brosnan, John. *The Story of Special Effects in Cinema.* New York: New American Library, 1974.

Burgin, Victor, James Donald, and Cora Kaplan, eds. *Formations of Fantasy.* London: Routledge, 1986.

Butler, Judith. *Gender Trouble: Feminism and the Subversion of Identity.* New York: Routledge, 1990.

Bibliography

———. "Gender Trouble, Feminist Theory, and Psychoanalytic Discourse." In *Feminism/ Postmodernism,* ed. Linda J. Nicholson. New York: Routledge, 1990.

Carr, Jay. "A Romantic 'Ghost' to Believe In." *Boston Globe,* July 13, 1990.

Carter, Margaret L. *Specter or Delusion? The Supernatural in Gothic Fiction.* Ann Arbor, Mich.: UMI Research Press, 1987.

Chodorow, Nancy J. *Feminism and Psychoanalytic Theory.* New Haven: Yale University Press, 1989.

Clover, Carol. "Her Body, Himself: Gender in the Slasher Film," *Representations* no. 20 (fall 1987): 187–228.

———. *Men, Women and Chain Saws: Gender in the Modern Horror Film.* Princeton: Princeton University Press, 1992.

Comolli, Jean-Louis. "Machines of the Visible." In *The Cinematic Apparatus,* ed. Teresa de Lauretis and Stephen Heath. London: Macmillan, 1985.

Corliss, Richard. "Giving Up the Ghost: Two Movies Trivialize Matters of Life and Death." *Time,* July 16, 1990, 86.

Corrigan, Robert W., ed. *Comedy: Meaning and Form.* San Francisco: Chandler Publishing, 1965.

Cowie, Elizabeth. "Fantasia." In *The Woman in Question,* ed. Parveen Adams. Cambridge, Mass.: MIT Press, 1990.

Creed, Barbara. "Horror and the Monstrous Feminine: An Imaginary Abjection," *Screen* 27 (1986): 44–70.

Cripps, Thomas. *Making Movies Black: The Hollywood Message Movie from World War II to the Civil Rights Era.* New York: Oxford University Press, 1993.

de Lauretis, Teresa. *Alice Doesn't: Feminism, Semiotics, Cinema.* Bloomington: Indiana University Press, 1984.

de Lauretis, Teresa, and Stephen Heath, eds. *The Cinematic Apparatus.* London: Macmillan, 1985.

Deleuze, Gilles. *Masochism: An Interpretation of Coldness and Cruelty.* New York: Zone Books, 1989.

Doane, Mary Ann. *The Desire to Desire: The Woman's Film of the 1940s.* Bloomington: Indiana University Press, 1987.

———. "The Voice in the Cinema: The Articulation of Body and Space." In *Narrative, Apparatus, Ideology: A Film Theory Reader,* ed. Philip Rosen, 335–48. New York: Columbia University Press, 1986.

———. "Ideology and the Practice of Sound Editing and Mixing." In *The Cinematic Apparatus,* ed. Teresa de Lauretis and Stephen Heath. London: Macmillan, 1985.

Doty, Alex. "Queerness, Comedy, and *The Women.*" In *Classical Hollywood Comedy,* ed. Kristine Brunovska Karnick and Henry Jenkins. New York: Routledge, 1995.

Dunn, Linwood G. and George E. Turner. *The ASC Treasury of Visual Effects.* Hollywood: American Society of Cinematographers, 1983.

Dutka, Elaine. "Women and Hollywood; It's Still a Lousy Relationship." *Los Angeles Times,* Nov. 11, 1990.

Dyer, Richard. "White," *Screen* 29, no. 4 (Autumn 1988): 44–64.

Ellis, David. "A Ghost With Legs." *Time,* November 5, 1990, 25.

Fabrikant, Geraldine. "The Media Business: Advertising Campaign Helps Sleeper Become a Hit." *New York Times,* Sept. 19, 1990.

Fainaru, Dan. "Lifeless *Ghost.*" *Jerusalem Post,* Oct 16, 1990.

Fischer, Lucy. "Sometimes I Feel Like a Motherless Child." In *Comedy/Cinema/ Theory,* ed. Andrew Horton. Berkeley: University of California Press, 1991.

Foucault, Michel. *Discipline and Punish: The Birth of the Prison.* Translated by Alan Sheridan. New York: Vintage Books, 1979.

———. *The History of Sexuality, Volume I.* Translated by Robert Hurley. New York: Vintage Books, 1990.

Freud, Sigmund. *Beyond the Pleasure Principle.* Trans. and ed. James Strachey. New York: W. W. Norton, 1961.

———. "A Child Is Being Beaten." In *Sexuality and the Psychology of Love,* ed. Philip Rieff. New York: Macmillan/Collier Books, 1963.

———. "The Economic Problem in Masochism." In *Sexuality and the Psychology of Love,* ed. Philp Rieff. New York: Macmillan/Collier Books, 1963.

———. *The Freud Reader.* Ed. Peter Gay. New York: Yale University Press, 1989.

———. "Instincts and Their Vicissitudes." In *The Freud Reader,* ed. Peter Gay. New York: W. W. Norton, 1989.

———. *Introductory Lectures on Psychoanalysis: The Standard Edition.* Trans. and ed. by James Strachey. New York: W. W. Norton, 1977.

———. "Three Essays on the Theory of Sexuality." In *The Freud Reader,* ed. Peter Gay. New York: W. W. Norton, 1989.

Fry, Christopher. "Comedy." In *Comedy: Meaning and Form,* ed. Robert Corrigan. San Francisco: Chandler Publishing, 1965.

Frye, Northrop. *Anatomy of Criticism: Four Essays.* Princeton: Princeton University Press, 1957.

———. "The Mythos of Spring: Comedy." In *Comedy: Meaning and Form,* ed. Robert Corrigan. San Francisco: Chandler Publishing, 1965.

Garner, Jack. "This 'Ghost' Story Is Played for Laughs." *Gannett News Service,* July 19, 1990.

Genelli, Tom, and Lyn Davis Genelli. "Between Two Worlds: Some Thoughts Beyond the 'Film Blanc,'" *Journal of Popular Film and Television* 12, no. 3 (fall 1984): 100–111.

"Ghost." *Wall Street Journal,* December 12, 1990.

Grant, Barry Keith. "Experience and Meaning in Genre Films." In *Film Genre Reader,* ed. Barry Keith Grant. Austin: University of Texas Press, 1986.

Grotjahn, Martin. "Beyond Laughter: A Summing Up." In *Comedy: Meaning and Form,* ed. Robert Corrigan. San Francisco: Chandler Publishing, 1965.

Guerrero, Ed. *Framing Blackness: The African American Image in Film.* Philadelphia: Temple University Press, 1993.

Hartl, John. "Summer's Golden 'Ghost'—Fantasy Romance Makes Hearts Beat, Cash Registers Ring." *Seattle Times,* August 30, 1990.

Haskell, Molly. *From Reverence to Rape: The Treatment of Women in the Movies.* New York: Penguin Books, 1974.

Hollinger, David A. *Postethnic America: Beyond Multiculturalism.* New York: Basic Books, 1995.

Bibliography

Honeycutt, Kirk. "Director Leaves Laughs Behind to Capture Spirit of 'Ghost.'" *Los Angeles Times,* July 13, 1990.

hooks, bell. *Yearning: Race, Gender and Cultural Politics.* Boston: South End Press, 1990.

———. *Black Looks: Race and Representation.* Boston: South End Press, 1992.

Horrocks, Roger. *Masculinity in Crisis.* New York: St. Martin's Press, 1994.

Horton, Andrew, ed. *Comedy/Cinema/Theory.* Berkeley: University of California Press, 1991.

Howe, Desson. "Death Takes a Holiday: Why Are We Just Dying to See Movies about the Afterlife?" *Washington Post,* August 26, 1990.

Irwin, W. R. *The Game of the Impossible: A Rhetoric of Fantasy.* Urbana: University of Illinois Press, 1976.

Jackson, Rosemary. *Fantasy: The Literature of Subversion.* New York: Methuen, 1981.

James, Caryn. "Ghosts Must Catch the Spirit of the Time." *New York Times,* July 29, 1990.

Jekels, Ludwig. "On the Psychology of Comedy." In *Comedy: Meaning and Form,* ed. Robert Corrigan. San Francisco: Chandler Publishing, 1965.

Jenkins, Henry, and Kristine Brunovska Karnick. "Acting Funny." In *Classical Hollywood Comedy,* ed. Kristine Brunovska Karnick and Henry Jenkins, 149–67. New York: Routledge, 1995.

Johnstone, Iain. "Haunted by a Lightweight Lover." *Sunday Times* [London], October 7, 1990.

Kaplan, E. Anne, ed. *Psychoanalysis in Cinema.* New York: Routledge, 1990.

Kehr, Dave. "Three Balanced Performances Spark 'Ghost.'" *Chicago Tribune,* July 13, 1990.

Kelleher, Terry. "'Ghost': Patrick Swayze as a Dead Hero." *Newsday,* July 13, 1990.

Kerr, Howard, John W. Crowley, and Charles L. Crow, eds. *The Haunted Dusk: American Supernatural Fiction, 1820–1920.* Athens: University of Georgia Press, 1983.

Klady, Leonard. "The Hopeful Dead." *American Film,* March 1990, 16–18.

Koelb, Clayton. *The Incredulous Reader: Literature and the Function of Disbelief.* Ithaca: Cornell University Press, 1984.

Kristeva, Julia. *The Kristeva Reader.* Ed. Toril Moi. New York: Columbia University Press, 1986.

Krutnik, Frank. "The Faint Aroma of Performing Seals: The 'Nervous' Romance and the Comedy of the Sexes," *The Velvet Light Trap* no. 26 (fall 1990): 57–72.

Kuhn, Annette. *Women's Pictures: Feminism and Cinema.* New York: Routledge and Kegan Paul, 1986.

Laplanche, Jean, and J.-B. Pontalis. "Fantasy and the Origins of Sexuality." In *Formations of Fantasy,* ed. Victor Burgin, James Donald, and Cora Kaplan. London: Routledge, 1986.

———. *The Language of Psycho-Analysis.* Trans. Donald Nicholson-Smith. New York: Norton, 1973.

Lacan, Jacques. "The Circuit." In *The Seminar of Jacques Lacan: Book II,* ed. Jacques-Alain Miller, translated by Sylvana Tomasell. New York: W. W. Norton, 1988.

———. *Ecrits: A Selection.* Trans. Alan Sheridan. New York: W. W. Norton, 1977.

Lane, Anthony. "High Spirits in the Happy Ever Afterlife," *The Independent,* October 7, 1990.

Langer, Susanne. "The Comic Rhythm." In *Comedy: Meaning and Form,* ed. Robert Corrigan. San Francisco: Chandler Publishing, 1965.

Laplanche, Jean. *Life and Death in Psycho-analysis.* Trans. Jeffrey Mehlman. Baltimore: Johns Hopkins University Press, 1976.

Lapsley, Robert, and Michael Westlake. "From *Casablanca* to *Pretty Woman:* The Politics of Romance," *Screen* 33, no. 1 (spring 1992): 27–49.

Lent, Tina Olsin. "Romantic Love and Friendship: The Redefinition of Gender Relations in Screwball Comedy." In *Classical Hollywood Comedy,* ed. Kristine Brunovska Karnick and Henry Jenkins. (New York: Routledge, 1995), 314–41.

Lyttle, John. "Raising the Spirits of the Age: Films about Ghosts Are Suddenly in Fashion." *The Independent,* October 4, 1990.

Maslin, Janet. "It's Tough for Movies to Get Real." *New York Times,* August 5, 1990.

———. "Looking to the Dead for Mirth and Inspiration." *New York Times,* July 13, 1990.

———. "Spiritual Rewards." *New York Times,* November 19, 1990.

Mathews, Jack. "A Trip Back in Time Again." *Newsday,* August 23, 1991.

———. "Hollywood's Feel-Good Fantasies." *Los Angeles Times,* August 5, 1990.

Mayne, Judith. *Cinema and Spectatorship.* New York: Routledge, 1993.

Messent, Peter B., ed. *Literature of the Occult.* Englewood Cliffs, N.J.: Prentice-Hall, 1981.

Metz, Christian. "The Imaginary Signifier" (excerpts). In *Narrative, Apparatus, Ideology: A Film Theory Reader,* ed. Philip Rosen. New York: Columbia University Press, 1986.

Modleski, Tania. "The Search for Tomorrow in Today's Soap Operas," *Film Quarterly* 33, no. 1 (fall 1979): 12–21.

Moi, Toril. *Sexual/Textual Politics: Feminist Literary Theory.* New York: Routledge, 1985.

Moretti, Franco. *Signs Taken for Wonders: Essays in the Sociology of Literary Forms.* Trans. Susan Fischer, David Forgacs, and David Miller. London: New Left Books, 1983.

Mulvey, Laura. "Afterthoughts on 'Visual Pleasure and Narrative Cinema' inspired by *Duel in the Sun.*" In *Psychoanalysis and Cinema,* ed. E. Anne Kaplan, 24–35. New York: Routledge, 1990.

———. "Visual Pleasure and Narrative Cinema." In *Narrative, Apparatus, Ideology: A Film Theory Reader,* ed. Philip Rosen, 198–209. New York: Columbia University Press, 1986.

Nachman, Gerald. "Love Doesn't Stand a 'Ghost' of a Chance." *The Chronicle,* September 9, 1990.

Bibliography

Neale, Steve, and Frank Krutnik. *Popular Film and Television Comedy.* New York: Routledge, 1990.

Nicholson, Linda J., ed. *Feminism/Postmodernism.* New York: Routledge, 1990.

Pacteau, Francette. "The Impossible Referent." In *Formations of Fantasy,* ed. Victor Burgin, James Donald, and Cora Kaplan. London: Routledge, 1986.

Parsons, Dana. "Ghost Film Taps into Some Spooky Regions of Us All." *Los Angeles Times,* October 21, 1990.

Penzoldt, Peter. *The Supernatural in Fiction.* London: Peter Nevill, 1952.

Polan, Dana. "The Lighter Side of Genius: Hitchcock's Mr. and Mrs. Smith in the Screwball Tradition." In *Comedy/Cinema/Theory,* ed. Andrew Horton. Berkeley: University of California Press, 1991.

———. *Power and Paranoia: History, Narrative, and the American Cinema, 1940–1950.* New York: Columbia University Press, 1986.

Pond, Steve. "The Women's Movement." *Washington Post,* September 21, 1990.

Propp, Vladimir. *Morphology of the Folktale.* Austin: University of Texas Press, 1968.

Radway, Janice A. *Reading the Romance: Women, Patriarchy, and Popular Literature.* Chapel Hill: University of North Carolina Press, 1984.

Ray, Robert. *A Certain Tendency in Hollywood Cinema: 1930–1960.* Princeton: Princeton University Press, 1985.

Reed, John R. "The Occult in Victorian Literature." In *Literature of the Occult: A Collection of Critical Essays,* ed. Peter B. Messent, 89–104. Englewood Cliffs, N.J.: Prentice-Hall, 1981.

Rodowick, D. N. *The Difficulty of Difference.* New York: Routledge, 1991.

Rohter, Larry. "Top Movie of the Year a Sleeper: It's 'Ghost.'" *New York Times,* November 3, 1990.

Rosen, Philip, ed. *Narrative, Apparatus, Ideology: A Film Theory Reader.* New York: Columbia University Press, 1986.

Rowe, Kathleen. "Comedy, Melodrama and Genre: Theorizing the Genres of Laughter." In *Classical Hollywood Comedy,* ed. Kristine Brunovska Karnick and Henry Jenkins. (New York: Routledge, 1995).

Rutherford, Jonathan. *Men's Silences: Predicaments in Masculinity.* London: Routledge, 1992.

Ryan, James. "Hollywood Hunts for What's Hot." *BPI Entertainment News Wire,* October 2, 1990.

Ryan, Michael, and Douglas Kellner. *Camera Politica: The Politics and Ideology of Contemporary Hollywood Film.* Bloomington: Indiana University Press, 1988.

Sarris, Andrew. "The Afterlife, Hollywood-Style," *American Film* 4, no. 6 (April 1979): 25.

Scarborough, Dorothy. "Modern Ghosts." In *Literature of the Occult: A Collection of Critical Essays,* ed. Peter B. Messent, 105–16. Englewood Cliffs, N.J.: Prentice-Hall, 1981.

Schatz, Thomas. *Hollywood Genres: Formulas, Filmmaking and the Studio System.* New York: Random House, 1981.

Seidman, Steven. *Romantic Longings: Love in America, 1830–1980.* New York: Routledge, 1991.

Shohat, Ella, and Robert Stam. *Unthinking Eurocentrism: Multiculturalism and the Media.* London: Routledge, 1994.

Sikov, Ed. *Screwball: Hollywood's Madcap Romantic Comedies.* New York: Crown, 1989.

Silverman, Kaja. *The Acoustic Mirror: The Female Voice in Psychoanalysis and Cinema.* Bloomington: Indiana University Press, 1988.

———. *Male Subjectivity At the Margins.* New York: Routledge, 1992.

Siskel, Gene. "'Ghost' an Appealing Blend of Thriller, Comedy, Romance." *Chicago Tribune,* July 13, 1990.

Slusser, George E., Eric S. Rabkin, and Robert Scholes, eds. *Bridges to Fantasy.* Carbondale: Southern Illinois University Press, 1982.

Snead, James. *White Screens Black Images: Hollywood from the Dark Side.* New York: Routledge, 1994.

Sobchack, Thomas. "Genre Film: A Classical Experience." Reprinted in *Film Genre Reader,* ed. Barry Keith Grant. Austin: University of Texas Press, 1986.

Sobchack, Vivian. *Screening Space: The American Science Fiction Film.* New York: Ungar Publishing Co., 1987.

———. *The Address of the Eye: A Phenomenology of Film Experience.* Princeton: Princeton University Press, 1992.

Studlar, Gaylyn. *In the Realm of Pleasure: Von Sternberg, Dietrich, and the Masochistic Aesthetic.* Urbana: University of Illinois Press, 1988.

———. "Masochism and the Perverse Pleasures of the Cinema." In *Movies and Methods: Volume II,* ed. Bill Nichols, 602–21. Berkeley: University of California Press, 1985.

Styan, J. L. "Types of Comedy." In *Comedy: Meaning and Form,* ed. Robert Corrigan. San Francisco: Chandler Publishing, 1965.

Sypher, Wylie. "The Meanings of Comedy." In *Comedy: Meaning and Form,* ed. Robert Corrigan. San Francisco: Chandler Publishing, 1965.

Tasker, Yvonne. *Spectacular Bodies: Gender, Genre and the Action Cinema.* New York: Routledge, 1993.

Todorov, Tzvetan. *The Fantastic: A Structural Approach to a Literary Genre.* Trans. Richard Howard. Cleveland: The Press of Case Western Reserve University, 1973.

Upchurch, Michael. "It's Gimmicky, But Comic Timing Gives Lively Spirit to 'Ghost.'" *Seattle Times,* July 13, 1990.

Valenti, Peter L. "The 'Film Blanc': Suggestions for a Variety of Fantasy, 1940–45," *Journal of Popular Film* 6, no. 4 (winter 1978): 295–303.

Varnado, S. L. *Haunted Presence: The Numinous in Gothic Fiction.* Tuscaloosa: University of Alabama Press, 1987.

Waggoner, Diana. *The Hills of Faraway: A Guide to Fantasy.* New York: Atheneum, 1978.

Wexman, Viriginia Wright. *Creating the Couple: Love, Marriage, and Hollywood Performance.* Princeton: Princeton University Press, 1993.

Williams, Linda. "Film Bodies: Gender, Genre, and Excess," *Film Quarterly* 44, no. 4 (summer 1991), 2.

Wloszczyna, Susan. "'Ghost,' More Teary Than Scary." *USA Today,* July 13, 1990, Life Section.

Bibliography

———. "Ghost Writer Presses All the Right Weep Buttons." *USA Today,* July 17, 1990.

Wollen, Peter. "Discussion." In *The Cinematic Apparatus,* ed. Teresa de Lauretis and Stephen Heath. London: Macmillan, 1985.

Wood, Robin. "Ideology, Genre, Auteur." Reprinted in *Film Genre Reader,* ed. Barry Keith Grant. Austin: University of Texas Press, 1977.

———. *Hitchcock's Films Revisited.* New York: Columbia University Press, 1989.

———. *Hollywood from Vietnam to Reagan.* New York: Columbia University Press, 1986.

Wurtzler, Steve. "She Sang Live, but the Microphone Was Turned Off: The Live, the Recorded, and the *Subject* of Representation." In *Sound Theory, Sound Practice,* ed. Rick Altman. New York: Routledge, 1992.

INDEX

Index

Index

BOOKS IN THE CONTEMPORARY FILM AND TELEVISION SERIES

Cinema and History, by Marc Ferro, translated by Naomi Greene, 1988

Germany on Film: Theme and Content in the Cinema of the Federal Republic of Germany,
by Hans Gunther Pflaum, translated by Richard C. Helt and Roland Richter, 1990

Canadian Dreams and American Control: The Political Economy of the Canadian Film Industry,
by Manjunath Pendakur, 1990

Imitations of Life: A Reader on Film and Television Melodrama, edited by Marcia Landy, 1991

Bertolucci's 1900: A Narrative and Historical Analysis, by Robert Burgoyne, 1991

Hitchcock's Rereleased Films: From Rope to Vertigo,
edited by Walter Raubicheck and Walter Srebnick, 1991

Star Texts: Image and Performance in Film and Television,
edited by Jeremy G. Butler, 1991

Sex in the Head: Visions of Femininity and Film in D. H. Lawrence,
by Linda Ruth Williams, 1993

Dreams of Chaos, Visions of Order: Understanding the American Avant-garde Cinema,
by James Peterson, 1994

Full of Secrets: Critical Approaches to Twin Peaks, edited by David Lavery, 1994

The Radical Faces of Godard and Bertolucci, by Yosefa Loshitzky, 1995

The End: Narration and Closure in the Cinema, by Richard Neupert, 1995

German Cinema: Texts in Context, by Marc Silberman, 1995

Cinemas of the Black Diaspora: Diversity, Dependence, and Opposition,
edited by Michael T. Martin, 1995

The Cinema of Wim Wenders: Image, Narrative, and the Postmodern Condition,
edited by Roger Cook and Gerd Gemünden, 1997

New Latin American Cinema: Theory, Practices, and Transcontinental Articulations, Volume One,
edited by Michael T. Martin, 1997

New Latin American Cinema: Studies of National Cinemas, Volume Two,
edited by Michael T. Martin, 1997

Giving Up the Ghost: Spirits, Ghosts, and Angels in Mainstream Comedy Films,
by Katherine A. Fowkes, 1998